Outstanding Women in Public Administration

Outstanding
Women in Public
Administration

Leaders,

Mentors, and

Pioneers

Edited by Claire L. Felbinger and Wendy A. Haynes

M.E.Sharpe
Armonk, New York
London, England

Library of Congress Cataloging-in-Publication Data

Outstanding women in public administration : leaders, mentors, and pioneers / edited by
Claire L. Felbinger and Wendy A. Haynes.
    p. cm.
  Includes bibliographical references and index.
  ISBN 0-7656-1368-9 (cloth : alk. paper) — ISBN 0-7656-1369-7 (pbk. : alk. paper)
    1. Women in public life—United States—Biography. 2. Women in civil service—United
States—Biography. 3. Women in politics—United States—Biography. I. Felbinger, Claire L.
II. Haynes, Wendy A., 1949–

HQ1391.U5O928 2004
305.42′092′273—dc22   2003028135

Printed in the United States of America

The paper used in this publication meets the minimum requirements of
American National Standard for Information Sciences
Permanence of Paper for Printed Library Materials,
ANSI Z 39.48-1984.

∞

| BM (c) | 10 | 9 | 8 | 7 | 6 | 5 | 4 | 3 | 2 | 1 |
| BM (p) | 10 | 9 | 8 | 7 | 6 | 5 | 4 | 3 | 2 | 1 |

We dedicate this book to our mothers,
Mary Ann Felbinger and Jenni Green.
They may not have been public administrators,
but they were most certainly
life administrators of the highest order.

Contents

Preface

The genesis of this book was a spirited discussion at an ordinary business meeting at the American Society for Public Administration (ASPA) shortly after the publication of Mary Ellen Guy's lead article in *Public Administration Review* (*PAR*) on Laverne Burchfield and her contributions to public service. Everyone at the meeting was impressed with the article. Mary Ellen told of how interesting and fulfilling the research had been—and she radiated enthusiasm for the venture as she spoke. Many of us were struck by the need for more of this type of research in order to capture the significant role of women in shaping the public service.

We were then members of the Publications Committee of ASPA and on the board of its Section for Women in Public Administration. We floated the idea of editing a book that would capture the research in progress on "outstanding women." Both the Publications Committee and the Section for Women in Public Administration encouraged us to pursue the project. At the next ASPA meeting, we organized a panel to discuss research on outstanding women in public administration, which included the lead presentation of Mary Ellen Guy. The room was filled with people who supported the project, wished to contribute to the project, and who suggested that the contributions of additional women in public administration should be documented in a shorter, vignette-based document so as to capture the essence of their work before it was forgotten.

With the momentum on our side, we examined the horizon to determine how our proposal would have an impact on the extant literature on women in public administration. Neither of us would be described as feminist theorists— in fact, we both conduct research in areas that are male-dominated. We were surprised to find no volume either on women in public administration or on women in political science. From that point forward, our goal would be to aggregate the existing research or encourage research that systematically and analytically examined the role of women in public administration.

Is this the definitive book on *the most* outstanding women and their contributions to public administration? No. It is a first effort to publish a compendium of research-based chapters on women who would be considered outstanding under any definition of the term. We sought to engage scholars who were actively involved in research on women in public administration and to excite those who—inspired by the impact those women had on their lives—expressed interest in documenting their contributions.

The eight substantive chapters here document the lives and contributions of very different women. They might consider themselves public administrators or not, academics or not. Some would proudly call themselves feminists; some did proudly call themselves suffragists; and at least one was praised for being feminine rather than a feminist.

By infusing a little of public administration's feminist theory into the mix, we hope our readers will come to understand why this book was not compiled years ago. In Part I we look at the founding pioneers who engaged in public administration, even though they might not have acknowledged it: Laverne Burchfield, Josephine Goldmark, Mary Livermore, and Nellie Tayloe Ross. Part II focuses on two women who attained prominent positions during a time when women were not ordinarily considered the leading candidates for administrative posts: Frances Perkins and Patricia Roberts Harris. Part III considers how latter-day women balance the competing claims of current lifestyles and still make substantial contributions to public administration as we know it—Naomi Lynn and Maxine Kurtz.

We would like to thank all the public administrators who offered support, suggested contributions, and conducted research on the lives of women who meant so much to them. We thank the people of ASPA who encouraged us to explore this project. We thank Mary Ellen Guy not only for her work on the Burchfield project, but also for her active support of this effort. We do not care whether the focus on her article came from her being a former ASPA president or a scholar outside the traditional realm of feminist theory; her good work beget what followed.

Finally, we would like to thank Harry Briggs and M.E. Sharpe for taking on this labor of love as they seek new ways to contribute to the service of celebrating public administration in its many forms.

Claire L. Felbinger and Wendy A. Haynes

Introduction

This is a book about individual women. Each woman made a significant contribution to public service. Each adds her own uniqueness to an eclectic mix of personalities and paths to service. Their contributions were so compelling that the men and women who contributed to this volume immersed themselves in very personal research—often working with methodologies far afield from their normal research endeavors.

This is a book about outstanding women. Although one may quibble with the representative nature of those chronicled in this volume, by most measures they would be judged as indicative of women who do what outstanding women do—whatever is necessary to get the job done. Most importantly, this book is about the evolution of public administration and the role of women in it.

Camilla Stivers (2000, 2002) has painstakingly developed the theoretical framework within which one can explain women's role in public administration and the role gender images contribute to the explanation. Historically, some careers were considered "male" or "female." On the one hand, maleness is equated with public and public-service ventures while femaleness is equated with private and familial service. Consequently, governance, objectivity, scientific method, and entrepreneurship are considered male domains. These careers were important to sustain a democratic society. The Wilsonian "politics-administration" dichotomy has its roots in this tradition. On the other hand, females served as wives and mothers and provided assistance to those who lacked such support. Social service and nursing are examples of such assistance. These careers supported the private and familial society. Presumably, this service was necessary but not as important as public, that is, higher, service. Consequently, male endeavors become equated with "important" and female ones with "unimportant."

Stivers argues that the reinforcement of the male approach to public service and administration as the best approach necessarily eliminates the perspective of the female gender and its unique contributions to a civil, democratic society. It also eliminates the contributions of other cultures and races. She indicates that the prevalence of a male-dominated image of "objective" public administration produces predictable policy implications having detrimental effects on identifiable portions of the population.

In the chapters that follow, note how the women viewed their contributions vis-à-vis men's. The serving nature of the earliest efforts moves to a recognition of direct contributions to public service and public management, and on to "having it all." Unfortunately, Stivers might argue, having it all still means "having it both" and performing two jobs. In other words, men can claim to put their emphasis on one role—the important one outside of the familial role—while women have no such choice. The outstanding women whose legacies are documented here made uncommon contributions in the context of the world of public service as was practiced in their eras.

References

Stivers, Camilla. 2000. *Bureau Men, Settlement Women: Constructing Public Administration in the Progressive Era.* Lawrence: University Press of Kansas.
———. 2002. *Gender Images in Public Administration,* 2d ed. Thousand Oaks, CA: Sage.

Outstanding Women in Public Administration

Part I

A Different Way of Serving, a Different Way of Seeing

There is an alternative to scientific management besides the ancien régime. The settlement workers and other social reformers have shown us so. Will we be wise enough to heed their call to a profession of public service? Constructing such a profession and field of study is, in my judgment, a worthy aim *for public administration's future* [emphasis added].

(Stivers 2000, 137)

A worthy aim, indeed. In the following chapters, the authors tell the riveting stories of four women, each one a part of the fabric of history that might have been forgotten had it not been for the devoted attention of our contributors. Each story illustrates the aptness of Mary Ellen Guy's observation early in the first chapter: "Gender was its own corset, defining 'appropriate' activities for women and for men." And in each story, our heroine slips the stays that bind and, in the process, contributes to the practice of public administration whether she would have seen it that way or not. It is in the beauty and toughness of their spirits that the stories and our lessons reside.

Introduction to Part I

Mary Ellen Guy revels in the life of Laverne Burchfield, "a woman passionately committed to the world of public service, the world of ideas, and, simply, the world in its natural splendor." Burchfield served as an early managing editor of *Public Administration Review*, now the premier journal in the field. Throughout her life, the amazing Miss Burchfield succeeded by "staying in the shadow, lacing her contributions with humility, and deflecting attention from her to the man with the title." Guy's contention that the "same forces that conspired to hide Mary Parker Follett's contributions to the field of management acted on Laverne Burchfield's career" provides a fitting segue to the second chapter.

Hindy Schachter continues, throughout her study of Josephine Goldmark, the theme of female progenitors to advancement of thinking in public administration. Goldmark "saw science as a weapon in the battle for justice" in the early-twentieth-century reform movement for protective labor legislation, particularly for women and children. Like Burchfield and Follett, Goldmark was not accorded the recognition from her contemporaries or, arguably, subsequent generations that her contributions warranted. Schachter presents a compelling argument for including Goldmark in "public administration's Progressive-era pantheon."

From the early-twentieth-century streets of New York, the third chapter moves back in time to the Civil War era. *Pat Shields* recounts the saga of Mary Livermore, Civil War nurse, nineteenth-century journalist, public administrator with the Sanitary Commission of the U.S. Army, and vocal proponent of women's rights. Shields weaves Livermore's writings into the saga and provides context for Livermore's statement that the Civil War provided a "stimulus of powerful appeal" that aroused women and acted to "fuse and weld them into unified action [where] barriers of sect, caste, and conventionalism, which had heretofore separated them, were burned away in fervid heat of their loyalty." In an era when women were thought to be incapable of unified action—fundamentally unequipped to administer in the public interest—Livermore and her cohorts gifted us with a legacy of caring and cooperative womanhood united in a common purpose, a legacy that would serve generations to come.

Reel forward several decades to 1924 Wyoming to find Nellie Tayloe Ross elected the first woman governor of an American state. *Teva Scheer* presents a biographical portrait of Ross, a woman who was thrust by the untimely death of her husband into public office. Described as "ever feminine, never a feminist"—reflective of the prevailing fear that the "immoral public sphere would render them coarse and mannish"—Nellie Tayloe Ross served as governor, vice-chair of the Democratic National Committee, leader in the campaign for the women's vote, and the first female director of the Mint in the U.S. Department of the Treasury. According to Scheer, "Nellie managed to strike a balance between her personal and business lives that most American women in the first decade of the twenty-first century are still struggling to pull off themselves."

1

The Amazing Miss Burchfield

Mary E. Guy

What goes around comes around: The woman who once solicited others to produce manuscripts for *PAR* [*Public Administration Review*] is now the subject of a manuscript. Laverne Burchfield was managing editor of this journal for 15 volumes, from 1943 to 1958, and in the ASPA's [American Society for Public Administration] early days before it had an executive director, she served as secretary/treasurer for the association, and she wrote the proposal that funded the first executive director. This is her biography—a woman passionately committed to the world of public service, the world of ideas, and, simply, the world in its natural splendor.

Even in those last days, after the stroke had left her too frail to live the independent life she loved, she could be found at the convalescent center surrounded by stacks of newspapers. A voracious reader who reveled in the world of ideas, she was in her element during the years she edited *Public Administration Review.* Long after she had left *PAR*, she looked back at her work and explained that her position had put her in a dialogue with the best thinkers of the age as their ideas came fresh off the typewriter (D. Webster 1999). She was a synthesis person who found connections among diverse ideas and places. But I am getting ahead of myself. First, who was she?

Who was this person that most of us know *of*, but few know *well?* Through library archives, Internet searches, e-mails, letters, and interviews with former colleagues and family, I have uncovered facts about her work that I wish I had known long ago. If the professionalization of public administration could be equated with a hurricane, she was at the eye.

I have read about Lewis Meriam, Leonard D. White, Louis Brownlow, Charles Merriam, Luther Gulick, David Lilienthal, Herbert Emmerich, Marshall E. Dimock, John M. Gaus, Donald C. Stone, William E. Mosher, and the other luminaries who carved the path that we follow. These figures worked at the Public Administration Service; created the Public Administration Clearing House; crafted the Report of the President's Committee on Administrative Management; breathed life into the Tennessee Valley Authority; created the American Society for Public Administration; and generally created the professional infrastructure that we enjoy today. These names I see in textbooks on the intellectual history of the field. The name that is missing is Laverne Burchfield.

She is the person who edited the Tennessee Valley Authority's earliest reports; she is the person who edited the Brownlow Committee report; she is the person who staffed ASPA until a full-time executive director came on board, funded by the Ford Foundation grant she had written; she is the one who . . . you get the picture. Working as a staffer rather than a director, her contributions, though enormous, have remained invisible to historians who never looked behind the door. This chronology, however brief, may help to set the record straight.

Not one to boast of her own accomplishments, if Laverne Burchfield were alive today, I suspect she would read this article, think about it, smile lightly, then never mention it unless directly asked—at which time she would recall every minute detail. She was a quietly proud person, aware that she was a pioneer for women in public service and committed to succeeding as a woman working in a man's world. Guided by her own star, her rewards came less through job titles and more through pride in work well done and the appreciation of friends whom she valued.

I will start at the beginning and relate the events of her life in as much detail as these pages allow. With a historical piece such as this, the reader is left, just as is the biographer, to fill in gaps with hunches. My imagination has curled around the amazing Miss Burchfield and will not let go. I hope that the paragraphs that follow will tease your imagination as well. Laverne insisted on having a scotch before dinner (never *with*; only *before*). I invite you to pour one for yourself; then read on.

From the Beginning

Adah Laverne Burchfield was born January 18, 1900, on a farm near Holland, Ohio, on the outskirts of Toledo. She was a pioneer in public administration, as her family was in settling the land. The farm, which remains in the family today, was deeded to Laverne's great-grandfather, John, who had moved west from Pennsylvania and homesteaded there, earning the property in 1834 through a government land grant.

The Burchfield family valued education, especially for women. Her father, Clarence Joshua, was the youngest of four siblings in his family. While he stayed on the farm, his three older sisters went to college and all became teachers. Her mother, Alyda Wood Burchfield, was also a teacher and sought the best education for her daughter. As a schoolgirl, Laverne wintered with her paternal grandmother and aunt in nearby Toledo, where she benefited from the superior schools. As bright students were allowed to do, Laverne skipped a couple of grades and graduated from high school around age 16. Just as her aunts had done a generation earlier, she headed to college while her one sibling, a brother named C.D. Burchfield, stayed home to farm.

During her childhood years, the move from farm to city was in full swing, and industrialization was carving a new urban landscape. The economy was in transition, with its roots in an agrarian past and its future in urban industry. Laverne took the path that many youth of her generation did—she moved to the city. Her first years of college were spent at a two-year institution, the University of Toledo, before going on to the University of Michigan to complete her baccalaureate degree, which she earned in 1921. This was two years after Congress had refused for the United States to join the League of Nations, one year after women had won the right to vote, one year after the League of Women Voters had been established, and smack in the middle of the Jazz Age and an era of newfound freedom for women.

Laverne Burchfield, a young woman of her time, matured into a woman ahead of her time. No doubt affected by the events of World War I and the debate over the League of Nations, Burchfield's early academic interests were trained on international affairs. A Phi Beta Kappa graduate, she remained at the University of Michigan to pursue doctoral studies in political science (Briston 1999). Twenty-eight years after her birth, in the midst of the Roaring Twenties, Laverne Burchfield was crossing the last *t* and dotting the last *i* of a 344-page dissertation, *The Theory of American International Law: Analysis and Criticism.* In the same year that Herbert Hoover became president, she earned the Ph.D. It was 1928, a year when only about 350 women in the nation received doctoral degrees (Ginzberg 1966). At the University of Michigan, she was one of 70 newly minted Ph.D.s and one of nine women (Bradley 1999).

But Burchfield's educational achievement was not as exceptional as one might think. Between 1920 and 1928, women began to go to college at the same rate as men; there would not be a rebound to this level until the late 1960s (Woloch 1994). The cultural icons of the time included writers Gertrude Stein and Ernest Hemingway, artist Georgia O'Keefe, and golfer Mildred

"Babe" Didrickson, who would play in the 1932 Olympics. Reformer Jane Addams had already met with national renown two decades earlier.

Despite the success of the suffrage movement and the creation of the League of Women Voters, political life in the early years of the century remained a man's business. Government and politics were to remain spectator, rather than participant, sports for women. Historian Richard Hofstadter reported that there was a cultural fear that "If women invaded politics, they would become masculine, just as men became feminine when they espoused reform" (1963, 190).

Gender was its own corset, defining "appropriate" activities for women and for men. The same forces that conspired to hide Mary Parker Follett's contributions to the field of management acted on Laverne Burchfield's career. Her choice of study had moved her into a man's world where, for the duration of her professional career, she would succeed by staying in the shadow, lacing her contributions with humility, and deflecting attention from her to the man with the title.

The Theory of American International Law: Analysis and Criticism

The text of her dissertation provides clues to how she framed issues; how she tempered idealism with pragmatism; and how she respected diverse peoples and diverse ideas. Reminiscent of Follett's belief in the value of citizenship and of Peter Drucker's earliest writings about international affairs, this work shows her grasp of connectedness and global context: "International law needs to be studied from the new point of view, taking into account diplomatic history and the political and economic life of states. This will bring out the principles universally admitted and show their greater or less precision or elasticity. For each matter and by the same method the deformations and special problems of each continent should be studied. This will show the real physiognomy of the international community and the ever-changing relations of civilized peoples" (Burchfield 1928, 21).

Her dissertation also demonstrated an impatience with theory for the sake of theory. Faulting outmoded solutions to newfound problems, she said, "it is ridiculous to proclaim today a rule for situations which have disappeared" (Burchfield 1928, 33). "The best ways to attain perfection and unity in international law is to be first of all realistic" (Burchfield 1928, 40). Neither is she duped by pandering: In a footnote about communications among international law experts, she said: "In this connection it must be kept in mind that the authors of these letters were writing to Dr. Sa' Vianna and might express more hearty or more general approval than they otherwise would" (Burchfield 1928, 35).

Although the study of international law can be abstract, she kept her focus on the ultimate benefactors of the laws—the citizens of the involved states. She said, "Inasmuch as the principles of International Law have their origin and foundation in the real necessities of the life of peoples, they are as varied as those necessities and follow them in their development and modifications" (Burchfield 1928, 276). Throughout her life, she preferred application to theory, hands-on experience to armchair speculation.

Burchfield had a wanderlust that drew her to new experiences, meeting people from diverse walks of life, and seeing sights firsthand. As if a research knowledge of international affairs could not equip her as well as she liked, she and her aunts toured England, France, Italy, Poland, Hungary, Czechoslovakia, Austria, and Germany, in 1930. The trip included the usual cruise ship to England but was spiced up by the more daring experience of crossing the English Channel by plane. She would repeat the trip by herself at the close of her ASPA years and would later explain to her niece that although she had enjoyed the trip with her aunts, she had enjoyed the trip by herself more because when traveling alone, "everybody talks to you" (J. Webster 1999).

The connections she had made at the University of Michigan catapulted her into the center of the political science discipline. Professor Thomas Reed, a member of the political science faculty, would soon tap her to write a book for the American Political Science Association. Her first job, for which she moved to New York City and lived in Fayerweather Hall at Columbia University, would begin the route that would bring her to Chicago, 1313 East 60th Street, and ASPA, a decade later.

Off to New York and a Career in Editing

A striking woman who measured 5 feet 8 inches, with dark eyes and a dry wit, she headed east as soon as she completed her doctoral work. The newly created *Social Science Abstracts* were headquartered at Columbia University. Under the auspices of the Social Science Research Council, the social science disciplines had joined in a project to compile abstracts of the best literature. The American Historical Association, American Sociological Society, American Geographical Society, American Political Science Association, American Economic Association, American Psychological Association, American Statistical Association, and American Anthropological Association were partners. From its first issue until its last, she worked as one of four assistant editors of the *Abstracts*, a reference publication similar in form to what is now published separately as *PAIS* [Public Administration Information Service], *Sociological Abstracts* and *Psychological Abstracts*. Her dissertation research had drawn from documents in English, Spanish, French, Portuguese, and German and had prepared her well for the job. The abstracts were a comprehensive abstracting and indexing of the world's periodical literature in the social sciences, containing in her words, "signed abstracts by specialists of important articles in more than 3,000 periodicals" from around the world (Burchfield 1935, 379). The abstracts were published in four volumes, 1929 through 1932; the 1933 volume was the index.

It was this editing job that brought Burchfield to work closely with the progenitors of contemporary public administration. Through the Social Science Research Council, she met members of the Council's Committee on Public Administration, which included William Anderson, George C.S. Benson, Louis Brownlow, Adele Clark, John Dickinson, Harold Dodds, Rowland Egger, George A. Graham, Luther H. Gulick, E. Pendleton Herring, Lewis Meriam, Lindsay Rogers, Harold Smith, Leonard D. White, John H. Williams, and George F. Yantis (Griffith 1948). She would cross paths with most of these members many times in the years that followed, to such a degree that several became like an extended family to her.

As a young professional who had proven her mettle with the sophisticated editing required by the *Abstracts*, Burchfield became the "go to" person when writing was required. Being pegged by Louis Brownlow, Pendleton Herring, Lewis Meriam, Charles Merriam, Luther Gulick, and Leonard White, among others, proved both a blessing and a curse. These luminaries cast long shadows that obscured her work to outsiders but endeared her to them. Such would mark the rest of her professional career until she would own and operate her own business—but more on that later.

Good Things Come in Threes

At about the same time the *Abstracts* were ceasing publication, Burchfield took the train from New York to Princeton to attend a conference. When she arrived at the meeting, she had no idea what the future would hold for her. It was the Depression and jobs were scarce. By the time she caught the train for the return trip, she had received three job offers. Ever the optimist, she told her niece, Joan Webster, that good things come in threes and told this as an example. She said the first offer, which she had received during the meeting, did not sound very interesting. As she stood on the platform waiting for the train, though, she received two more. The record is unclear here, but it is likely that she accepted both of the platform offers: one to write a book for the American Political Science Association and one to work for the Tennessee Valley Authority.

Student's Guide to Materials in Political Science

The nation was in a depression, Franklin D. Roosevelt was president, and the nation looked to government for help. Interest in political science and public administration was intense. A grant by the Carnegie Corporation funded the American Political Science Association's Committee on Policy, chaired by Thomas H. Reed from her alma mater. Its Subcommittee on Research "was able to make a very advantageous arrangement with the Social Science Research Council for the services of Dr. Laverne Burchfield" to produce a handbook of research that would be "an important tool for the work-bench of every apprentice to the trade of political science. It can be very useful, too, to not a few of the graybeards whose heads are too full of a number of things to keep in memory the daily commonplaces of their professional activity" (Reed 1936, 144–145). The members of the subcommittee included Charles A. Beard, Arnold Bennett Hall, James Hart, Charles E. Merriam, Edward S. Corwin, and W.F. Willoughby. During the same time frame, Luther Gulick, John M. Gaus, Marshall Dimock, and C.B. Gosnell were active on other subcommittees of the Policy Committee. Thus, Burchfield found herself nested among the best and brightest of the field as professionalization was beginning.

The *Student's Guide to Materials in Political Science* was a compilation of reference materials pertaining to political science, national, state, and local government, allied fields in the social sciences, directories, handbooks, newspapers, encyclopedias, and dissertations. In its foreword, Leonard White, Edward Corwin, and H.P. Seidemann, among others, are credited for rendering "invaluable service to Miss Burchfield and the Sub-Committee in matters of editorial advice and helpful criticism" (Burchfield 1935, iv). This project, coupled with her dissertation research and *Social Science Abstracts*, gave her a firsthand look at the social science literature worldwide. This experience, with the familiarity she developed with members of the Policy Committee, set the stage for the contributions she would make to public administration a few years later.

The American Political Science Association's Subcommittee on Research, in addition to hiring Burchfield to produce the *Student's Guide*, held two conferences in Knoxville, Tennessee, while she was working on the *Guide*. The purpose of the meetings was to focus on the problem of research in connection with the activities of the Tennessee Valley Authority (Reed 1936, 145). It was not unusual, then, that as David Lilienthal and others realized the need to conduct social research and to craft annual reports and other documents, they turned to Laverne Burchfield.

Tennessee Valley Authority [TVA]

Once the abstracts had concluded publication in 1933 and she had completed the book for the American Political Science Association in 1935, she was off on her next adventure. She loved living in New York and was an ardent fan of the theater, but she also liked to travel and to experience new places firsthand. She packed her bags, said goodbye to the physician she was dating, and moved from New York City to TVA headquarters in Knoxville, Tennessee. Not wanting to give up her own career, she maintained a long-standing relationship with him for years afterward but chose not to marry. She explained to her niece that his work was too different from hers, and "his life would never have meshed with mine." She looked forward to years of adventures that she knew would conflict with marriage (J. Webster 1999).

The Tennessee Valley Authority, which had been established by Congress in May 1933, was in its infancy as she joined David Lilienthal, Floyd Reeves, Gordon Clapp, Herman Pritchett, and others in Knoxville in 1935. Despite her familiarity with rural living from her childhood, Knoxville was a challenge. The rural town with a rapidly growing industrial core provided beautiful mountainous scenery, but little in the way of theater and big city amenities she had enjoyed in New York. The escape route for her and her chums was her automobile. In fact, Herman Pritchett, who would later serve on the faculty of the University of Chicago and publish a history of the TVA's early days, was in Knoxville during this time and would tell the story of their getaways, always prefacing with "Thank goodness Laverne had a car!"(J. Webster 1999).

While she was at the TVA, she worked in the Social and Economic Division, which was under the Planning and Demonstration Services Unit. Her job title was "economist," and she applied her writing skills to the Authority's early reports. The 1936 annual report shows that she earned $3,200, an amount equal to many of the engineers. The director, David E. Lilienthal, earned the maximum salary of $10,000; Gordon R. Clapp, director of personnel, earned $7,200; civil engineers earned $2,600; research aides earned $2,000; and secretaries earned $1,800 (Tennessee Valley Authority 1936). According to Pritchett (1943), the Division had two major policies. One was to work through established local governments and organizations to strengthen them and to minimize resentment of "outsiders" to the TVA. The other was to limit planning projects and activities to those areas which were clearly within the jurisdiction and competence of TVA.

Gordon Clapp, who later would be named to *PAR*'s first editorial board and would become *PAR*'s second editor-in-chief, rose to general manager in 1939, a couple years after Burchfield had left TVA and headed to Washington, DC, at Louis Brownlow's behest. He had called upon her to assist in the preparation of the report of the President's Committee on Administrative Management. It is likely that Burchfield's experience with the TVA, coupled with her childhood on the farm, kindled her interest in rural public adminis-tration. But, again, I get ahead of the story. First, to the Brownlow Report.

Editing the Brownlow Committee Report

Louis Brownlow had chaired the Public Administration Committee of the Social Science Research Council, the organization that produced the *Social Science Abstracts*. He had met Laverne Burchfield while she was on her first job, editing the *Abstracts*. He had also preceded Burchfield's years in Knox-ville, serving as city manager there from 1923 to 1925. Thus, they knew of each other's work, plus they had the common experience of having lived in Knoxville (Brownlow 1955, 1949). Other members of the President's Com-mittee, Luther Gulick and Charles Merriam, were also familiar with Burchfield's work through Social Science Research Council connections. It is no surprise, then, that they came to her to craft the report.

In 1937, the President's Committee on Administrative Management, tagged the Brownlow Committee, issued a report to Congress linking democracy with good management. At the tail end of 1936, the Committee was hard at work trying to meet the deadline for getting the report to press. Brownlow (1958) described the process of writing the Committee report: He said that the three committee members, he, Luther Gulick, and Charles E. Merriam, had written the principal parts of the report. When it came to editing the supporting documents, they relied

> . . . directly on the aid of Dr. Joseph P. Harris, chief of the research staff, on his assistant, John Miller, and, for meticulous editorial scrutiny, on Miss Laverne Burchfield, whom we had borrowed from the editorial staff of the Tennessee Valley Authority . . . On the very last night, Dr. Harris was at home ill and was endeavoring to talk to Miss Burchfield between seizures of laryn-gitis. Merriam, Gulick, and I had our heads together going over every sen-tence and every revision suggested by the staff. About three o'clock in the morning we were startled by an outburst of laughter in the next room. It came from the mild-mannered John Miller, who . . . was very much in love and was engaged to be married. He wrote to his fiancee every day. The day before had been strenuous, but he had finally gotten his letter written and addressed. He looked at the envelope and exploded. All three of us rushed in to see what was the matter. He had addressed the letter to his sweetheart, "Miss Management." We decided to call it a day, or a night, or a morning, or something, and told Miss Burchfield to put the whole bunch of documents in

an envelope and see that they got to the printer early the next morning. There were no more revisions. (Brownlow 1958, 383)

One fellow is writing to his girl friend, all the men are tired and go home, and Laverne Burchfield is the one who puts the finishing touches on the report, does the final proof, and gets it to the printer.

On the heels of the Brownlow Report, she edited the final report and supporting studies of the President's Committee on Federal Relations to Education. Then, in 1939, she moved from Washington to Chicago to work on the Rural Education Project, an initiative formed jointly with the University of Chicago and the Public Administration Clearing House and headed by Floyd W. Reeves. She found an apartment near the university in Hyde Park, where she would live for 20 years until she would commission an architect to build a state-of-the art house in nearby Chesterton, Indiana.

Public Administration Clearing House

The first decade of her professional life behind her, the next two decades would be spent circulating between the University and 1313 East 60th Street, where the Public Administration Clearing House and Public Administration Service were located. These years would be consumed by working on the Rural Education Project, serving as an assistant to the director of the Public Administration Clearing House, as secretariat for the American Society for Public Administration, as managing editor for *Public Administration Review*, and as publications director for the Public Administration Service. Most of the time she wore several hats, working on multiple projects concurrently. It was during these years that she traveled the country and prepared numerous reports for the Public Administration Service, published a book for the Rural Education Project (1947), and edited *Public Administration Review* (1943–1958).

The connection between Charles Merriam, Louis Brownlow, and Laverne Burchfield that had started years earlier was cemented at Merriam's brainchild, the Public Administration Clearing House (Brownlow 1958). The Clearing House began operations in 1931 to facilitate the establishment and work of organizations focused on public administration and to provide office space for them so that a synergy would develop and information would be exchanged easily and quickly. The work of the Clearing House was supported by grants from philanthropic foundations for 25 years until it was dissolved in 1956. Upon dissolution, the building at 1313 East 60th Street was turned over to the Public Administration Service (Brownlow 1958). During the Clearing House's 25-year lifespan, it facilitated or spawned at least 22 public interest organizations. Included among these were the American Public Welfare

Association, American Public Works Association, American Society for Public Administration, American Society for Planning Officials, Council of State Governments, Federation of Tax Administrators, Governors' Conference, National Association of Assessing Officers, International City Managers' Association, National Institute of Municipal Clerks, Municipal Finance Officers' Association, National Association of Attorneys General, National Association of Housing and Redevelopment Officials, National Legislative Conference, National Association of State Budget Officers, Public Personnel Association, Public Administration Service, and others (Toulmin 1999). Working out of the director's office, Burchfield worked closely with the leaders of all these organizations.

Laverne Burchfield's life coincided with the transition of a nation moving to an administrative state capable of dealing with complex national and global challenges. Referring to the reform movement of the late 1800s and early 1900s, Stivers (1995) makes the point that although some men were active as social policy advocates, as a group they were more attracted to efforts aimed at making government agencies function in an efficient, business-like way. Civil service reform, administrative improvements, and the formation of municipal research bureaus absorbed their attention. "Whether women were uninterested in such efforts or actually discouraged or barred from them, there is little evidence of their involvement" (1995, 525). Burchfield's role with the Public Administration Clearing House, the Public Administration Service, and the American Society for Public Administration, provides a case in point. She was at the eye of the movement, yet she was invisible.

The 1930s, 1940s, and 1950s were fecund years for the professionalization of the field. Many future leaders traveled through "1313," coming to know Laverne and she them. Elmer Staats (1999) was at the 1939 meeting when ASPA was founded. He recalls meeting Burchfield shortly after she had arrived from Washington. He was working at the Public Administration Service, a not-for-profit organization established in 1933 to provide technical assistance to governments; Donald C. Stone directed its research and consulting arm (Public Administration Clearing House 1936; Toulmin 1999). As a young intern from 1937 to 1939, Staats and his fellow interns worked on projects for which Burchfield would edit the reports. Upon her early arrival in Chicago and throughout her tenure at 1313, Staats and others recall that she developed relationships easily, was good to work with, and was the consummate professional, dedicated to the highest ideals of public service.

Samuel Gove (1999) recalls working with her about a decade later, 1948–49. He, as others, describes her as a woman ahead of her time. But it was not all work and no play. She enjoyed entertaining at her Hyde Park apartment and would do so often for her 1313 colleagues. She also enjoyed sports and was good at athletic events. She played tennis, rode horseback, and loved the outdoors. She was also a good bowler—better, in fact, than Samuel Gove. He and Laverne both bowled on his team, Gove's Gophers. He recalls that she consistently outscored him. Her real passions, though, were theater-going and playing the stock market, at which she was quite successful.

Our Rural Communities: A Guidebook to Published Materials on Rural Problems

During the time that Laverne worked at the Clearing House and edited reports for the Public Administration Service, she also wrote a book about rural problems. Similar in style to the *Student's Guide*, it was a compendium of reference material. In the book she provides a narrative on the problems that plague rural communities. It reflected her emphasis on active citizenship and political participation at the grass roots. When Burchfield first moved to the University of Chicago and worked as a research associate with Floyd W. Reeves, she developed a digest that would eventually turn into this book. In the foreword, Reeves wrote: "At its meeting in April, 1944, the Board of Directors of the American Country Life Association expressed the opinion that the digest should be greatly expanded and prepared for publication in the form of a book. It requested that Miss Burchfield do this work. Because of the interest of the Rural Education Project in assembling background materials for use in connection with research, instructional, and service activities, Miss Burchfield undertook this revision, and the present monograph is the result" (Burchfield 1947, vi, vii).

Unlike her dissertation and the *Student's Guide*, Burchfield put more of herself into this book. Her comments reflect the work of someone who is giving voice to more of her own views than her earlier works do. She hoped "that the monograph may prove helpful to many leaders and groups desirous of gaining an over-all view of rural life and of pursuing major problems with a view to helping in their solution" (ix). Moreover, "In a democracy decisions must be made and action taken by the people at the grass roots. The user of this book is urged to investigate the resources of his own community—What groups are interesting themselves in local problems? What are the county, town, township, and village governments doing and what can they do?" (ix). The chapters included materials on the status of rural schools, services provided by the Agricultural Extension Service, public libraries, churches, health care, welfare, housing, recreation, youth services, land use, local government, and community organization.

Each chapter begins with an explanation of the nature of the problem and then proceeds to list resources that will help the reader address the problems.

In regard to schools, she says: "The quality of education provided in rural areas is a matter of state and national interest. Each decade several hundred thousand young persons educated in rural schools migrate to cities in their own and other states to find work opportunities. State and federal aid for the support of schools is essential if the children in rural and urban areas are to have comparable educational opportunities" (2). In the chapter on local government, she emphasizes the importance of citizens determining what they want and making it happen: "Large cities, generally, have won a large measure of home rule. In many states, however, counties and other comparable local units lack the powers necessary to provide one or another badly needed service. In considering whether it is desirable for their local government to undertake a new function, citizens must first determine whether this government is permitted to do so. They may have to put their first efforts into securing necessary constitutional changes or enabling legislation to permit the local unit to embark upon the desired program" (155). About local government, she said, "There has been a steady increase in the functions that citizens wish their governments to perform. The activities of governments during the depression and war periods, especially, have served to give the individual citizen a feeling of being close to his government, whether local, state, or nation" (155). In a section that foretells today's issues, she said: "The term 'neighborhood' is coming to mean only a group of houses fairly near to each other. In many cases the neighborhood provides a unit for certain purposes of social organization such as school district or church parish, but it cannot function in the same way as the community, which unites people in several of their chief interests" (173). These excerpts reflect her values in regard to active, informed participation and the value of community.

The book may have helped to reconnect her with her roots. The longer she lived in the city, the more she would take holidays at the farm near Toledo, Ohio, where she grew up and where her brother, C.D., farmed. She enjoyed visiting and helping out, not because she had to, but because she liked it; she enjoyed farming, and it provided a grounding for her (Phillips 1999).

The ASPA Years

Let there be no doubt about it: Laverne Burchfield was an important, powerful figure while ASPA was headquartered in Chicago. At the same time that she was editing Public Administration Service reports and writing the book on rural problems, she was steering the American Society for Public Administration during its early years. To provide a sense of history, by the time Dwight Waldo wrote *The Administrative State* in 1948, Laverne Burchfield had been working for 20 years; had crafted the nascent TVA's reports; had edited the Brownlow Committee Report; and had been serving as managing editor of *PAR* for five years.

Miss Burchfield Shapes the Future

ASPA was created in 1939, shortly after Burchfield had arrived in Chicago to work on the Rural Education Project. In 1943, she was named managing editor of *PAR*. Between 1940 and 1958, while the position of editor-in-chief changed hands seven times, the managing editor's job had only two incumbents—Don K. Price from 1940 to 1943 and Laverne Burchfield from 1943 to 1958. Leonard White was the first editor of *PAR*, followed by Gordon Clapp. Laverne had already worked with White on projects of the Social Science Research Council and had worked with Clapp at TVA. Thus, the comfort level between her and the first two editors was high. Both of these men had already relied on her writing and editing for previous projects. When Burchfield became managing editor, this announcement appeared in *PAR:*

> Miss Laverne Burchfield, assistant to the director of the Rural Education Project at the University of Chicago, has been appointed managing editor of Public Administration Review to succeed Don K. Price, who is awaiting orders to active service in the United States Naval Reserve. Miss Burchfield, a Ph.D. in political science from the University of Michigan, has been assistant editor of *Social Science Abstracts*, a staff member of the Social and Economic Research Division of the Tennessee Valley Authority, editor of the reports of the President's Committee on Administrative Management, editor for the Advisory Committee on Education, and more recently research associate of Public Administration Service. (*Public Administration Review* 1943, 378)

The third editor-in-chief with whom she worked, E. Pendleton Herring, said: "My title of Editor-in-Chief was purely formal. Laverne edited the *Public Administration Review* and did it very well. Her personality was pleasant, even-tempered and calmly effective. My memories of her are altogether happy and admiring. I felt then and still do that she should have been titled as she truly was the real Editor-in-Chief" (Herring 1999). Following Herring's tenure as editor-in-chief, Rowland Egger, Fritz Morstein Marx, Wallace S. Sayre, Frederick C. Mosher, and York Willbern followed.

Burchfield was a stabilizing force for ASPA, serving as its secretary/treasurer as well as the managing editor of *PAR*. She had the ability to work well with many different temperaments coupled with an uncompromising commitment to scholarship. It was this latter characteristic, an uncompromising commitment to scholarship, that would produce one of the few significant disputes she would have with any of the men with whom she worked. It was also this dispute that resulted in her leaving ASPA to work full-time with the Public Administration Service. Here I go, jumping ahead again. First, a look at her editorial inclinations.

Laverne's grandnephew, Donovan Webster (1999) remembers her as someone who never stopped making connections between disciplines. From her earliest work editing the *Abstracts*, she enjoyed editing because it let her work with ideas coming from all different directions. She was a synthesis person, finding connections before others could see them. She did not fit into an ideologue's box; rather, she liked assessing all views, which is precisely what she had done in her dissertation. She valued balance and critique and warned others not to cede their judgment to someone else. "Never read the Op-Ed page until you have your own opinion on the subject," she would say, emphasizing that the purpose of op-ed writers is to persuade, not to report (D. Webster 1999).

She was neither a liberal nor a conservative. People respected her views because she was informed and thoughtful and because she did not feel compelled to persuade them to her way of thinking. Her frame of reference for evaluating public policy was that she believed people should be able to work toward a better life, and she believed that every situation demands a unique solution. She was for the right kind of government—not necessarily more government, not necessarily less government. For example, to prevent today's solution from becoming tomorrow's problem, she suggested that social programs be reconsidered every four years.

PAR published several of Herbert A. Simon's papers during Burchfield's tenure (Simon 1944, 1946, 1947, 1953). Simon (1999) recalls that "Laverne was a very competent and energetic editor of the *Review*, at a time when editors did much of the selecting of papers for publication instead of passing that task to referees; hence, although she was labeled 'managing editor,' she had much to do with setting the tone of the journal in its early years." He credits her with being "a person of considerable executive talent, and a friend who, like the whole '1313' crowd, was dedicated to the improvement of the public service, and who filled her *PAR* office with energy and ability and was especially concerned that it have real impact on the practice of management."

Laverne hired Beverly Blersch Phillips to assist with her ASPA duties, which included editing *PAR* and serving as secretary/treasurer of the association. Phillips worked for Laverne from June 1950 to May 1956, when she married and moved to Florida. Burchfield started her out performing secretarial duties. By the time she left, Laverne had mentored, groomed, and trained her to the point that Beverly was not only performing secretarial tasks, but had also learned to produce a monthly newsletter, copyedit manuscripts, and write grants, plus she had learned a lot about succeeding in an office directed by powerful men. Although Burchfield did not have the title, Phillips (1999) recalls, "of course she ran the organization; she was the CEO."

In Phillips' assessment of Burchfield's workstyle, she described her as an optimist. She says that Burchfield "put up with an awful lot" but that "she never let being a woman get in the way." She credits Burchfield with teaching her not "to be afraid of any of those men; she's the one who made me think that being a woman was not a problem." She recalls that when "Brownie" (Louis Brownlow) was in town, he enjoyed coming into Laverne's office to sit and tell stories. She also recalls that Laverne got along well with Herb Emmerich, who succeeded Brownlow as director of the Clearing House. In fact, "all the people in that building had high regard for her; she knew everybody in the field. They all liked her and they respected her; she just was a neat lady; I learned so much from her." Phillips would go on to win a seat on the Dade County Board of Commissioners in Miami, Florida, and to serve as executive director of the Dade County YWCA. She credits Burchfield with teaching her early in life to stand up for herself and to take pride in her work. They remained lifelong friends, visiting with one another long after Burchfield had retired.

James A. "Dolph" Norton (1999), who served as ASPA president in 1968–1969 remembers that "For me she was, even in the 1950s, an impressive person, devoted to public administration, the source of more information than anyone else around, and important to the Public Administration Service and ASPA." Ferrel Heady (1999), who served as president (1969–1970), remembers her "as being modest and self effacing." James Mitchell (1999) recalls that when he was president of ASPA (1952–1953), Burchfield sought his advice upon receiving a scorching letter that criticized her editorship. It had been written by an author whose manuscript had been rejected. Normally unflappable, the letter was particularly vicious, and Laverne came to him to seek advice about whether she should resign. He remembers telling her "Absolutely not!" No more was said of it.

During her last years at ASPA, Phillips (1999) recalls that she and Laverne learned that the Ford Foundation was offering grants for which ASPA might be eligible. "We heard they had some grants so we sat down and wrote a grant for $245,000. We didn't know anything about grant writing but we wrote it; we got the grant because a lot of people had a lot of connections." Ironically, it was implementation of the conditions of the grant that resulted in Burchfield's distancing herself from ASPA and from *PAR*.

Letting Go

The grant required that an executive director be named. Phillips recalls that everyone thought that ASPA could and should be bigger, better, and stronger.

A formal executive director to replace the looser structure of a secretary/ treasurer was the solution. Although Burchfield had been fulfilling the secretariat function, there is no evidence that she was considered for the director post. In 1956, Robert Matteson, then senior staff member of the Institute of Public Administration, was named executive director. Although his tenure was short compared to Burchfield's, turmoil erupted during his years, causing him to leave the post earlier than planned. He initially wanted to convert *PAR* to a format more in keeping with a trade magazine, but Burchfield insisted that it remain a scholarly journal. Uncomfortable with her degree of influence over the content of the journal and wanting to bring all ASPA activities under his control, conflict was inevitable.

Matteson locked horns with the senior staff at 1313, most of whom had worked with Laverne since the early Social Science Research Council days. According to Don L. Bowen (1999), Matteson's assistant director, Burchfield won the battle to keep *PAR* as it had been—a scholarly publication with content applicable to practice—but it was a Pyrrhic victory. She had more clout than Matteson because of the support from the Clearing House leadership. The outcome of the dispute resulted in the journal remaining scholarly, as Burchfield had developed it. The difference in style between Burchfield and Matteson, however, was so great that neither wanted to work with one another. She left the post of managing editor and went to work full-time for the Public Administration Service [PAS], focusing her energy and attention there until her retirement in 1965. Phillips (1999) recalls that PAS welcomed her with open arms. "All those people were friends and they had worked together for years, long before ASPA had consumed so much of her time." Phillips left ASPA to move to Florida shortly after Matteson was hired. Although not being in the office to experience the fireworks firsthand, she speculates that Burchfield was hurt by the events but "was the kind who wasn't going to make a fuss and PAS was delighted to get her, anyway." Bowen, who was in the office at the time, believes that Burchfield would rather have worked with *PAR*, but it was more important to her that the journal continue in its scholarly vein than that she remain the managing editor.

Matteson hired a managing editor, William Shore, to work as staff officer in charge of ASPA publications. To ensure continuity in *PAR*, Matteson contracted with the Public Administration Service to retain Burchfield as a consultant to Shore on the journal—a role she filled until 1958. One can imagine the tension inherent in that relationship. Nevertheless, William Shore (1999) describes Laverne as a lovely person. In terms of how the transition from Burchfield to himself took place, he says, "I strongly suspect she was pushed and was unhappy about it." He remembers that while she was a friend and friendly, he and she were not close, largely because their offices were far apart and they did not cross paths often.

The first editor-in-chief under the new regime was James W. Fesler. It was during Fesler's tenure that the transition from Burchfield to Shore occurred. Fesler (1999) recalls that Burchfield had high standards and was highly competent at what she did. He also recalls that the journal retained its scholarly bent: "William B. Shore, the remarkably able Managing Editor, proved as academic in taste as I." He credits Burchfield with the book review essay. From his point of view, this venue was an excellent way to procure thoughtful essays. "Why? Because a busy scholar or author-bent practitioners who predictably would decline her invitation to do an article would agree to do a book review, in their past experience just four or five paragraphs of prose. Too late her captive would learn from Laverne that the review-essay should approach an article's length."

To commemorate Burchfield's contributions to *PAR*, the Burchfield Award was established in the early 1960s. It is presented for the best book review or TOPS [other political science] article published during the volume year. The award was first given in 1963 to Frank Sherwood for his review essay "View from the Outside," which appeared in the December 1963 issue of the journal (Hamilton 1999). Sherwood remembers Burchfield and describes her this way: "She was a thoroughly fine person. In the 1950s she really was *PAR*, regardless of who was listed as the editor. Nothing got into the journal that she had not carefully reviewed and improved. In addition, during most of the 1950s she was really the executive director of the organization. That changed in 1956 when ASPA received a Ford grant and imported an executive director and a much larger staff. The grant resulted in a big change in the organization, and Laverne more or less got shoved aside" (Sherwood 1999). Sherwood goes on to say that "the book review award fitted very well with her concern to see that *PAR* reviews were really quality essays, hopefully covering several books, and not just those little blurbs you see in many journals. I don't know whether it was an approach taken by other professional journals; but I well remember thinking that the book review essay was the best piece of (the) journal . . . I think we have to give Laverne credit for a part of *PAR* that is still one of its best features" (Sherwood 1999).

Intent on commemorating Burchfield's contributions to *PAR*, York Willbern drafted a tribute to her. It was signed by all the editors with whom Laverne had worked prior to the transition to Shore. "As I remember, I wrote the first draft of the piece, and Fritz Marx, with Germanic thoroughness, revised it" (Willbern 1999). The editors whose names appear at the end of the tribute are Gordon Clapp, Rowland Egger, Pendleton Herring, Fritz Morstein Marx, Frederick C. Mosher, Wallace S. Sayre, and York Willbern.

On the Contributions of Laverne Burchfield

Laverne Burchfield became managing editor of *Public Administration Review* in 1943, three years after its beginning, and held that post until 1958. During those 15 years she was a strong and steady influence in forming and maintaining the character of the *Review*.

Her influence ranged widely. She stimulated the production of papers which were published in the *Review*, guided by her wide knowledge of who was doing what and which things needed recognition in the rapidly developing field. She showed keen and discriminating judgment about the merit and importance of manuscripts. She helped many an author to trim his copy and to bring into better focus matters that were significant. She had a rare capacity for stimulating members of the editorial board to provide fresh ideas and find themselves refreshed by the process. She maintained the highest standards of editorial work, insisting on accuracy and clarity in the words and sentences which the *Review* printed. To those who worked with her, she proved herself a warm and understanding friend.

> While she has now moved from her responsibility for the *Review* into full-time work for Public-Administration Service, we know that she will remain a valuable counselor to the editorial board and to the staff. But her completion of fifteen years as managing editor of *Public Administration Review* seemed to the former editors in chief to require a public acknowledgment of her immeasurable services. We are sure that Leonard D. White, the first editor-in-chief, would have wanted to join in this statement, and that he would be particularly happy to acknowledge Laverne Burchfield's distinguished part in achieving a publication of the high standard at which he aimed. (Clapp et al. 1958)

As fate would have it, Matteson ran into difficulty on many sides over many issues, and there were sighs of relief when he left and his associate director, Don Bowen, rose to the directorship. Bowen (1999) describes Burchfield as "a highly intelligent person; a woman professional in a man's world; well-liked and broad gauged; I don't think you'll find anyone who will speak ill of her—she worked in a terrain that was difficult and she did it well; she was a woman and was in a sense a victim of that."

"Victim" is not a word used often when describing Laverne Burchfield, but as one traces her career, it is likely that had she been male, she would have been ASPA's first executive director. To put the naming of Matteson as executive director in context, a survey of college-educated women whose careers would have coincided with Burchfield's is instructive. Ginzberg (1966) quotes a respondent: "A Ph.D. economist who works for a leading oil company reported that it would not allow women economists to make formal reports to directors. All had to be relayed through a man" (104). York Willbern (1999) captures her work for ASPA and *PAR*:

> She was the backbone of both—officers came and officers went, editors came and editors went, but Laverne was there and did the bulk of the work. Officers and editors didn't delegate chores to Laverne; Laverne delegated chores to them. She knew the public administration people all over the country, and who ought to be on programs and write articles. After leaving her job with the Review, she continued for some years on the staff of Public Administration Service, at 1313. But for those of us who were active in the community in those years, she was one of the greatest of its leaders, even though she never occupied a high-ranking public office or a major professorship.

Nothing kept Burchfield down for long. She was resilient, enjoyed her work and hobbies, and lived a full, fun life despite hurdles. She was a voracious reader and kept up with events around the world by reading three or four newspapers a day; she was curious about everything. She had a busy home life, made fast friends, and enjoyed entertaining colleagues at her Hyde Park apartment. She also loved gardening and, partly as a Victory Garden and partly because she simply enjoyed it, she rented space on the lakefront and grew a garden. She also enjoyed the piano and played daily, as Beverly Blersch Phillips recalls. But what about family ties, you may be asking. Devoted to her family, she helped to raise her niece, Joan Webster.

When Joan was six years old, her mother died. Just as her aunts had done for her, Laverne helped to raise Joan. She lived with Laverne during the summers from 1941 to 1946 and lived with her year-round for four years while she attended the University of Chicago Lab School, where Laverne had been instrumental in arranging her enrollment. When Joan moved in with her, Aunt Laverne instructed her "On the sideboard is a bowl and I will put $20 in it at the first of the week; you are to spend it on bread, milk, and other groceries. Keep track to the penny of the money you spend. At the end of the week if the account is right, you get to keep the left over money." Joan learned to keep accurate accounts and to spend wisely so as to have money left over.

Joan has fond memories of family friends, Charles Merriam, John "Corky" Corcoran, Herb Emmerich, "Uncle" Leonard White, and others of the 1313 crowd. She would stay with Leonard and his wife when Laverne had to be away on trips. In the family tradition, Aunt Laverne encouraged her to complete college and go on for graduate work, which she did. After Joan married and had a family, her children became like grandchildren to Laverne. Her grandniece, Susan Webster (1999), recalls that Laverne would care for her and her siblings when her parents would be away. She also recalls that her aunt would often spend Sunday afternoons with them, sitting in the living room and reading. From this, she learned the value of reading. Two of Joan's children, Susan and Donovan, are now writers, and the youngest, John, lives with his family in Chesterton, Indiana, and owns an import business—an enterprise that Laverne is probably smiling over for reasons that will become obvious in the next few pages.

On to the Next Chapter

In the post-ASPA years, Burchfield worked at 1313 as director of publications for the Public Administration Service. PAS's field representatives helped to establish city charters, budgeting systems, and management processes for governments in the United States as well as around the world. Shortly after she had switched to a full-time assignment with PAS, Laverne took a second trip around the world, this time alone. From her days at 1313 she knew so many people in government around the world that she hopscotched from country to country, visiting with old friends along the way. Years later she would relate a lesson she had learned on the trip. She was on a bus in Pakistan, when a man with objectionable body odor sat down beside her. When she asked the driver to have him move, the driver responded that "your perfume smells as bad to him as his odor does to you." She told the story as a lesson about accepting others (Roth 1999).

When she returned from the trip, she soon joined other Chicago workers who were moving out of the city. She bought a lot next door to her colleague, John "Corky" Corcoran and his wife, in a Chicago suburb, Chesterton, Indiana, about 50 miles to the east. Corky was associate director of the Public Administration Service. Several other colleagues lived there as well, including Herb Emmerich, who had succeeded Louis Brownlow as director of the Clearing House, and Herman Pope, who directed the Public Administration Service. They would carpool to and from Chicago.

It was around 1960 when she commissioned renowned Chicago architect and good friend George Fred Keck to design a house that would blend into the wooded riverbank and have large open spaces for entertaining. Situated at the end of a gravel road overlooking the Calumet River, the walls were glass, permitting a full view of the outdoors. Just as she was ahead of her time, so was the house, which was unlike any other home in traditional Chesterton. The furnishings were top notch, with bleached birch cabinets, plenty of library space, and furnishings she had collected from her travels abroad. Solar heat was achieved by the sitting of the house and its overhangs, making it economical to heat and cool.

By the time ASPA moved its headquarters from Chicago to Washington, DC, in 1964, Laverne was about to close the professional chapter of her life and start the entrepreneurial chapter. She retired from the Public Administration Service in 1965 at the age of 65 (*PA Times* 1987). The National Academy of Public Administration [NAPA] got under way and started appointing fellows around 1967. The early appointments sought to name both active members and to recognize distinguished persons in the field who had retired before NAPA's formation. Because she was already retired, she was named an Honorary Fellow in 1975 (Dean 1999). By this time, she was consumed by another passion: gardening and running the Chesterton Feed and Garden Center. Now comes the last chapter.

Business Owner

Around 1962, while Laverne was still working at 1313 but had begun to turn her sights toward retirement, she purchased the Chesterton Feed and Garden Center (Roth 1999). As town lore had it, the store had been run by four brothers. It consisted of a garden center that sold livestock feed and gardening supplies. The brothers quarreled, and the hours that the store was open became irregular. This was where she purchased the wild bird seed that she fed the birds at her house. She went in one day to make her usual purchase and learned from the brothers that they might be closing. She asked, "Where will I buy my bird seed?" You can guess the rest. Very shortly, she was the owner of the store.

One of the conditions of the sale was that Virginia, a sister-in-law to one of the brothers, would be allowed to continue working at the store. This arrangement was advantageous to Laverne, since she was not yet ready to retire, and to the store, because customers knew and liked Virginia and she was a reliable employee. Her popularity with the townspeople eased the transition in ownership and retained the customer goodwill the brothers had built. She would remain at the store throughout the years that Laverne owned it.

Just as she had done throughout her career, Laverne put herself on a crash course, learning all she could about running a retail store, displaying products, and marketing. Her years of following the stock market and studying corporate successes provided the business acumen she needed. She redesigned and upgraded the building and put a greenhouse on the front end. She sought training to learn how to do store design and how to stock shelves in an attractive manner. Garden centers were just coming into vogue in the suburbs, and the Chesterton Feed and Garden store rode the fashion wave. She catered to the traditional rural market with livestock feeds and catered to the new suburbanites by selling gardening supplies, cedar mulch, bulbs, seed, and plants. The store grew its own flowering perennials and had show gardens, meaning plots that demonstrated how gardens would look with various flowers and different types of landscaping. No other garden centers in the area had such displays. Again, Laverne Burchfield was on the mark and ahead of her time—but this time, it was her show.

After a few years, she retired from the Public Administration Service to devote her full attention to the store. Those who visited her recall that she maintained an enormous garden of fruits and vegetables at her home; that she enjoyed the vista provided by her glass-walled house and the wild birds that frequented there to take advantage of daily feedings; and that she was happily immersed in store operations (Sherwood 1999). As her friends from the 1313 days passed away or moved, she entertained less. Rather than recreating those friendship bonds with the locals around Chesterton, she became self-contained: "[S]he may have been a mystery to others, but she knew herself quite well—she just didn't feel a need to pass it on" (D. Webster 1999). She stayed abreast of news from around the world, kept up with her correspondence, and stayed busy planning her next adventure and managing the store.

When she was 78 and her energy flagged, comparatively speaking, she began to consider selling the store. Doing so, she reckoned, would provide more time for her travels. Although she had several offers from prospective purchasers, she chose to sell the store to Chuck Roth, who had worked for her since 1973, when he had started as a teen, weeding the gardens and carrying purchases to customers' cars. As grandmother to grandson, there was a fondness between them and she could trust that he would continue to maintain the quality she had developed. She delayed the sale for a couple of years so that Roth could go away and complete horticultural training. The store actually changed hands in 1980.

She had made plans to travel extensively following the sale. As an 80-year-old she planned to take a trip down the Amazon, but had to cancel at the last minute when she faced the fact that she would have difficulty getting into dugout canoes (Roth 1999). [No, kind readers, I did not make this up.] She stayed on as an advisor at the store until fate played its hand and her health failed. When she was 81, she had a bout with breast cancer that weakened her, and a series of strokes followed. She insisted on living by herself, but soon became so frail that she finally agreed to find an assisted living center near where she had grown up and her brother still farmed. While she was looking for a place in May 1981, she had a stroke that left her hospitalized. She went from the hospital to the convalescent center. In September, her brother and his wife took her for a drive to see the autumn leaves. Another driver ran into their car and C.D. was killed. Though Laverne sustained no serious injuries, she lived only one month longer.

As quietly as cat's feet, at the age of 81, her work done, her life fulfilled, her store safely in someone's hands, surrounded by newspapers that informed her of the world she loved, she slipped away. She died October 27, 1981, near the farm where she was born.

Epilogue—A Computer Named Laverne

If you walk into the Chesterton Feed and Garden Center today, you will find a computer with the name "Laverne" pasted on it. When Chuck Roth bought the first computer for the store, shortly after Laverne had passed away, he loaded software on it and mused to himself that the machine would become the brain and guts of the store. With little thought, he wrote "Laverne" on a label and pasted it on the computer. Each new computer since then receives the same label. Roth chuckles that "half the people who work here now don't know why it is named Laverne."

If you walk into her grandnephew Donovan's house, you will find signed first editions of books she cherished. If you walk into her grandniece's office, you will find a thesaurus she still uses, given to her by Aunt Laverne to help in copywriting. If you visit Chesterton, you may encounter her grand-nephew John's import business as well as the Feed and Garden Center. If you write a book review for *PAR*, you will be eligible for the Burchfield Award. If you follow ASPA history, you now know that she is the one who wrote the proposal that built the staff. Her footsteps were light but true, firm yet unassuming. Her legacy rests in your hands.

Acknowledgments

Preparation of this manuscript was made possible by the work of my research assistant, Aubrey Mayo, and the research, guidance, clues, and recollections of the Bentley Historical Library, Brookings Institution, Erik Bergrud, Don Bowen, Alan Dean, Mel Dubnick, James Fesler, Pat Florestano, George Frederickson, Samuel Gove, Mary Hamilton, Ferrel Heady, E. Pendleton Herring, Jan Hitchcock, Barbara Judd, John P. Keith, Rosslyn Kleeman, Melvin Manis, Tex McLain, James Mitchell, Chester A. Newland, James A. "Dolph" Norton, Beverly Blersch Phillips, Darrell Pugh, Chuck Roth, Frank Sherwood, Phyllis Shocket, William Shore, Herbert A. Simon, Elmer B. Staats, Larry Terry, the Toledo Public Library, Harry Toulmin, York Willbern, Dwight Waldo, Donovan Webster, Joan Webster, and Susan Webster. I am grateful to each.

References

Bowen, Don L. 1999. Personal communication, September 24, October 23.

Bradley, Jeffrey. 1999. Letter on behalf of the Bentley Historical Library, University of Michigan, September 2.

Briston, Heather. 1999. Letter on behalf of the Bentley Historical Library, University of Michigan, October 7.

Brownlow, Louis. 1949. *The President and the Presidency.* Chicago: Public Administration Service.

―――. 1955. *A Passion for Politics.* Chicago: University of Chicago Press.

―――. 1958. *A Passion for Anonymity.* Chicago: University of Chicago Press.

"Burchfield Hailed for Early ASPA Service." 1987. *Public Administration Times* 10, no. 3: 5.

Burchfield, Laverne. 1928. *The Theory of American International Law: Analysis and Criticism.* Ph.D. diss., University of Michigan.

―――. 1935. *Student's Guide to Materials in Political Science.* New York: Henry Holt.

―――. 1947. *Our Rural Communities: A Guidebook to Published Materials on Rural Problems.* Chicago: Public Administration Service.

Clapp, Gordon, Rowland Egger, Pendleton Herring, Fritz Morstein Marx, Frederick C. Mosher, Wallace S. Sayre, and York Willbern. 1958. "On the Contributions of Laverne Burchfield." *Public Administration Review* 18, no. 4: 369.

Dean, Alan. 1999. Personal communication, September 23.

Fesler, James W. 1999. Re: Do You Remember Laverne Burchfield? E-mail to author, September 16, 17.

Ginzberg, Eli. 1966. *Life Styles of Educated Women.* New York: Columbia University Press.

Gove, Samuel. 1999. Personal communication, September 20, 21.

Griffith, Ernest S. 1948. *Research in Political Science.* Chapel Hill: University of North Carolina Press.

Hamilton, Mary. 1999. Letter to author, August 25.

Heady, Ferrel. 1999. Re: Burchfield. E-mail to author, September 17.

Herring, E. Pendleton. 1999. Laverne. E-mail to author, September 21.

Hofstadter, Richard. 1963. *Anti-intellectualism in American Life.* New York: Alfred A. Knopf.

Mitchell, James. 1999. Personal communication, October 1.

"New Managing Editor." 1943. *Public Administration Review* 3, no. 4: 378.

Norton, James A. "Dolph." 1999. Re: Do You Remember Laverne Burchfield? E-mail to author, September 24.

Phillips, Beverly Blersch. 1999. Personal communication, October 1.

Pritchett, C. Herman. 1943. *The Tennessee Valley Authority: A Study in Public Administration.* Chapel Hill: University of North Carolina Press.

Public Administration Clearing House. 1936. *A Directory of Organizations in the Field of Public Administration.* Chicago: Public Administration Clearing House.

Reed, Thomas H. 1936. "Report of the Committee on Policy of the American Political Science Association for the Year 1935." *American Political Science Review* 30, no. 1: 142–165.

Roth, Chuck. 1999. Personal communication, October 5, 6.

Sherwood, Frank. 1999. Laverne Burchfield. E-mail to author, September 6.

Shore, William. 1999. Re: Laverne Burchfield. E-mail to author, September 21, 22.

Simon, Herbert A. 1944. "Decision-making and Administrative Organization." *Public Administration Review* 4, no. 1: 16–30.

———. 1946. "The Proverbs of Administration." *Public Administration Review* 6, no. 1: 53–67.

———. 1947. "A Comment on 'The Science of Public Administration.'" *Public Administration Review* 7, no. 3: 200–203.

———. 1953. "Birth of an Organization: The Economic Cooperation Administration." *Public Administration Review* 13, no. 4: 227–236.

———. 1999. Laverne Burchfield. E-mail to author, September 23.

Staats, Elmer. 1999. Personal communication, September 29.

Stivers, Camilla. 1995. "Settlement Women and Bureau Men: Constructing a Usable Past for Public Administration." *Public Administration Review* 55, no. 6: 522–530.

Tennessee Valley Authority. 1936. *Annual Report of the Tennessee Valley Authority.* Washington, DC: Government Printing Office.

Toulmin, Harry T. 1999. *A Life's Memoir.* Daphne, AL: Village Press.

Waldo, D. 1948. *The Administrative State.* New York: Ronald Press.

Webster, Donovan. 1999. Personal communication, October 1.

Webster, Joan. 1999. Personal communication, September 30.

Webster, Susan. 1999. Personal communication, October 4.

Willbern, York. 1999. Re: Do You Remember Laverne Burchfield? E-mail to author, September 19, 26.

Woloch, Nancy. 1994. *Women and the American Experience*, 2d ed. New York: McGraw-Hill.

2

Josephine Goldmark

Champion of Scientific Management and Social Reform

Hindy Lauer Schachter

Several academic fields claim Josephine Goldmark as a progenitor. Histories of American social work and industrial relations praise her research on labor conditions. Nursing histories cite her 1923 report on public-health nursing. Law textbooks see her as an avatar of legal realism. The American Psychological Association awarded her a 2003 posthumous distinguished leadership award for her occupational-health psychology research.

But her name rarely appears in public administration texts. This article is almost certainly her first biographical sketch in the public administration literature. Readers of the piece have a chance to see why so many disciplines claim her as a founder and to explore how her work meshes with the output of people who are in public administration's Progressive-era pantheon.

Early Life

Josephine Clara Goldmark was born on October 13, 1877, into a family she came to believe was "possessed by the passion for liberty" (Goldmark 1930, 289). In 1848, her father, Joseph Goldmark, a Hungarian-born physician and chemist, had been a leader in the liberal revolt against Metternich in Vienna. With the revolt's failure, the Austrian authorities accused Joseph of treason and murder. He fled to Switzerland. Afraid that he might be extradited as a common criminal on the murder charge, he left for America and arrived in New York in July 1850.

Joseph Goldmark prospered in his new home. He developed a factory to manufacture his chemical inventions, which included percussion caps and red phosphorous, items useful to the Union Army in the Civil War. With his profits, he was able to amass significant property. He married Regina Wehle whose once-wealthy Prague family had also fled to America after the abortive 1848 uprising. Josephine later noted that both her parents "loved liberty and democratic institutions with the enthusiasm of adoptive sons and daughters" (Goldmark 1930, 289).

The Goldmarks lived a comfortable life first in Brooklyn and later on the upper west side of Manhattan. Regina and Joseph had ten children of whom Josephine, or "Do" as she was called, was the youngest (Paper 1983, 154). After her father died in 1881, her siblings became especially important in her upbringing. They brought varied experiences and insights into the home. Her brother Henry was a civil engineer who designed and constructed the lock gates for the Panama Canal. He brought home talk of rationality and the importance of mastering technique. Her oldest sister Helen married Felix Adler, who had founded the Ethical Culture Society in 1876. Since Ethical Culture is a nontheistic religion that urges people to create a more humane world, the Adlers' conversations probably stressed the importance of social justice. Josephine's work would incorporate both messages. Her contribution to reform would be to show the benefits technique can bring to the quest for justice.

For recreation, the Goldmarks were strong on exploring the outdoors. Beginning in 1883, Josephine spent summers with her mother and siblings in the Keene Valley region of the Adirondacks, a place of virgin forests and mountaintops. Josephine fished in Chapel Brook using grasshoppers for bait. With her siblings she climbed mountains and crossed streams on logs, not easy feats when the hiker had to wear skirts that reached the ground (P. Goldmark n.d.).

The Adirondack lodge welcomed visitors. In the summer of 1890, a young lawyer, Louis Dembitz Brandeis, a second cousin on the Wehle side, often joined the family.[1] Soon he and Josephine's sister, Alice, were engaged (P. Goldmark n.d.). Their marriage in March 1891 would have important consequences for Josephine's future work.

At the end of the nineteenth century, new educational opportunities blossomed for wealthier women in the form of elite, private women's colleges. The Goldmark family took advantage of these institutions. When Josephine finished the Brackett School, a private academy in Brooklyn, she followed her sisters Susan and Pauline to Bryn Mawr, a Quaker-endowed university in suburban Pennsylvania that had opened its doors in 1885 with a mission to offer women rigorous intellectual training.

The Goldmark women entered Bryn Mawr at a time when Jews, even secular Jews such as themselves, were not always fully accepted in American higher education. Bryn Mawr had a de facto admissions quota for Jews and housed Jewish and Christian students separately (Novey 1997). Nevertheless, Josephine thrived at the school. She majored in English and acquired a reputation among her peers for maturity, disciplined thinking, and a love of the outdoors (Park 1951). After her graduation in 1898 she followed Pauline's trajectory of studying for a year at Barnard where she then served as a tutor. At that point she was drawn into the orbit of the National Consumers League (NCL).

The National Consumers League

In 1899 Florence Kelley left the Hull House settlement in Chicago to become executive secretary of the National Consumers League in New York. This female-run and female-funded organization was set up to convince shoppers to restrict purchases to goods made in stores which offered employees humane work conditions. Under Kelley's leadership it also became a key player in the campaign to enact protective labor legislation, particularly for women and children (e.g., Muncy 1991).

Impressed with Kelley's enthusiasm, Pauline Goldmark took a position as assistant secretary of the New York Consumers League, one of the NCL's state affiliates, in 1899 (Carter 1986). Shortly afterward Josephine started work at the NCL as a volunteer. She traveled cross-town from her family's home at 270 W. 94th Street to the League office in the United Charities Building at 105 E. 22nd Street. This journey took her to an area at the heart of midtown but close to a small urban park and the first Madison Square Garden.

In 1903 Josephine accepted a paid position as publication secretary. Her main function was to compile yearly handbooks on child labor laws throughout the United States. Data on various individual state laws existed in innumerable separate archives. This data had to be amalgamated and assembled in readable form. As Kelley explained, society needed "full, consecutive, trustworthy information" (1908, 1). Only if the information was available, could people use it to limit the employment of child workers.

Between 1903 and 1908, Josephine produced a series of handbooks identifying the applicable laws in each state. She showed considerable research grit and ingenuity in editing and classifying legislation. She categorized the laws as to their approach to age limits, maximum permissible hours, educational requirements, excluded occupations, and other employment-related variables. She identified each state's factory inspectors. She listed penalties—generally fines—for breaking each law.

Because the handbooks identified Goldmark as their compiler—rather than author—readers may assume that the material was a simple compendium rather than an expression of the publication secretary's values (Goldmark 1907, 1908, front cover). Nothing could be further from the truth. While she did an exhaustive job of tracking down and recording laws, she made no pretense at value neutrality. She analyzed laws in terms of which were "best" and "effective" (Goldmark 1908, 19 and 58). She argued that society and its institutions would have to change if the laws were to have an impact on children, saying at one point, "No law enforces itself" (Goldmark 1908, 58). She discussed how education would have to shift; schools needed to offer a curriculum "which appeals to the parents as worth having, in lieu of the wages which the children are forbidden to earn" (Goldmark 1908, 58).

Goldmark's work made her part of a reform network that also included several other members of her family. At the New York Consumers League, Pauline, the sibling closest to her in age, was trying to limit child labor in canneries. Her brother-in-law Felix Adler was chair of the newly formed National Child Labor Committee whose offices also were located at 105 E. 22nd Street.

Her work honed Josephine Goldmark's belief in the importance of enacting laws to create just employment systems. She also discovered a methodology to reach that goal. Her approach was through experimentation and empirical fact-finding that would convince legislators, judges, and other authoritative decision makers of the need for change. In a 1904 article on working children, she argued that child labor was bad for children and bad for society. She noted that some people believed that selling newspapers helped build a boy's character. Although it is clear she did not agree, she did not recoil from that assertion. Instead, she suggested that people needed to test the assumption with empirical evidence. She studied the percentage of former newsboys, messengers, and peddlers in reformatories as compared with their rate in the population as a whole to see if it was higher or lower. When she found that the percentage of such boys in reformatories was high, she considered that one piece of evidence to rebut the character assertion. She believed that eventually if enough evidence showed the problems created by youthful employment, legislation for change would come. She assumed investigation yielded usable knowledge to produce a win-win solution for the poor and society at large (Goldmark 1904).

The need to gather facts was a given among Progressive-era reformers. Kelley stressed the importance of gathering facts in the campaign for child-labor laws (e.g., National Child Labor Committee 1909). Jane Addams wrote to Josephine to agree with her "view of the value of the wide-spread evidence" (1909).

But a stress on gathering facts was not unique to the NCL and its allies in the war against child labor. Empirical fact-finding was also central to Frederick Taylor's (1947) then hot-off-the-press theory of shop management. He believed that investigation of work routines would produce usable knowledge to increase efficiency and fashion a win-win solution for business and labor. Starting in 1908, Goldmark would amalgamate insights from both NCL and shop-management techniques in her next—and most important—labor-law assignment.

In Defense of Labor

In fall 1907, the Oregon Consumers League contacted Kelley about the need to work on a case defending an Oregon law that prohibited women employed in factories and laundries from working more than ten hours a day. Because Josephine was Kelley's "most trusted adviser at this time," she was consulted on what strategy to use (Paper 1983, 162).

The facts of the case were simple and uncontested. The state of Oregon arrested Curt Muller who ran a laundry where women worked more than ten hours a day. After losing his case in state court, Muller appealed to the United States Supreme Court on the grounds that the state law interfered with his workers' rights to make whatever contracts they chose.

Muller had some precedent on his side. Two years previously the Court had struck down a New York law prohibiting bakers—male or female—to work more than ten hours a day. Citing a doctrine of substantive due process, the majority of the justices had affirmed that workers had a constitutional right to make whatever contracts they chose to sell their labor. As bakers were no stupider than other people, the state could not decide for them which contracts to make. It could not limit their choices (*Lochner v. New York* 198 U.S. 45).

For Josephine, this argument lacked any connection to the real world of manual labor where worker options were few. Yet she was optimistic that the line of reasoning need not prevail if defenders of protective legislation took the right approach. Immediately after the Lochner decision, she had written an article for the *American Journal of Sociology* in which she made two important points. She noted that the Court had not found New York's law to violate individual contract rights per se but rather the law had "been held to infringe upon the individual right of contract *without good cause*" [italics in the original] (Goldmark 1905, 322). In addition, four justices had dissented from the majority view, showing that difference of opinion existed on the Court itself. She saw the proper strategy as convincing at least one justice that states had good cause to restrict hours. That could be done by collecting material demonstrating a connection between long hours and danger to workers' health and safety. Factual evidence about long hours' real-world consequences would win the day. As Goldmark noted later, the health impacts of fatigue had not protected workers, "just because they have been unknown to those persons who could have benefited most directly: the legislators who frame the law" (1912, 10).

For counsel, Josephine recruited her brother-in-law, Louis Brandeis. On November 14, 1907, she and Kelley went to Massachusetts to meet with him. He and Alice were then living at 6 Otis Place near the Charles River. He agreed to take the case if Oregon's attorney general would identify him as the state's counsel and if Goldmark would research the brief with the approach she had suggested in her article (Sklar 1997; Paper 1983).

Kelley contacted Oregon, which accepted Brandeis as state counsel. Josephine began research in the New York Public and Columbia University libraries—the very same locales where much of the preparation for this article was done.

The Goldmark-Brandeis Brief

Early-twentieth-century legal thought conceived the law as an enclosed system of axioms derived primarily from judicial precedent. Using these axioms, judges could deduce specific rules for each case, thus creating an internally complete system (Fisher et al. 1993). Into this elegant fiction, Goldmark introduced real-world chaos. She showed what actually happens when women endure long hours at monotonous physical labor. Her work on the child-labor handbooks had taught her how to track and report statutes. Now she amassed over 100 pages of quotations from physicians, state labor bureaus, legislative committees, and other people and institutions who had explored the consequences of long hours in England, France, Germany, and Denmark as well as America. Her quotations spanned the years from the early part of the nineteenth century to her own day.

The thrust of this evidence was that long hours were problematic both for women and society at large. They robbed women of their health by causing eyestrain, leg problems, miscarriages, and a general lowering of resistance to disease. They fostered accidents. Their negative impact on women was even stronger than on men because of female physiognomy, a connection between overwork during pregnancy and infant mortality, and woman's double burden—when she returned from work, she still had to complete her domestic chores (Goldmark 1912, 135–260).

The picture of laundry work was brutal (Goldmark 1912, 490–493). Workers stood throughout their twelve- or even thirteen-hour labor in a hot, humid room, causing feet and legs to swell. After several hours repeating the same motions, fatigue set in. At that point the women had to be constantly on their guard not to relax their concentration for a moment. If they did, the machines might catch their fingers, causing horrible burns.

The irony was that long days were a losing proposition. They were necessary neither for profits nor for adequate wages. Efficiency would actually rise with shorter hours; the quality of goods would improve leading to fewer spoiled items (Goldmark 1912, 345–395). Higher efficiency would bring higher profits and greater compensation even with shorter labor time.

For modern readers, two caveats must be noted about the brief. When Goldmark liberally sprinkled her work with talk of facts, she did not mean results of random experiments comparing worker health in ten- and twelve-hour laundries. Such evidence did not exist. By facts, she meant the opinions of people who had investigated life in low-skill occupations. Sometimes her sources used statistical analysis as in a discussion of accidents tending to occur at the end of shifts (Goldmark 1912, 192). Sometimes her sources were anecdotal. Josephine had a broad conception of the kind of data that might be useful to her case. By facts, she meant moving from "the purely legal defense of these laws" to "the empirical testimony of the working woman's physician, the factory inspector, and the economist" (Goldmark 1912, 249–250). Modern readers with a penchant for quantitative research would find her evidential standards a tad too lenient. She explicitly noted that in getting facts "the cumulative recorded social experience of mankind plays as great a role as the more exact definitions and laws of the sciences" (Goldmark 1918, A19).

In addition, her talk about female weakness is bound to grate on contemporary ears as a reinforcement of gender stereotypes. A comparison of female and male knee physiognomy for purposes of ascertaining who can stand for eleven hours sounds strange today. What shall we make of the anachronistic tenor of the argument from physique? First, it shows the short shelf-life of some social expertise. Second, in Goldmark's defense, readers must remember that she was not writing an intellectual tract. She was engaged in defending a law that singled out women for protection. Part of her task was to show that this restriction made sense. Some of the evidence she offered did come from the experience of male workers and it is clear from her presentation that she preferred that men too had shorter work days. That outcome was not on the table; in Oregon the justices could either protect women or nobody.[2]

In February 1908, a unanimous Supreme Court ruled that Oregon's ten-hour law was constitutional. Although Goldmark's evidence had not formed part of the original trial-court record and Curt Muller had had no opportunity to cross-examine her sources, the Court accepted the arguments in Goldmark's research. The decision paved the way for other states to pass laws protecting working people.

Goldmark was now chair of the NCL's newly created committee on legislation and legal defense of labor. With a grant from the Russell Sage Foundation, she prepared an even longer brief defending in state court Illinois' ten-hour law designed to protect women in factories and laundries (*Ritchie v. Wayman, et al.*, 244 Ill., 509). Once again a court faced with one of her evidential briefs upheld a statute restricting permissible labor time. In an article urging the Illinois legislature to extend the law to women who worked in shops, Goldmark (1910) attributed this victory to the strength of the evidence she had put before the court. The opinion itself noted that judges could not ignore in court facts they knew to be true outside the judicial setting.

The Factory Investigating Commission

On March 25, 1911, 146 workers—most of them young women—died when fire broke out in their littered workplace at the Triangle Shirtwaist Company in downtown Manhattan. In response to one of the worst industrial tragedies in New York's history, the state created a nine-person commission to investigate factory conditions. State Senator Robert F. Wagner and state Assembly member Alfred E. Smith were designated chairman and vice-chairman, respectively. In fall 1911, the commission held fifty-nine hearings in cities throughout the state. Because these hearings afforded an unprecedented opportunity for reformers to catch policymakers' attention, people close to the NCL—including Josephine and Pauline Goldmark, Florence Kelley, and Felix Adler—gave testimony on how the authorities could improve worker health and safety. Among the many other witnesses were Lillian Wald of the Henry Street Settlement and Henry Bruere of the New York Bureau of Municipal Research.

Josephine's testimony centered on the need for a flat prohibition on working more than ten hours a day and a ban on factory work by women after 9 P.M. She was particularly emphatic that laws should not allow any exemptions such as for busy seasons. Such exemptions made it almost impossible to police firms adequately (New York State 1912, 1605). Along with her remarks she gave the commissioners copies of her Oregon and Illinois briefs. In response to her testimony, the commission recommended that the New York State legislature pass a law prohibiting female factory employment between 10 P.M. and 6 A.M.

Scientific Management

In 1912, Goldmark prepared a book to present the modern study of fatigue as a basis for labor legislation. This book, *Fatigue and Efficiency*, would not only encapsulate the various opinions on the health dangers she had quoted in the court briefs; it would also address the role of efficiency in halting long hours. She showed the manuscript to her sister Pauline and to Florence Kelley, both of whom made editing suggestions.

Josephine agreed with Louis Brandeis (1913) that increased efficiency was the only way out of the overwork problem. Brandeis had become aware of the possibilities inherent in Frederick Taylor's shop management when he used its insights to argue against a rate increase for eastern railroads in 1910. He contended that efficient railroads would not need a rate increase. American railroads could become more efficient if they adopted Taylor's system, which Brandeis coined "scientific management" (Mason 1946, 240–241).

Goldmark devoted a whole chapter to the new science of management. Her analysis in chapter seven presented a guardedly optimistic picture of how Taylor's work could ameliorate worker fatigue. Shop management gave empirical evidence that speed and long hours were not the keys to productivity as business owners had thought for so long. At the Simonds plant and elsewhere, Taylor (1947) found that forcing workers actually decreased productivity while rest periods increased their efficiency. Goldmark realized that some managers could pervert shop management's mechanical devices, such as timing work, to exploit employees. While she was not always happy with how factories used shop management, she believed the theory in the right hands had enormous potential for good. She embraced this system that was attempting to move away from traditional strategies of driving workers and instead was taking employee health and long-term efficiency into account. She believed that shop management showed that efficiency was "no obstacle or check" to shorter hours "but rather an incentive" (Goldmark 1912, 210). Scientific study of work operations had already changed machinery in ways that minimized fatigue while increasing output. In a 1913 article, Goldmark discussed how a scientific-management study of work in thirty-one Milwaukee laundries led to lowering the treadles of ironing machines which accomplished both the result of less fatigue and increased productivity—thus creating a win-win situation for owners and employees.

Her book received keen attention and high praise in the reform community. Kelley pronounced it a "fundamental work" (1914, 71). Columbia University economics professor Henry Seager, a leading proponent of social insurance programs, crowed that her argument was hard to refute because it was "so exhaustively fortified with facts" (1912). Progressive business leaders cited her work in explaining their shift to shorter hours and rest periods (e.g., Feiss 1916).

The Schweinler Case

In 1913, with Robert Wagner and Al Smith's leadership, the New York State legislature passed a number of laws the factory investigating commission had proposed. These statutes mandated fire drills and automatic sprinklers as well as a prohibition on employing women in factories between 10 P.M. and 6 A.M. (New York State 1914).

Shortly after the passage of these laws, Charles Schweinler was arrested for assigning women to night work at his bookbinding plant, Schweinler Press (*People of the State of New York v. Schweinler Press,* 214 N.Y. 395). When he appealed his conviction on right-to-make-a-contract grounds, Brandeis (1913) and Goldmark sprung into action, he as a lawyer and she as author of another brief with masses of opinion, this time on the deleterious health effects of long night work for women. Her depictions of the hard life and frequent unemployment of women in the bookbinding industry relied on research done by the Russell Sage Foundation's Mary Van Kleeck (1913). When the court ruled against Schweinler, Goldmark declared, "Facts have won again" (1914, 450).

Members of the reform community agreed that Goldmark's work had been crucial in sustaining protective labor legislation. The economist Henry Raymond Mussey (1910) said that only her remarkable work made possible sustaining the Oregon and Illinois laws. The secretary to the New York State Factory Investigating Commission praised Goldmark's splendid evidential contributions to the campaign to limit worker hours (Pike 1912, 271–299).

Yet on the cover of the briefs she wrote, Goldmark did not get all the recognition that her contribution warranted. One problem in researching early-twentieth-century public administration women is that many of them held staff rather than line positions; their names did not appear on work in which they played a major part. A woman's contribution was often presented in a way that deflected attention from her and onto "the man with the title" (Guy 2000, 8).

Goldmark faced an attenuated version of this problem with her briefs from Muller to Schweinler. She had formulated the strategic direction needed to win the cases. She researched the evidence. Yet as Brandeis was the attorney, the title page of the brief identified its authors as "Louis Brandeis assisted by Josephine Goldmark" (1908, 1913).

A more accurate statement of authorship would omit the phrase "assisted by." Goldmark's (1912) own book on fatigue identified the briefs' authors as Brandeis and Goldmark without any "assisted by" added. In our day, many analyses refer to the authors as Brandeis and Goldmark (e.g., Alchon 1992; Fisher et al. 1993, 237–241; Greenwald 1980, 259) although some writers speak simply, if erroneously, of the Brandeis briefs (e.g., Paper 1983, 165). In this case, part of the problem in gaining Goldmark proper twenty-first-century recognition may stem from Brandeis's name already having popular resonance from his service as a Supreme Court justice.

Labor in Wartime

When America entered World War I in 1917, some business owners argued that the time of sacrifice required rescinding shorter hours in the name of maximum productivity. The federal Council of National Defense in cooperation with the United States Public Health Service asked Goldmark to investigate the actual relation of hours and efficiency in wartime factories. She worked with Mary Hopkins, a friend since Bryn Mawr days who had helped her translate and arrange materials for the Schweinler brief.

They concluded that factory experiments showed that shorter hours did not erode production. They actually increased efficiency if companies instituted change as part of a scientific overhaul of work. Companies could cut hours and yet overall productivity per worker still rose. Hopkins noted that "maximum output is attained only by fresh and vigorous workers" (1917, 159). A return to eleven- or twelve-hour days would hurt rather than help the war effort!

The wartime study showed Goldmark once again a link between shop management and labor reform. The connection led her to join the Taylor Society, an organization formed shortly after Taylor's 1915 death to disseminate his ideas. She was one of a group of reform women who were inducted in 1919. Among the first nonengineers to enter the organization, the group of women included her sister Pauline, Florence Kelley, and Mary Van Kleeck. Harlow Person, the society president, welcomed them by stating explicitly that the organization needed more than engineers. It needed all "those whose general interests . . . lead them to develop an interest in scientific management as a factor in industrial and social progress" (1919, 2). In the 1920s, the Taylor Society became a venue for exploring labor reform and the use of legislation limiting hours and night work to protect women workers.

Public-Health Nursing

After World War I, Josephine turned her attention to improving the administration of nursing. In December 1918, the Rockefeller Foundation called a conference on how to develop public-health nursing in the United States. An eighteen-member committee, chaired by Dr. Charles Winslow, professor of public health at Yale University, was appointed to explore the topic. The committee asked Goldmark to conduct the investigation because of her eminent social-research achievements (Committee for the Study of Nursing Education 1923). She received her appointment in June 1919 and started work in October of that year.

Once again Goldmark's research was "prompted by the desire to obtain authentic, impartial information" as a prelude to improving a social situation (1923, 33). This time her strategy involved intensive study of how 164 public-health nurses in 49 different organizations performed their work. She recruited other nurses to follow her selected sample and record their actions as they visited low-income families in rural and urban settings. Her ensuing report included rich narratives on specific visits along with statistical generalizations, such as number of nurses per supervisor and hours worked per day. Roberts (1954) noted that even thirty years after it appeared, Goldmark's report remained the definitive study in the area, the only broad-based analysis of public-health nursing based on observation of a large group of nurses going about day-to-day activities.

An interesting point in the report involved the relationship between physicians and public-health nurses, a relationship that offered nurses greater autonomy than they had in any other specialization. In hospitals, nurses worked under a doctor's supervision. They followed physician orders rather than telling patients what kind of care was appropriate for them. The public-health nurse, however, faced a wide range of situations where it was her job to suggest which hospital or what kind of help a client should seek. One duty was even to protect patients from lapses in preventive care by doctors. As Goldmark noted "in teaching prevention of disease . . . and in arousing community interest in public health measures . . . a wide range of opportunities has been opened up . . . in which the ordinary rules of professional etiquette do not apply" (1923, 128–129). The public-health nurses—at that time almost certainly 100 percent female—had a rare chance to be autonomous professionals.

Because Goldmark often stressed the importance of efficiency, it is useful to note that, for her, this concept entailed responsiveness to the situation rather than a blind reliance on providing more of a given action. At one point in the report, she compared two nurses—one who made five visits a day and the other who made twelve—and concluded that the first woman gave more efficient service. The second saw additional patients but spent too little time to teach them how to care for themselves and improve their situation; to Goldmark she provided "a parody of public-health nursing" (1923, 112).

The study concluded that America would benefit from better-educated public-health nurses and the creation of a second tier of trained subsidiary nurses to handle routine chores. Nurse education programs needed university affiliations with public-health courses to prepare practitioners in that field. A direct outcome of the report was the creation of Yale University's nursing school, which from its start emphasized public-health nursing (Benson 1987). Most nursing programs, however, continued to have hospital, rather than university, affiliations.

Later Years

In the 1920s, the NCL's influence and membership declined. One reason was that in the immediate aftermath of World War I, politicians "red-baited" it along with other Progressive organizations. But the group also sealed its own fate by failing to broaden its membership base beyond the socioeconomic elite (Wolfe 1975). The organization's coordinators, such as Goldmark, wanted to help unskilled labor but, unlike trade-union leaders, they were not themselves factory operatives. As trade unions grew, they produced indigenous worker-leaders who took over some of the League's lobbying functions.

One of the last NCL projects on which Goldmark worked with Florence Kelley was to publicize the problem of radium poisoning among women dial painters at U.S. Radium Corporation in New Jersey. Although laboratory chemists at the plant protected themselves from radium with screens, no care was given to shield the factory workers from what Goldmark called a "lethal, industrial poison" (1953, 203–204). On the contrary, managers told the women to use their lips to guide their brushes in painting dials with the substance. Kelley and Goldmark publicized the heartless treatment the firm meted the women as their bones dissolved from radium poisoning. In 1928, they helped to get a settlement for five very ill former workers who had sued the firm. The ability of an outraged public opinion to prod the settlement pleased Goldmark as an expression of a kind of democracy.

In the last decades of her life, Josephine retired to live with her sister Pauline in Hartsdale, a Westchester County suburb located about an hour's drive from New York City. The two women shared an unusual number of interests—family, labor reform, hiking in the Adirondacks. Neither woman had ever married—a common occurrence at that time among women with lifelong careers. But Josephine's exit from full-time employment hardly equaled a retirement from the life of the mind or the sphere of public service. On a 1937 Bryn Mawr alumnae survey she answered yes to the question: Do you administer the household? She answered no to the question: Is it your chief occupation?

Volunteer activities became one path for service. In 1937, she was a NCL vice-president, a member of the board of directors of the Henry Street Visiting Nurse Service and chair of the board's education committee, and an advisory council member of the American Association for Labor Legislation. She was also an alumna member of the board of directors of the Byrn Mawr

Summer School for Women Workers. Through this program, the university made $250 stipends available to female factory workers to study liberal arts for a summer at the college. Inaugurated in the 1920s, the summer school was later attacked by the university's board of trustees as too radical and petered out in 1938 (Heller 1984).

Equally likely her chief occupation was writing—the only leisure-time activity she listed on the alumnae survey. In the Depression decade, at a time when many people were turning to the extremes of communism or fascism, her two major books dealt with the human passion for democracy. In 1930, Yale University Press published *Pilgrims of '48,* her account of her father's fight for freedom in 1848 Austria. In 1936, Goldmark wrote a survey of *Democracy in Denmark.* She chose this topic because she felt a kinship with decisions the Danes had made about their society. In particular she appreciated their path for creating an educated citizenry in all economic strata. She stressed the importance to their democracy of affording ample educational opportunities even where people had to leave the regular school system to earn a living in farms and factories. In aim, the Danish folk schools had similarities with Bryn Mawr's summer school for workers where she served as an alumna representative. She saw the difference in the fate of the Bryn Mawr summer school project and the folk school network which Danish society embraced.

Her picture of Danish life gave some sense of the kind of polity she would have welcomed in the United States—a society that eliminated extreme disparities of income and provided basic social security to all citizens. For such a society she had labored all her life.

Josephine Goldmark died in White Plains Hospital of a heart attack on December 15, 1950. At the time of her death, she was writing a biography of Florence Kelley. The University of Illinois Press published the book posthumously in 1953 under the title *Impatient Crusader.*

Legacy

Narratives on the birth of public administration as an academic offering stress that the field emerged, at least in part, from people who deployed Frederick Taylor's shop-management insights in the public sector. The fledgling Progressive-era field expanded Taylor's assertion that scientific research could improve work into public agencies, keeping shop-management's high valuation of efficiency and rationality. The New York Bureau of Municipal Research (BMR), an early organization that tried to use shop-management insights to improve public agencies, is often cited in present-day texts as a progenitor of the public administration field.

Goldmark used shop-management insights to change the scope of the public sector, particularly in showing how organizational research could affect legislation and judicial decisions. Like other NCL administrators, Goldmark published in the same journals and appeared at the same conferences as leaders of New York's BMR; she championed a facts-based approach to social investigation that was similar to theirs. She might therefore seem a natural addition to public administration histories. Indeed, her inclusion would have two consequences for chapters on Progressive-era origins of the field.

First, including her endeavors with those of the BMR would portend greater understanding on which people used shop management in the Progressive era and for what purposes (Schachter 2002). Goldmark's interests clash with a popular picture of scientific management as a theory of economic motivation or worker disenfranchisement. The BMR published material on how to improve agency accounting as well as how to expand social functions such as school health. Public administration narratives that want to separate shop management and social reform can highlight the first type of publication and still feature the BMR in the Progressive-era pantheon. But all Goldmark's early research centered on social reform. Adding her endeavors to public administration texts would show a clear nexus between scientific management and social change. Indeed, the few times when public administration narratives do mention her work, the aim is sketching a relationship between Taylorism and Progressive politics (e.g., Martin 1989, 197).

Adding her biography would also broaden the demographic canvas in our accounts of Progressive-era public administration. Stillman (1998) has described the Protestant influence on several key reformers, including Frederick Taylor, who shaped the modern administrative world. While Goldmark did not follow traditional Jewish ritual, she did learn about and reflect on Jewish history and theology with members of her family (e.g., T. Goldmark 1912). Her inclusion in the Progressive pantheon would add a moral reformer from the Jewish tradition with its own social-justice fulcrum.

Josephine Goldmark had great optimism about the gains research could bring the poor. She saw science as a weapon in the battle for justice. She believed efficiency and justice were complementary goals; industrial societies could have both or neither. First, scientific inquiry would augment efficiency. Next, increased efficiency would then produce industrial justice.

For many people today those claims sound naïve—as naïve as her insisting that people of good will should agree on the facts as she presented them and that these facts would dictate a particular policy outcome. But her vocabulary and reasoning should be evaluated in relation to her purpose as well as the philosophical underpinnings of her methods. Goldmark could not conjure change by fiat. To spur reform she needed to convince decision makers to support her proposals. Her recourse to a vocabulary of facts and science brought recognition from decision makers such as legislators and judges whose actions she needed to propel reform. Her appeals to what we may see as a naïve science gave political figures a reason to approve change at a time when business leaders argued that they needed eleven- to thirteen-hour work days to produce profits. Her approach to research may have been epistemologically naïve but it was incredibly successful in spurring social reform. She hit the right buttons to set change in action. Perhaps only a naïveté as deep as hers could have confronted a system where companies demanded long days of labor and convinced a panel of justices that the time had come to sanction change.

Notes

1. Born in Louisville, Kentucky, in 1856, Brandeis became a prominent Boston lawyer with significant trade-union sympathies. In 1916, President Woodrow Wilson appointed him to the United States Supreme Court, where he was a strong advocate of individual rights. He retired from the bench in February 1939.

2. By the 1920s, reform ranks were split on the benefits of women-only protective laws. The National Women's Party opposed them on the ground that they compromised equality. Most trade-union women, the National Consumers League, and the Taylor Society supported such legislation. See, for example, Gilbreth et al. (1926).

References

Addams, Jane. 1909. Personal communication to Josephine Goldmark, December 10. Available in the Josephine and Pauline Goldmark Papers, Schlesinger Library, Radcliffe Institute for Advanced Study, Harvard University, Cambridge, MA.

Alchon, Guy. 1992. "Mary Van Kleeck and Scientific Management." In *A Mental Revolution: Scientific Management since Taylor,* ed. Daniel Nelson, 102–129. Columbus: Ohio State University Press.

Benson, Evelyn. 1987. "Josephine Goldmark (1877–1950): A Biographical Sketch." *Public Health Nursing* 4, no. 1: 48–51.

Brandeis, Louis. 1913. Personal communication to John Graham Brooks. June 3. Available in John Graham Brooks Papers, Schlesinger Library, Radcliffe Institute for Advanced Study, Harvard University, Cambridge, MA.

Brandeis, Louis, assisted by Josephine Goldmark. 1908. *Women in Industry: Brief for the State of Oregon.* New York: National Consumers League.

Brandeis, Louis, assisted by Josephine Goldmark. 1913. *Court of Special Sessions of the City of New York. The People of the State of New York against Charles Schweinler Press: A Summary of "Facts of Knowledge" Submitted on Behalf of the People in Support of Its Brief on the Law.* New York: R.H. Tyrrel.

Carter, Irl. 1986. "Goldmark, Pauline Dorothea." In *Biographical Dictionary of Social Welfare of America,* ed. Walter Trattner, 330–332. Westport, CT: Greenwood Press.

Committee for the Study of Nursing Education. 1923. *Nursing and Nursing Education in the United States.* New York: Macmillan.

Feiss, Richard. 1916. "Scientific Management and Its Relation to the Health of the Worker." *Bulletin of the Taylor Society* 2:11–13.

Fisher, William III; Morton Horowitz; and Thomas Reed, eds. 1993. *American Legal Realism.* New York: Oxford University Press.

Gilbreth, Lillian; Pauline Goldmark; and Mary Van Kleeck. 1926. "The Women's Industrial Conference." *Bulletin of the Taylor Society* 11, no. 1: 40–42.

Goldmark, Josephine. 1904. "Street Labor and Juvenile Delinquency." *Political Science Quarterly* 19, no. 3: 417–438.

———. 1905. "The Necessary Sequel of Child-Labor Laws." *American Journal of Sociology* 11, no. 3: 312–325.

———. 1907. *Child Labor Legislation.* Philadelphia: American Academy of Political and Social Science.

———. 1908. *Child Labor Legislation.* Philadelphia: American Academy of Political and Social Science.

———. 1910. "The Illinois Ten-Hour Decision." *Academy of Political Science Proceedings* I, no. 1: 185–187.

———. 1912. *Fatigue and Efficiency: A Study in Industry.* New York: Charities Publication Committee.

———. 1913. "Waste." *The Survey* 30 (December 6): 273–274.

———. 1914. "New York Nightwork Law for Women Upheld." *The Survey* 32 (August 1): 450.

———. 1918. "Introduction." In Brandeis, Louis, assisted by Josephine Goldmark. *Court of Special Sessions of the City of New York. The People of the State of New York against Charles Schweinler Press: A Summary of "Facts of Knowledge" Submitted on Behalf of the People in Support of Its Brief on the Law: The Case Against Night Work for Women.* New York: National Consumers League.

———. 1923. "Report of a Survey of Nursing and Nursing Education." In Committee for the Study of Nursing Education, *Nursing and Nursing Education in the United States*, 33–585. New York: Macmillan.

———. 1930. *Pilgrims of '48: One Man's Part in the Austrian Revolution of 1848 and a Family Migration to America.* New Haven, CT: Yale University Press.

———. 1936. *Democracy in Denmark. Part I: Democracy in Action.* Washington, DC: National Home Library Foundation.

———. 1953. *Impatient Crusader: Florence Kelley's Life Story.* Urbana: University of Illinois Press.

Goldmark, Pauline. n.d. "Keene Valley Reminiscences." Unpublished manuscript available in the Goldmark Family Papers, Rare Book and Manuscript Library, Columbia University, NY.

———. n.d. "The Summer of 1890." Unpublished manuscript available in the Goldmark Family Papers, Rare Book and Manuscript Library, Columbia University, NY.

Goldmark, Theodore. 1912. Personal communication to Josephine Goldmark, December 10. Available in Goldmark Family Papers, Rare Book and Manuscript Library, Columbia University, NY.

Greenwald, Maurine Weiner. 1980. *Women, War and Work: The Impact of World War I on Women Workers in the United States.* Westport, CT: Greenwood Press.

Guy, Mary. 2000. "The Amazing Miss Burchfield." *Public Administration Review* 60, no. 1: 6–19.

Heller, Rita. 1984. "Blue Collars and Bluestockings: The Bryn Mawr Summer School for Women Workers, 1921–1938." In *Sisterhood and Solidarity: Worker's Education for Women, 1914–1984*, ed. Joyce Kornbluh and Mary Frederickson, 109–145. Philadelphia: Temple University Press.

Hopkins, Mary. 1917. "An Experiment in Hours." *New Republic* 11, no. 136 (June 9): 157–159.

Kelley, Florence. 1908. "Introduction." In *Child Labor Legislation*, compiled by Josephine Goldmark, 1–4. Philadelphia: American Academy of Political and Social Science.

———. 1914. *Modern Industry in Relation to the Family, Health, Education, Morality.* New York: Longmans, Green.

Martin, Daniel 1989. *The Guide to the Foundations of Public Administration.* New York: Marcel Dekker.

Mason, Alpheus. 1946. *Brandeis: A Free Man's Life.* New York: Viking.

Muncy, Robyn. 1991. *Creating a Female Dominion in American Reform, 1890–1935.* New York: Oxford University Press.

Mussey, Henry Raymond, ed. 1910. *The Economic Position of Women.* New York: Academy of Political Science in the City of New York.

National Child Labor Committee. 1909. *The Federal Children's Bureau: A Symposium.* New York: Author.

New York State. 1912. *Preliminary Report of the Factory Investigating Commission.* Albany: Argus.

———. 1914. *Third Report of the Factory Investigating Commission.* Albany: J.B. Lyon.

Novey, Joelle. 1997. "'One Aim and Concentrated Purpose': M. Carey Thomas as Daring Visionary and Flawed Reformer." *Concord Review* 7, no. 3: 181–207.

Paper, Lewis. 1983. *Brandeis.* Englewood Cliffs, NJ: Prentice-Hall.

Park, Marion Edwards. 1951. "Josephine Goldmark." *Bryn Mawr Alumnae Bulletin* 31, no. 2: 16–17.

Person, Harlow. 1919. "The Opportunities and Obligations of the Taylor Society." *Bulletin of the Taylor Society* 4, no. 1: 1–7.

Pike, Violet. 1912. "Women Workers in Factories in New York State." In State of New York, *Preliminary Report of the Factory Investigating Commission.* Albany: Argus.

Roberts, Mary. 1954. *American Nursing: History and Interpretation.* New York: Macmillan.

Schachter, Hindy Lauer. 2002. "Women, Progressive-Era Reform and Scientific Management." *Administration and Society* 34, no. 5: 563–578.

Seager, Henry. 1912. Personal communication to Josephine Goldmark, August 20. Available in the Josephine and Pauline Goldmark Papers, Schlesinger Library, Radcliffe Institute for Advanced Study, Harvard University, Cambridge, MA.

Sklar, Kathryn Kish. 1997. "Josephine Goldmark." In *Jewish Women in America,* ed. Paula Hyman and Deborah Dash Moore, 531–532. New York: Routledge.

Stillman, Richard. 1998. *Creating the American State: The Moral Reformers and the Modern Administrative World They Made.* Tuscaloosa: University of Alabama Press.

Taylor, Frederick. [1903] 1947. *Shop Management.* New York: Harper and Row.

Van Kleeck, Mary. 1913. *Women in the Bookbinding Trade.* New York: Russell Sage Foundation.

Wolfe, Allis Rosenberg. 1975. "Women, Consumerism, and the National Consumers League in the Progressive Era, 1900–1923." *Labor History* 16, no. 3: 378–392.

3

Mary Livermore

A Legacy of Caring and Cooperative Womanhood in Service to the State

Patricia M. Shields

Introduction

Two years before her death in 1905, Mary Ashton Rice Livermore addressed the New England Anti-Imperialist League in words that rang with the passion of a life lived in service to the public:

> I have for half a century been slowly, with the company of other women, trying to obtain for women the . . . right to vote, to have a voice in representation, and to effect something. . . . I ask that the Declaration of Independence shall be exercised upon me and upon women generally—that we may be allowed to be represented. Then, my brothers, we could help you men. We cannot do much now.[1]

Livermore's life belied the notion that women had not been able to "do much." She had been helping men (and women) all her life.

Although best known by some for her contributions as a nineteenth-century American journalist, lecturer, and suffragist, others knew Livermore best for her significant contributions to the public welfare as a nurse in hospitals on the front lines of the Civil War and a public administrator with the Sanitary Commission of the U.S. Army. Indeed, her experiences while serving as the associate director of the commission's Northwestern Branch during the Civil War would birth her passionate devotion to women's rights. Her work would hone her ability to make distant events come alive for her audience, and provide an opportunity for her to lead what she would later describe as "the first example of cooperative womanhood serving the state" (Livermore 1891, 186).

In her four years at the Sanitary Commission, Mary Livermore ran the Chicago office, supervised the delivery of supplies to Civil War battlefield hospitals, and participated in policy and planning at the national level. Presidential fiat created the commission in response to the need for an administrative logistical arm to collect medical supply donations, transport them to warehouses, transform them into bedding and bandages, and move the supplies from warehouses to the front lines. But it was the women's aid societies that provided the supplies and it was women at the commission branch offices who managed the logistical machinations from source to battlefront. Mary Livermore ranked high among the leaders at the commission and the caregivers in the field. She would then and later tell the story of what she saw and the profound effect of the war on the society that shaped her and that she would, in turn, shape.

Livermore also raised money through speaking engagements to support the effort. Her gift for describing remote hospital conditions and her compelling depiction of the needs of the soldiers made her a popular and effective fundraiser. In fact, the work of "the ladies" touched the heart of President Abraham Lincoln so deeply that he was moved to contribute the original Emancipation Proclamation document to an auction Livermore spearheaded to support the relief efforts.

Mary Livermore would later reflect on the significance of the Civil War—and the commission's work—as a catalyst for new perceptions about women's ability to act in concert with each other for a common public purpose. Though the precise words "public administration" permeated neither her writing nor her life, the nobility of a caring attention to those in need of assistance certainly did.

To appreciate her contributions and courage in the face of society's narrow view of women's role in the public realm requires a look at her life and times. And it is to her early life that we now turn.

Early Years

Mary Ashton Rice Livermore was born in 1820 in Boston to Timothy Rice, a Welsh laborer, and Zebiah Ashton, the daughter of an English sea captain. Her father's strict Calvinistic religion instilled in Mary a powerful faith and motivated her to "search for something that freed her from the haunting specter of eternal damnation" (Silber 1995, vi).

She received more schooling than was typical for a woman of her era. At sixteen, she graduated from a female seminary and taught there for two years. At nineteen, she became a tutor to several children on a Virginia plantation. In Virginia, she experienced literature, refinement, and the barbarity of sla-

very. Three years later she returned to New England a "pronounced abolitionist" (Silber 1995, vi).

She subsequently met and married Daniel Parker Livermore, an ardent
abolitionist and minister in the Universalist Church. She was attracted to his
religion of hope and love, which contrasted sharply with the pessimistic vision of her father. The couple traveled throughout the Northeast working for
the church, raised three daughters, and in 1858 moved to Chicago. Here,
Daniel owned and edited *The New Covenant,* a Universalist journal. Mary
contributed as an associate editor and reporter (Bolton 1886, 55).

At the start of the Civil War, the forty-year-old Mary was well poised to
administer the Chicago branch of the Sanitary Commission. For her time,
she was better educated and more widely traveled than her female peers.
Moreover, her reporter experience had exposed her to national politics. She
was passionately committed to the Union cause. Her husband and life partner encouraged her to step outside traditional female roles and enter the fray.

Birth of the Sanitary Commission

During the days that followed September 11, 2001, distraught Americans
generously gave money, time, and talent to relieve the suffering of the vic-
tims. This impulse to help in times of national crisis also pervaded the early,
dark days of the Civil War. Throughout the country, spontaneous gifts of
supplies poured forth. The uncoordinated relief efforts were a mixed blessing; although they brought some needed supplies, they often interfered with
the military's larger mission.[2]

The Army's Medical Bureau was ill prepared for the size and scope of the
battlefield medical crisis. During the Civil War, the Union Army had 650,000
casualties. Thirteen years earlier during the Mexican War, the United States
had 17,000 casualties. Thus, Union casualties were 38 times greater than
U.S. casualties during the Mexican War (World Almanac 2003, 209). Given
this order of magnitude, it is not surprising that the medical logistics system
for delivering personnel (nurses, doctors) and supplies proved woefully inadequate[3] and plagued by corruption.[4] The Sanitary Commission emerged to
address the dual problems of uncoordinated popular relief efforts and the
crisis created by an army overwhelmed by wounded and sick soldiers.

Early in the spring of 1861, relief organizations in New York met and
devised a plan to address both pressing problems. They conceived of a commission that would work with the Army Medical Bureau to coordinate relief
efforts and independently inspect army field medical facilities. They modeled their plan after the sanitary commission concept developed by the British after the Crimean War (Sanitary Commission [1864] 1972, 22).

The New York group, led by H.W. Bellows, traveled to the nation's capital and met, in May of 1861, with Medical Bureau Chief R.C. Wood. Although skeptical at first, Wood worked with the group and by June, President Lincoln had signed a document that ordered creation of a "Commission of Inquiry and Advice, in Respect of the Sanitary Interests of the United States Forces" (Sanitary Commission [1864] 1972, 7).

Among other tasks, the newly created commission was responsible for logistics functions that today reside as an essential activity in the military bureaucracy.[5] The Sanitary Commission was eventually responsible for the lion's share of the non-weapon-systems-related logistics.[6] And, remarkably, it "received no pecuniary support from the government" (Sanitary Commission [1864] 1972, 22).

Dr. Bellows, president of the Sanitary Commission, organized the agency into a decentralized system of eleven regional and state branches, which coordinated local relief efforts. Among other things, the branch offices became storage depots and distribution centers for the supplies provided by the 12,000 ladies' aid societies that were scattered throughout the Union (Sanitary Commission [1864] 1972, 261–283).[7]

Although the national leaders of the Sanitary Commission were men, all branch offices were "managed by women" (Livermore 1895, 588). Mary Livermore and her longstanding friend, Jane Hoge,[8] served as associate managers of the Northwestern Branch of the Sanitary Commission in Chicago (Sanitary Commission [1864] 1972, 279). In her work with the commission, Mary Livermore gained experience as a public administrator and contributed to the war effort.

Prior to the Civil War, the "ratio of soldiers killed in battle to died by disease was 1:4." The members of the Sanitary Commission were motivated by concern about the high death by disease rates during the Crimean War where "seven eights of the mortality of British troops were due to disease." The commission leadership believed that lack of sanitation and miserable field hospital conditions contributed to the unacceptably high mortality rate from disease. During the Civil War, "for every soldier that fell in battle only two died of disease—the splendid result of the [Sanitary] commission, which knew neither sect nor section, parties nor nationalities, in its life-saving and life-preserving activities" (Livermore 1895, 587). Today's performance measurement advocates would deem the Sanitary Commission an astounding success!

Headquarters

Although the public administration literature seldom describes the office environment of administrators, it is fundamental to the experience. Her Chi-

cago office was both the hub and depot for procuring and transporting supplies to the front lines of the Civil War. Mary Livermore shares the sights,
sounds and smells of her office in *My Story:*

> The headquarters of the Chicago, or "Northwest Sanitary Commission," as
> it was correctly re-christened . . . were the least attractive rooms in the city.
> . . . [The rooms] seemed smaller than they were, because they were gener-
> ally crowded with boxes and packages, huddled together to suit the conve-
> nience of those who opened, unpacked, assorted, stamped and repacked
> the contents. Drays were continually unloading and reloading with a furi-
> ous racket . . . the din was further increased by incessant hammering and
> pounding within, caused by opening and nailing of boxes. (Livermore
> [1887] 1995, 55–56)

In the crowded, sometimes chaotic, environment hundreds of volunteers
worked under their leaders' direction, coordinating and organizing activities
that redirected supplies to the field. Arriving fabric had to be transformed to
bedding, clothing for the sick, and bandages; important bulletins were written and sent.

> [Hence] The sewing rooms of the Commission were located in the room
> above us, where between 30 and 40 sewing-machines ran all day. The odors
> of the place were villainous and a perpetual torment. Codfish and sauer-
> kraut, pickles and ale, onions and potatoes, smoked salmon and halibut,
> ginger and whiskey . . . tobacco, kerosene . . . benzene . . . paint. . . . We
> called it the "perfume of the sanitary" and at last got used to it, as we did to
> the noise.
>   In these uninviting quarters the work of the Northwest Sanitary Com-
> mission was outlined or performed. Here were packed and shipped to the
> hospitals or battle-field 77,660 packages of sanitary supplies, whose cash
> value was $1,056,192.16. Here were written and mailed letters by the ten
> thousand, circulars by the hundred thousand, monthly bulletins and re-
> ports. (Livermore [1887] 1995, 156–157)

Field Work

The Chicago office was hundreds of miles from the war front and the hospitals that served the wounded. In order to gather information and ensure that
the correct supplies were reaching the sick and wounded, Mary Livermore
often went into the field. From the front lines, she sent to her husband vivid
reports, which were subsequently published.[9]

When the Union took the Mississippi in 1863, soldiers were encamped "amid the swamps, lagoons, bayous, and sloughs of the abominable portion of that country, known as the 'river-bottoms' " (Livermore [1887] 1995, 281). The camps soon became filled with sickness and suffering. Some 12,000 men were sick at one time; Chicago's location made it the hub for these relief efforts. Mary Livermore recounts: "Immense shipments of supplies were sent down on the sanitary boats, with men and women of executive ability, who attended to their safe transmission and equitable distribution. Accompanying these were special corps of relief accustomed to the work in hospitals, and possessed of physical endurance, able to encounter any horror of army life without blenching" (Livermore [1887] 1995, 281–282).

She was one of the relief workers who accompanied the 3,500 boxes of supplies. "It was with one of these shipments of sanitary stores, and as one of the relief corps, that I went down the Mississippi in March of 1863" (Livermore [1887] 1995, 282). She describes the work that was expected of the relief workers: "The programme marked out for us was this. We were to visit every hospital from Cairo to Young's Point opposite Vicksburg; relieve such needs as were pressing; make ourselves useful in any way among the sick and wounded, co-operating harmoniously as far as possible with medical and military authorities" (Livermore [1887] 1995, 282).

The Sanitary Commission was also the eyes and ears of the public: "From every point we were to report our movements, the result of our observations, what we had accomplished, and what we found needing attention, employing the Chicago Press and the bulletins of the Sanitary Commission as our mediums of communication" (Livermore [1887] 1995, 282–283).

Discovering New Missions

The Sanitary Commission's role grew during the Civil War to fill previously unrecognized and unmet needs, including transporting (often sick) soldiers from the battlefield to their home or new unit. On the 1862 trip to Washington, DC, she describes encounters with these sick soldiers.

> It was with heavy hearts that Mrs. Hoge and myself started from Chicago. All along the route furloughed or discharged soldiers were taken aboard. . . . On their way home, most of them maimed, crippled, pale, thin, weary and shabby. Unobtrusive, patient, and submissive, they took whatever accommodations chanced to fall to them. (Livermore [1887] 1995, 235, 237)

It was scenes such as these that induced Livermore, Hoge, and others to develop programs that provided food and lodging for returning soldiers.

Fundraising

The Sanitary Commission of the U.S. Army operated completely on donations. In 1862, funds were so low that the commission considered disbanding. Mary Livermore and Jane Hoge's fund-raising ideas and efforts may literally have saved the commission. They came up with the idea of staging a fair in Chicago:

> At last, Mrs. Hoge and myself proposed a great Northwestern Fair. . . . We were sure that a grand fair, in which the whole Northwest would unite, would replenish the treasury of the Commission. . . . We knew, also that it would develop a grateful demonstration of the loyalty of the Northwest to our beloved but struggling country. That it would encourage the worn veterans of many a hard-fought field, and strengthen them in their defence of our native land.
>
> Accordingly, we consulted the gentlemen of the Commission, who languidly approved our plan, but laughed incredulously at our proposition to raise twenty-five thousand dollars for its treasury. (Livermore [1887] 1995, 410–411)

In spite of the laughter of the "gentlemen of the Commission" the women persisted. Indeed, the first Sanitary Fair (October 1863) raised nearly $90,000 and, more important, served as a successful model that was emulated throughout the North (Sanitary Commission [1864] 1972, 280). Subsequent fairs in New York and Philadelphia raised $1 million each. Livermore later recalled that the first Sanitary Fair, "was an experiment, and was pre-eminently an enterprise of women, receiving no assistance from men in its early beginnings" (Livermore [1887] 1995, 412).

On October 27, 1863, the fair opened its door. Each day for two weeks 5,000 people paid 75 cents to get a meal served by prominent women of Chicago, view exhibit halls and purchase donated items such as pianos, agricultural equipment, artwork, furniture, flowers.

Perhaps the most unique and important item for auction was the original document of the Emancipation Proclamation. Lincoln sent this document to his beloved Illinois with this dedication: *To the Ladies having in charge the Northwestern Fair for the Sanitary Commission.* In closing the accompanying letter, he noted that he "had some desire to retain the paper; but if it shall contribute to the relief or comfort of the soldiers, that is better" (Livermore [1887] 1995, 430). The Emancipation Proclamation sold for $3,000. Lincoln's gesture reflects the country's heartfelt commitment to paying for the care of sick and wounded soldiers, and reveals his trust and esteem for the "ladies" of the Northwest Sanitary Commission.

National Public Policy

Mary Livermore and Jane Hoge also represented the Northwest in national policy and planning meetings. In late 1862, the Sanitary Commission of the U.S. Army called a council to Washington, DC, because "sanitary supplies were rapidly on the decrease, while the increasing demand for them was pitiful." Further, "the people lacked confidence in the ability of the Commission to carry to the suffering soldiers the supplies entrusted to its care." She notes that the Sanitary Commission policymakers had not communicated to the public their role nor the "dire necessities of the hospital and battle-field. . . . It was a time of great depression and discouragement. In the East there were only reports of disaster to our Armies" (Livermore [1887] 1995, 232).

Once Mary Livermore and Jane Hoge arrived at the actual meeting, much was accomplished.

> Of the prolonged meetings of the Sanitary Commission held during the week, no account need be given. They resulted in the formation of wise plans of work, which faithfully carried out, soon swelled the amount of sanitary stores to an extent never anticipated. Several agents were appointed, and a thorough system of canvassing was adopted. Monthly bulletins were issued by the various branches to their tributary aid societies, containing latest accounts of actual work, compiled receipts of sanitary stores up to date, and a statement of the immediate necessities of the hospitals. (Livermore [1887] 1995, 248)

While the Sanitary Commission was given authority by Lincoln to coordinate relief efforts with the army, not all relief organizations were interested in joining. Hence, the Sanitary Commission needed to convince other relief organizations to coordinate their efforts: "Earnest and successful efforts were made all along the lines to induce all organizations working for the relief of the army to adopt the Sanitary Commission as the almoner of their bounty" (Livermore [1887] 1995, 248).

To Public Administration: A Legacy of Caring

In *Bureau Men, Settlement Women*, Camilla Stivers (2000) contrasts the public-service perspective of men and women during the Progressive era. Stivers argues persuasively that the municipal research bureau men's "scientific" approach to public administration prized efficiency and businesslike practices, and regarded citizenship as oversight. In contrast, women working in the settlement houses viewed science as experiential, focused on improved living conditions, and viewed citizenship as involvement (Stivers 2000, 16). "Women referred to their work as 'public motherhood' and 'municipal house-keeping'" (Stivers 2000, 9). Caring was emphasized over efficiency (Stivers 2000, 126). These themes run deep in the work of the Sanitary Commission women in the office and in the field; indeed, nursing represents the epitome of caring. In retrospect, there is good reason to believe that the "motherly" nurses and the "caring" women administrators of the Sanitary Commission preceded and led the way for their Settlement daughters.

During the world wars of the twentieth century, the most visible role for women in uniform was nursing (Maning and Wright 2000). During the Civil War, the most recognized role for women was also nursing. As Mary Livermore traveled to the battlefield hospitals, she embraced the mantle of nurse whenever she encountered sick and wounded soldiers. Nursing may have been a lone "caring" component of what otherwise might be character-ized as a "killing" enterprise.[10]

During the Civil War, Dorothea Dix, the superintendent of nurses, prohib-ited young and attractive women from nursing the wounded soldiers (Wood 1972, 200). As a middle-aged woman, Mary Livermore was welcomed to serve as one of the mature, passionately caring nurses who regarded the help-less, very young Union soldiers as their sons.

Historian Ann Wood wrote about the mother-son bond that grew between these nurses and their young patients. The sick and dying men missed the embrace, sound, and scent of their mothers. They welcomed the maternal presence. The nurses used the mother-son bond as a moral wedge to protect their "boys" by advocating for change in senseless military regulations and side-stepping drunk or corrupt surgeons (Wood 1972). In addition, at a time before the connection between poor sanitation and disease was widely known, the Union nurses of the Sanitary Commission stressed the "motherly" virtues of cleanliness and good nutrition and in so doing saved countless lives (Silber 1995, xi). Mary Livermore's writings show how the caring "nurse" Liver-more is ever present and the compelling nature of the "mother-son" bond.

> [During a train trip to DC she fell asleep and] was awakened by a peculiar noise, like that of an animal in distress. [Mrs. Hoge asked the conductor about the distressing sound.] "A drunken soldier on the platform of the rear car, Madam!" [The women investigated and found a man lying] coiled in a heap on the platform of the rear car, writhing in the fierce throws [sic] of convulsions. With the assistance of bystanders, we brought him in, arranged a rough bed with the seats, unbuttoned his military overcoat, brushed off the snow that covered him and then looked into the pale face of a delicate lad of eighteen.

[Mary and Jane tended the convulsing boy for several hours.] We were rewarded for our efforts by seeing the young soldier relieved from pain, his muscles relaxed, his breathing became regular, and he was conscious. Gazed at us wondering for a few moments, he covered his face with his thin finger, through which the tears trickled. "Excuse me, ladies! *I thought I was at home with my mother.*" He was a convalescent soldier, going from the hospital to his regiment, and altogether too much of an invalid for the exchange. The cold, exposure, fatigue, and improper food of the journey had nearly bereft him of life [italics added]. (Livermore [1887] 1995, 242–243).

The work of the women on the home front, who ran the ladies' aid societies and managed branch offices of the Sanitary Commission, also reflected a caring and motherly orientation.

National Recognition

Mary Livermore's early communications with the public were through newspaper articles from the war front. Subsequently, she began raising money through speaking engagements. She spoke to large audiences and sometimes raised as much as $8,000 per speech, a considerable sum (Horton 1914, 161) that in the 1860s would have educated 889 high school students for a year (Derks 1999).[11]

Her popularity as a speaker continued after the war ended. According to historian Nina Silber (1995, v), Mary Livermore was one of the "most visibly active women of the nineteenth century." She was considered the "foremost of women orators" (Horton 1914). In 1886, Sarah Bolton noted that people were so eager to hear her speak that at the close of the war "she entered the lecture field and has for years held the foremost place among women as a public speaker. She lectures five nights a week for five months, traveling twenty five thousand miles annually" (Bolton 1886, 63). Her dual agenda during these presentations was to share her experiences as a nurse and manager for the Sanitary Commission, and to use these stories as a lever to lobby for women's rights.

Her Civil War memoir, *My Story*, was read by tens of thousands of nineteenth-century Americans (Silber 1995, v).[12] *My Story* gave vivid accounts of a wide range of Civil War experiences seldom discussed. Here was a beloved mother figure whose efforts and energy had saved countless sons of the Union. She was a trusted woman who had nursed the sick and successfully brought capable executive ability to redress a national tragedy. Mary Livermore had captured the nation's heart and mind and she now wanted the nation's commitment to women's rights.

Livermore and the Commission: Genesis of Cooperative Womanhood

It is not surprising that our historical sense of the Sanitary Commission is dim. At the close of the war, the Sanitary Commission was no longer needed and quickly disbanded. Its primary function—medical logistics—is now well funded and imbedded in contemporary military mission and structure. The unglamorous world of Civil War battlefield supply logistics is ignored and the role of women and the Sanitary Commission largely forgotten. Furthermore, most Civil War literature focuses on generals, strategies, victories, and defeats.[13]

Mary Livermore's writing reveals the Sanitary Commission's legacy to public administration. In 1891, when Mary Livermore was 71 years old, she wrote "Cooperative Womanhood in the State" for the *North American Review*. Here she explains how women's participation in the Sanitary Commission changed their view of themselves and their collective role in society.

Many of us are familiar with "Rosie the Riveter" and the fact that women during World War II took jobs traditionally performed by men. The experience women gained doing traditional men's work is often linked to the women's rights movement in the latter half of the twentieth century (Denman and Inniss 1999). Mary Livermore makes a persuasive case that the management and administrative experience women gained during the Civil War influenced the women's rights movement in the latter half of the nineteenth century.

In the rural economy of the 1860s, few questioned that women could contribute labor by spending long hours in the field. On the other hand, prior to the Civil War, there was "almost universal consensus" that only men were "fit" to organize effectively or had the ability to "combine specialized facts" for a "definite purpose." Women, in contrast, both individually (too sensitive and emotional) and as a group (too contentious) were innately unable to organize to achieve a larger purpose (Livermore 1891, 283). Mary Livermore describes this perception.

> It was commonly believed in the near past that only half the human race possessed a fitness for organization; that only men knew how to specialize facts, combine for a definite purpose, and so to translate feebleness into associated strength without splitting into antagonisms that would defeat their aim. It was declared, ex cathedra, that women lacked this power, that they were emotional and sensitive, segregated by rivalries and unfaith in one another, unable to subject selfhood to efforts for the general well being; and that therefore, solidarity of sentiment was not possible to them, nor unification of effort. There was almost universal consensus of opinion among men on this point. The facts superficially considered justified this belief. (Livermore 1891, 283)

She argued that the Civil War provided a "stimulus of powerful appeal" that aroused women and acted "to fuse and weld them into unified action" (Livermore 1891, 284). Further, during the Civil War, "barriers of sect, caste, and conventionalism, which had heretofore separated them, were burned away in fervid heat of their loyalty." At that time, approximately 12,000 women's aid societies banded together, "auxiliary to one Sanitary Commission." The organization and its effectiveness at meeting pressing national needs proved to all (especially women) that women were capable of organizing for the public good on a scale and scope previously considered impossible (Livermore 1891, 285).

Perhaps Mary Livermore exaggerated, yet not by too much, when she said: "This was the first example of cooperative womanhood serving the state the world had ever witnessed." Organizing cooperative efforts in the service of the state is what public administrators do. Thus, the activities and experiences of administering programs for the public good, led to an awakening of sorts. "While they were working for the relief of the army, women studied the policy of government, and learned what tremendous issues were at stake." Further, they recognized that they were good at the administrative activities previously considered the exclusive purview of men (Livermore 1891, 285).

> Not only did these women broaden in their views; they grew in practical and executive work. They learned how to cooperate intelligently with men; became an expert in conducting public business, in calling and presiding over public meetings, even when men made a large part of the audience; learned how to draft constitutions and bylaws, to act as secretaries and committees; how to keep accounts with precision and system; how to answer indorse [sic], and file letters; how to sort their stores and keep accurate account of stock; they attended meetings with regularity and promptness, and became punctilious in observance of official etiquette; in short, they developed rapidly a remarkable aptitude for business, on which men looked and wondered. "Where were these superior women before the war?" [italics added]. (Livermore 1891, 286)

The Sanitary Commission also provided women with personal experiences that motivated them to work for women's rights. Mary Livermore describes an encounter with a contractor (as part of her Sanitary Commission's duty) that radically changed her position on women's rights.

> Here was a revelation. We two women [Livermore and Hoge] were able to enlist the whole Northwest in a great philanthropic, money-making enter-

prise in the teeth of great opposition, and had the executive ability to carry it forward to a successful termination. We had money of our own in bank, twice as much as was necessary to pay the builder. But by laws of the state in which we lived, our individual names were not worth the paper on which they were written. Our earnings were not ours, but belonged to our husbands. Later in the conversation, we learned that we had no legal ownership in our minor children, whom we had won, in anguish, in the valley of death. They too were the property of our husbands.

We learned much of the laws made by men for women, in that conversation with an illiterate builder. It opened a new world to us. We thought rapidly, and felt intensely. I registered a vow that when the war was over I would take up a new work—the work of making law and justice synonymous for women. I have kept my vow religiously. (Livermore [1887] 1995, 437)

Thus, one can conclude that the women's rights movement of the latter nineteenth century was directly related to the public administration experience and contributions made by the women of the Sanitary Commission. Mary Livermore delivered the message of "cooperative womanhood serving the state" in print and through a career in public speaking.

Conclusion

The Sanitary Commission of the U.S. Army was the first federally authorized, large organization that used women extensively in an executive capacity. Mary Livermore was part of the pioneering group of "cooperative womanhood" that served the state during the Civil War. As manager of the Chicago office, she directed essential, emergency medical logistics for the Union Army.

Through her eclectic public service she encountered dying soldiers in dirty hospitals, determined relief workers on Mississippi steamships, dedicated ladies' aid society volunteers, and Abraham Lincoln in the White House. Much of what the world knows about the Sanitary Commission and the remarkable women who managed it comes through her books and articles. She contributed to our public administration heritage through her dedicated service and publications. She is truly an outstanding woman of public administration.

Notes

1. The quote was excerpted from Livermore, Mary A., "Remarks at the Annual Meeting of the New England Anti-Imperialist League," available at: www.boondocksnet.com/ai/ailtexts/livermore.html (August 24, 2003).

2. Mary Livermore describes a few of the problems with the uncoordinated relief efforts. Relief supplies were collected.

> But numerous difficulties and failure soon brought these methods [uncoordinated single relief agencies] into disrepute. The accumulation of perishable freight for the soldiers became fearful. It demanded instant transportation, and the managers of freight trains and expresses were in despair. Women rifled their store-rooms and preserve closets of canned fruits and pots of jam and marmalade, which they packed with clothing and blankets, books and stationery, photographs and "comfort bags." Baggage cars were soon flooded with fermenting sweetmeats, and broken pots of jelly. . . . Decaying fruit and vegetables, pastry and cake in a demoralized condition, badly canned meats and soups . . . were thrown away *en route*. And with them went the clothing, and stationery saturated with the effervescing and putrefying compounds which they enfolded. (Livermore [1887] 1995, 121–122)

3. In the early days of the Civil War, news about conditions often reached the public through the letters of soldiers that found their way to newspapers. Conditions were dreadful. The following are a few excerpts from an 1861 letter:

> As yet we have done little fighting, but have lost a large number of men. They are dying daily in the camps and hospitals from pneumonia, dysentery, and camp diseases, caused by severe colds, exposure and lack of proper food when ill. . . . In the hospital the sick men lie in rotten straw. . . . In the hospital the nurses are "convalescent soldiers," so nearly sick themselves that they ought to be in the ward, and from their very feebleness they are selfish and sometimes inhuman in their treatment of the patients. . . . We need beds and bedding, hospital clothing and sick-diet, proper medicines, surgical instruments, and good nurses. (as cited in Livermore [1887] 1995, 126–127)

Furthermore, the Union logistics system was eroded by the manpower (officers and enlisted men) that left the Union to serve the Confederacy.

4. Chapter 24 of Livermore's ([1887] 1995) *My Story* documents in vivid detail how Union nurses supplied by the Sanitary Commission fought corruption.

5. According to an Army Command and Management text, logistics systems "support the soldier in the field and in the garrison with what is needed, when, where, and in the condition and quantity required" (Department of the Army 1991, 18–19). Supply, maintenance, and transport are common logistics activities. Logistics is a specialized facet of public administration. Effective logistics entails careful planning, management, financial transactions, coordination, and mechanisms to ensure accountability. Sound logistical support requires procuring and moving materials to the field. Responsible administrators often must travel and engage in oversight to ensure plans are implemented.

6. Letters documented that such basic items as blankets were in short supply. This in turn led to pneumonia and other problems (Livermore [1887] 1995, 126).

7. Mary Livermore began her association with the Sanitary Commission as a president of a Chicago ladies' aid society (Livermore [1887] 1995, 136).

8. Mary Livermore describes Jane Hoge, another outstanding woman of public administration, in *My Story:*

> We were personal friends and had long been associated in the charitable work of the city. She was a practical woman, and her executive ability was marked. Her

power of patient, persistent work was seemingly limitless. Her force of character was irresistible, and bore down all opposition. Her energy was simply tremendous. . . . Her largeness of heart . . . united to her keen sense of justice, led her into the charitable and reform work of the time. She was concerned for the public welfare, and gravitated instinctively towards public work.

She was married for fifty years and the mother of seven children (Livermore [1887] 1995, 160).

9. In the preface to *My Story*, Mary indicates that during trips to the field,

I always corresponded with the press. And no issue of my husband's paper appeared when I was thus engaged, that did not contain long letters from the front, packed with narrations of facts and events, for which I knew its readers were eagerly looking. I sent similar letters to other periodicals in the Northwest, wrote war sketches for magazines struggling for existence. (Livermore [1887] 1995, 10)

She also notes that *My Story* was written using these articles that were carefully and chronologically preserved by her husband.

10. What distinguishes a soldier from other public-sector workers like policemen and firemen is not that they will risk their lives for their fellow citizens, but that they have agreed to kill for their country. Ethical issues about when such killing is justified are beyond the scope of this paper.

11. At that time it cost on average $9.00 a year to educate a high school student. Again, she received $8,000 for the speech ($8,000/$9 per student = 889 students). Today, it would cost $5.2 million to educate the same number of students. A comparison of 1860 prices and today's can be misleading. For example, a piano lesson in the 1860s was $3.00. Today an hour piano lesson is about $60, and it costs approximately $5,900 to educate a high school student for a year (Derks 1999).

12. Historians also regard *My Story* as one of the few source books on Civil War hospital and supply conditions. (Conversations with historians at Texas State University.)

13. The author spent 30 minutes in the large "Civil War" section of her local Barnes and Noble bookstore. Most books dealt with battles, generals, and strategies. The author looked in the index and table of contents of all the books whose titles suggested a "big picture" orientation. There was one short mention of the Sanitary Commission. One book gave a day-by-day report of the war and mentioned that Lincoln had spoken at the New York Sanitary Fair.

References

Bolton, S. 1886. *Lives of Girls Who Became Famous.* New York: Thomas Crowell.

Denman, J., and L. Inniss. 1999. "No War without Women: Defense Industries." In *Gender Camouflage: Women in the Military*, ed. F. D'Amico and L. Weinstein, 187–200. New York: New York University Press.

Department of the Army. 1991. *Army Command and Management: Theory and Practice.* Carlisle Barracks, PA: U.S. Army War College.

Derks, S, ed. 1999. *The Value of a Dollar: Prices and Incomes in the United States 1860–1999.* Lakeville, CT: Grey House.

Higginson, T., ed. 1895. *Massachusetts in the Army and Navy during the War of 1861–65*. Boston: Wright and Potter.

Horton, E. 1914. *A Group of Famous Women: Stories of their Lives*. New York: D.C. Heath.

Livermore, M. 1891. "Cooperative Womanhood in the State." *North American Review* 153, 418 (September): 283–295.

———. 1895. "Massachusetts Women in the Civil War." In *Massachusetts in the Army and Navy during the War of 1861–65*, ed. T. Higginson, 586–602. Boston: Wright and Potter.

———. [1887] 1995. *My Story of the War: The Civil War Memories of the Famous Nurse, Relief Organizer and Suffragette*. New York: Da Capo Press.

Maning, L., and V. Wright. 2000. *Women in the Military: Where They Stand*, 3d ed. Washington, DC: Women's Research and Education Institute.

Sanitary Commission of the United States Army. [1864] 1972. *A Succinct Narrative of Its Works and Purposes*. New York: Arno Press and the *New York Times*.

Silber, N. 1995. "Introduction." In *My Story of the War: The Civil War Memories of the Famous Nurse, Relief Organizer and Suffragette*, ed. M. Livermore, i–xxi. New York: Da Capo Press.

Stivers, C. 2000. *Bureau Men, Settlement Women: Constructing Public Administration in the Progressive Era*. Lawrence: University Press of Kansas.

Wood, A. 1972. "The War Within a War: Women Nurses in the Union Army." *Civil War History* 18, no. 3 (September): 197–212.

World Almanac. 2003. *The World Almanac and Book of Facts: 2003*. New York: World Almanac Books.

4

Feminine Pioneer

Nellie Tayloe Ross, First Woman Governor

Teva J. Scheer

Introduction

Less than a year after going down to defeat in her bid for reelection, the first woman governor of an American state reflected, "It does seem passing strange, when one considers the countless women who are well fitted to fill the office of governor, that I should have been the pioneer."[1] Passing strange, indeed. When she was elected Wyoming's governor in November 1924, few women in America could have had less qualifying experience or have been less prepared to become the first female chief executive of a state. Had it not been for the untimely death of her husband, Governor William Bradford Ross, Nellie Tayloe Ross would have spent the rest of her life as a contented political wife, whose personal ambitions extended no further than someday to be elected president of the Cheyenne Woman's Club.[2]

When Nellie died in 1977, the *New York Times* obituary described her as "ever feminine, never a feminist; a woman in politics who had not lost her womanliness."[3] Nellie's image as a dignified lady served her well in the male-dominated political world in which she made her career. Working-class women had always been present in the workforce, but when increasing numbers of upper- and middle-class women began to enter colleges and seek employment during the first decades of the twentieth century, many Americans became deeply concerned that women's emergence from the home would degender them. Their exposure to the immoral public sphere would render them coarse and mannish, and make it difficult if not impossible for these women to lead "normal" lives as feminine, and happily heterosexual, wives and mothers.[4] Nellie's demeanor allayed those fears and helped her to be accepted and respected, both by the male politicians who surrounded her and by the hundreds of wives and mothers in local Democratic clubs and organizations across the country who saw her as one of their own. Emily Newell Blair, who preceded Nellie as a vice-chair of the Democratic National Committee, said of her: "Few women have known more women or been beloved by so many. . . . Women recognize in her a woman who, when called on, can meet any and every situation with distinction, yet remain always feminine."[5]

Nellie always thought of herself as a wife and mother who had been thrust by circumstances into a career—and what an astonishing career it was! Nellie's 1924 gubernatorial election, which was covered in newspapers from coast to coast, made her one of the most famous political women in America during the late 1920s and early 1930s. Following her defeat for reelection in 1926, she embarked on a career of writing and speechmaking on the national Chautauqua circuit. In 1928, Al Smith appointed her vice-chair of the Democratic National Committee (DNC). She was drafted to make one of Smith's nominating speeches at the national convention that same year, and she even received thirty-one votes herself for the position of vice-president.[6] She directed the DNC Women's Division for the next four years, and she helped to direct the campaign for the women's vote in 1928 and 1932. In 1933, Franklin Delano Roosevelt appointed her as the first female director of the Mint. She was renominated to the Mint post three more times by Roosevelt and Truman. In 1953, after having completed a full federal career of twenty years, she retired at age seventy-six.

Childhood

Nellie Davis Tayloe was born in 1876 outside St. Joseph, Missouri, on what was left of the family plantation. Her family had been wealthy slaveowners who backed the secessionists and who lost everything but their land as a result of the Civil War. Nellie spent her first seven years on the farm until her father, facing a large mortgage and unpaid taxes, decided to make a new start in the small prairie town of Miltonvale, Kansas. Nellie's family would remain in Miltonvale until she graduated from high school in 1892, but the last few years in Miltonvale were difficult ones. Nellie's mother died when she was thirteen, and her father lost both the family home and his grocery business when the crippling drought of the late 1880s wiped out dozens of small farming communities. The family's economic misfortunes left permanent scars on Nellie's personality, affecting equally her personal life and her management practices. Both as governor and Mint director, Nellie made strict economy a cornerstone of her administrations. In Wyoming, one of Nellie's legislative priorities was a reduction in state expenditures to eliminate a persistent state overdraft.[7] At the Mint, Nellie took pride in underspending the annual appropriation; one year, she returned more than 20 percent of the Mint appropriation to the Treasury.[8] Always seeking ways to hold down or reduce expenses, she personally reviewed and signed off on all the bureau's requisitions. She also held salary increases to a minimum. "She was good at giving people special recognition," remembers one of her managers at the Mint, "but she wasn't overly generous on promoting people."[9]

Although Nellie's mother died when Nellie was still a young girl, Elizabeth Green Tayloe had a profound impact on Nellie's character. "Lizzie" Tayloe was a refined and traveled woman who had completed her education at an exclusive boarding school in Richmond, Virginia. Reared to become the cultured wife of a planter, Lizzie Tayloe trained her eldest daughter to be a southern lady despite the family's financial circumstances. During the years on the farm, cash was tight, and with little money to pay for hired help, Lizzie became her husband's economic partner. In addition to keeping house and bearing a succession of children, it is likely that Lizzie tended a garden, raised chickens, milked the cows, churned butter, and made cheese; she may also have sold butter, eggs, and honey to bring in cash. The result was that in her early years, Nellie experienced a true working mother who was substantively contributing to the family enterprise.

After the family moved to Miltonvale, Nellie had the opportunity to observe a mother who demonstrated leadership for women, but always within the careful confines of socially accepted activities. Lizzie could have chosen to retire to the private sphere of home and family that bounded the lives of most middle-class Victorian wives, but instead she became involved in the principal activities that were open to respectable women: She taught a Sunday school class and she also became a founding member of the Miltonvale chapter of the Women's Christian Temperance Union (WCTU), the largest organization of women in the nineteenth century. With Lizzie's life as a model, it is little wonder that Nellie emphasized her own feminine nature. However, Nellie never let her deference to social propriety get in the way of something she really wanted to do; instead, she used charm as a weapon. Her secretary at the Mint recalled that in her dealings with male politicians as well as her superiors and subordinates, Nellie always practiced the adage that "honey caught more [flies] than vinegar."[10]

Marriage

After Nellie's father lost his Miltonvale business, the family moved to Omaha. Nellie contributed to the family coffers by teaching piano while she completed her education in a two-year teacher training program. Subsequently, she taught kindergarten for four years in the Omaha public schools. As the only woman in the family, Nellie learned how to juggle a career while managing a household. In 1900, Nellie traveled to Tennessee to visit relatives. There she met a young lawyer named William Bradford Ross and, after her return to Omaha, the couple began to court by mail. Shortly after meeting Nellie, William moved west to establish his own practice in Cheyenne, Wyoming. In September 1902, he traveled to Omaha to claim his bride. Nellie arrived in the small frontier town of Cheyenne to find that William's outgoing personality had already won him many friends in Cheyenne. Moreover, his new practice was prospering. While William built up his legal practice and became increasingly involved in the state Democratic party, Nellie concentrated on her home and her four sons.[11] However, Nellie was just as substantive a partner in her marriage as Lizzie had been in hers; William valued Nellie's judgment and common sense, and he increasingly sought her counsel on legal and political matters.[12]

In 1922, William campaigned as a progressive Democratic candidate for governor. In an astonishing political upset, he was elected by a margin of less than 1,000 votes. Nellie had opposed his candidacy; always concerned with the family income, she wanted him to concentrate on his law practice, which had suffered as a result of his political activities. However, she came to enjoy her position as Wyoming's first lady, both the social aspects and her role as William's advisor. As events turned out, the couple's intellectual partnership became Nellie's tutelage for the governorship.

In September 1924, William was taken ill with appendicitis; the surgeons operated to remove his severely infected appendix, but his condition continued to deteriorate. On October 2, William died; he was buried in a quiet neighborhood cemetery of Cheyenne, next to his son Alfred, who had died in infancy. William's death devastated Nellie; she and William had become one of those rare couples whose mutual affection, respect, and passion had grown with each passing year. "Few women in the world have been blest with [what I have] lost—for however unworthy I have been, never was woman more loved and admired," mourned Nellie.[13]

Governorship

Nellie was still in a state of shock from William's sudden death when she was approached by the chair of the state Democratic Committee just a few days after the funeral, asking whether she would consider running for governor to complete the last two years of William's term. After a brief period of deliberation with party officials and her brother, who had traveled to Cheyenne to support her during William's illness and death, Nellie said yes. She later attributed her decision to run to an altruistic desire to carry out her husband's unfinished agenda. While this factor undoubtedly played a part in her deliberations, it was also a politically astute strategy. Nellie capitalized on the image of the wife in mourning who sacrificed her privacy to further her husband's legacy. The truth was that Nellie suddenly awoke to personal ambition. Nellie's brother, who watched her handle meeting after meeting with Democratic officials on the nomination question, wrote his wife that

> Nellie is as keen a politician as any of them. She wants to run and the Democrats want her but there is a great question as to her winning. . . . She will certainly take a chance if she finally thinks she could probably win. No one ever wanted it more.[14]

On November 4, 1924, Nellie defeated her Republican opponent by more than 8,000 votes of the 79,000 votes cast—of Wyoming's 23 counties, Nellie carried 20. She won by the largest margin of any statewide race, and she was the only Democrat to be elected to state office. Her opponent's association with the oil business cost him votes, since Teapot Dome[15] was still fresh in the minds of Wyoming's voters, but undoubtedly sympathy for the bereaved widow played a deciding role in her election. Nellie was elected the same day that Texas voters chose Miriam "Ma" Ferguson to carry on the legacy of her husband, who had been impeached and was ineligible to run for reelection as governor; however, Nellie was sworn in about 20 days earlier than Mrs. Ferguson. Newspapers around the country struggled to assess the import of the two women's elections as state chief executives. Opinions ranged from positive endorsements that were supportive of women's abilities to scandalized predictions of eminent failure. Sexism inevitably colored many of the editorials, even the supportive ones. For example, the *Birmingham News* observed that since women were "natural-born housekeepers," the "infinite detail of a Governor's office" should interest any woman; her homemaking responsibilities provided her with excellent training to be governor or mayor.[16]

"The way laid out for me was not exactly a bed of roses," Nellie wryly remembered.[17] Nellie faced a Republican majority in both houses; she was a political neophyte and a woman to boot. It seemed a perfect opportunity for the legislature to strengthen its political power at the expense of the governor. From the moment she was inaugurated, the courtly treatment that Nellie had received from the state's Republican leaders after William's death evaporated, and she was plunged into partisan politics. There would be times over the next two years when she would look up from her desk and gaze upon the portraits of former governors, taking strength from their supportive presence; it comforted her to know that all of them, including her beloved William, had faced their own crises, but somehow each had survived.[18]

After a brief but feverish few weeks of study and sessions with William's former advisors, on January 15, 1925, Nellie faced the assembled senators and representatives to present her legislative proposals. Nellie outlined eleven areas of proposed legislation, only three of which—the need for strict state economy, extension of a loan program for farmers, and determined enforcement of prohibition—derived directly from her husband's own legislative program. The remaining eight of Nellie's legislative proposals were her own. Among her initiatives was a call for legislation requiring Wyoming's counties, cities, and school districts to develop systems of executive budgeting; the discipline of the planning process would help them to identify and eliminate "waste and extravagance." As a result of several recent bank failures, Nellie also endorsed legislation to strengthen the bank examination program and provide insurance for individual depositors. She urged the legislature to consider her proposals for strengthening mine health and safety provisions, and she also endorsed protective legislation to support female employees in industry. Finally, she asked the legislature to ratify a pending federal constitutional amendment that would have curbed the use of children in the labor force.[19]

Partisan battles between the governor and the Republican-controlled legislature characterized the Eighteenth Legislature. By the end of the forty-day session, their duel had ended in a draw. While the legislators had acted favorably on only five of Nellie's proposals, she had successfully used her veto power to block their attempts to curb the governor's authority. Among her eight vetoes, all of which were sustained, was one bill that would have limited the governor's appointment of water division superintendents and another that would have transferred supervision of interstate water negotiations from the governor to the state engineer. While the legislature had failed to enact most of Nellie's proposals, it also failed to develop and enact many of its own. The state's editors, even many from Republican newspapers, branded the Eighteenth Legislature as one of the least productive in Wyoming's history.[20]

"The governor is the most visible state official," noted one political scientist in the 1960s. "There is little assurance that he will always be able to influence public opinion but there is little doubt that he has ample opportunity to be heard."[21] For Nellie, the first woman governor and, therefore, something of a national celebrity, this statement was doubly true. Through her words and her acts, and for better or worse, she had the opportunity to cast more national attention on Wyoming politics than it had ever received. Nellie's first invitation to step onto the national stage arrived less than two weeks after her inauguration; she was invited to deliver the keynote speech at a Washington banquet for the Democratic Party's top leadership. The thought of speaking before the Party luminaries might be "a little appalling at first thought, I know, . . . [but] I am sure you could make a wonderful success of it. . . . Don't forget that you belong to the whole world now, not only Wyoming," the dinner's organizer counseled.[22] More than 300 persons attended the dinner, at which Nellie spoke on her early impressions and experiences as governor. The next day, the *Washington Star* declared the dinner a brilliant affair and Nellie was launched as a national figure in the Democratic Party.[23]

After returning from the excitement of Washington, Nellie's days fell into the predictable if frenetic pattern experienced by all governors. Most mornings, she left the Governor's Mansion between nine and ten o'clock for her short walk to the Capitol building. She tried to leave by six each evening so that she could spend her evenings with her youngest son, who was still at home, but inevitably, she often spent her evenings devoted to the reading and staff work that she could not get done between office appointments.[24] Nellie's crowded office bustled with the noise of constant visitors and she found herself scheduled for back-to-back meetings and interviews. The Wyoming governor shares power with four other officials elected statewide; many of the state agencies are headed by boards or commissions comprised of these five individuals. The first week of every month, Nellie devoted most of her time to these board meetings. Since she was the only Democrat, she was reluctant to miss any of the monthly meetings. Her diligent, businesslike performance earned her a positive early assessment from a neighboring state. After she had held office for three months, the *Denver Post* observed, "One of the surprising and edifying circumstances of her governorship has been the fact that she has conducted her office not like a gentle-faced, soft-voiced appealing woman in the mourning of a widow, but as an intelligent, tactful, resourceful individual."[25]

Nellie had several opportunities to represent Wyoming on the national stage. Based on the positive assessments of her participation at the 1925 annual Governors' Conference in Maine, Nellie was successful in her bid to convene the 1926 conference in Cheyenne. She hosted the governors of Montana and Idaho at the opening of Yellowstone Park's western gate. The governors, members of Congress, and state engineers of Colorado, Wyoming, and Utah elected her presiding officer of an August 1925 meeting in Denver to discuss water rights of states in the upper Colorado River basin. She also represented Wyoming at a subsequent water rights hearing convened in Washington by the Federal Power Commission, where the commission ruled favorably in the dispute between the upper- and lower-basin states.

When it came time for Nellie to run for reelection, she was determined to stay focused on the issues rather than responding to or indulging in personal attacks. She also refused to play the woman's rights card, asking instead that voters judge her solely on her accomplishments. On the Republican side, the campaign was nasty. Nellie was criticized for her vetoes, accused of spending excessive time outside the state, labeled a mere figurehead for her male advisors, and condemned for failing to support women for state positions. Juggling her board meetings with her campaign appearances, Nellie set out in June 1926 to crisscross the state. It was a rare day that she did not participate in at least three events, and sometimes as many as seven; she spoke in community centers, schools, churches, and even private homes. Wherever she went, she was greeted by record crowds. Despite Wyoming's Republican majority, it was clear that Nellie's sincere affinity for people and her excellent interpersonal skills had made her very popular with Wyoming's citizens. However, her popularity was not enough; on election day, the Republicans achieved a clean sweep of the statewide offices. Nellie's race was by far the closest; of the 70,000 votes cast, she lost by less than 1,400. Her loss can be attributed to superior Republican organization and funding and the impact of the Republicans' negative allegations. Also, once the novelty of a woman governor and sympathy for her widowhood had passed, an estimated 2,000 to 4,000 reportedly voted against her simply because she was a woman—a relatively small number, but one that was decisive in such a close election.[26]

Postmortems on Nellie's effectiveness as governor ran the spectrum from extraordinarily accomplished to inconsequential, but almost all assessments agreed that she had worked hard and had discharged her duties with dignity. To evaluate her performance with benefit of hindsight, it is useful to divide a governor's responsibilities into three categories: policy development, administration, and public relations.[27] In the policy area, which includes a governor's legislative proposals, his or her success in gaining passage, and the subsequent implementation of those policies, Nellie's performance was respectable, if not spectacular. The adversarial nature of her administration's relationship with the Republican legislature hindered her ability to achieve her policy objectives. In fairness, however, her success rate was comparable to that of other Democratic governors in Wyoming, including her husband's. Nellie's lack of experience affected her performance most in the area of administration; for those agencies solely under her supervision, it appears that she exercised little or no leadership or oversight. Nellie was fortunate that the management aspects of her position were not nearly as important in the 1920s as the other two components of her responsibilities. Nellie served as governor during the period when the position was in a transition from a mere figurehead role, generally limited to public relations responsibilities, to that of a substantive, modern chief executive. Fifteen years later, her lack of administrative experience would have been a much greater handicap, because the administrative and managerial demands of a modern governor would have demanded knowledge and expertise that Nellie lacked when assuming office, expertise that she would not have had time to develop during her short tenure of two years.

In the third area of gubernatorial responsibility, public relations, Nellie excelled. She was extremely popular with Wyoming's citizens, and it is likely that no other Wyoming governor has ever brought the state more beneficial national publicity and acclaim. Thanks to Nellie, Wyoming also enhanced its reputation as a bastion of equal rights. Public relations effectiveness is dependent on good people skills, communication ability, and innate astuteness in handling the press, and in these areas, Nellie was superbly talented. The opening wedge of Nellie's public relations success may have been her unique status as the first female governor; however, one should not discount her excellent public relations performance simply because she took advantage of her unique status. The female governor angle, clumsily handled, could just as easily have worked against her. In sum, Nellie gave little attention to the administrative area, she performed acceptably in the policy area, and she excelled in the public relations area. Thanks to her intelligence, hard work, and interpersonal skills, her tenure was far more successful than one would have predicted, based on her experience. Her proficient performance helped to pave the way for aspiring female politicians across the nation who followed her.

National Politician

Within a few weeks of her defeat, Nellie's anxiety about financial security had led her to capitalize on her gubernatorial fame by signing contracts to write articles for the popular press and join the Chautauqua summer lecture tour.[28] The ten-week Chautauqua contract alone would earn her more than her annual salary as governor.[29] Chautauqua was founded in rural New York in 1874 as an educational summer camp for adults, but it quickly spread across America in the form of "circuit" Chautauquas that traveled from town to town and provided a brief diversion for small-town residents who were starved for entertainment and self-development. At its zenith, 40 million men, women, and children flocked to the Chautauqua tents each summer to hear famous speakers like Nellie, William Jennings Bryan, Mark Twain, and Susan B. Anthony, and to enjoy their first taste of professional music, theater, and other first-class performers. Nellie, who became known for her exceptional diction and delivery, was an extraordinarily popular speaker. She stayed on the Chautauqua circuit until it withered away around 1930, a victim of the Depression and other forms of mass entertainment, notably the radio and the cinema. Nellie spoke on her gubernatorial experiences, on politics, and on women's rights. In one speech, "Woman's Work New and Old," she declared,

Slowly and one by one the barriers have fallen that excluded [woman] from long coveted paths until now she walks unchallenged into almost any field of endeavor she chooses, even invading those most desirable ones that from time immemorial were traditionally supposed to constitute the exclusive preserves of men. And whether in the sciences, progressive business or public service, her success is indisputable. She has brought to her new responsibilities . . . that same fidelity and devotion to duty that has characterized her as wife and mother throughout the ages.[30]

By the spring of 1928, Nellie had begun to juggle her speaking engagements with her campaign activities on behalf of Al Smith, who was seeking the Democratic nomination for president. Nellie used her connections with local Democratic women's clubs and other women's organizations to promote Smith's progressive accomplishments as governor of New York. Once Smith received the nomination, Nellie was rewarded with her appointment as a vice-chair of the Democratic National Committee (DNC). John J. Raskob, Smith's choice as DNC chair, also offered Nellie a paid position as director of the Woman's Division. Nellie and Eleanor Roosevelt were to develop a partnership, lasting through the end of the 1932 campaign, in which Eleanor ran the office activities and Nellie campaigned intensively across the nation. When Franklin Delano Roosevelt won the presidential election in 1932, he acquiesced to the Woman's Division's pressure to appoint women to key positions in his administration. He was interested in appointing a woman to a cabinet-level position, and Nellie received a significant number of endorsements for secretary of the interior; however, he settled on Frances Perkins, who had worked for him in New York as industrial commissioner, to be his secretary of labor.[31] Nellie was tapped instead to be director of the Mint. She was the first woman appointed to lead a "masculine" Treasury bureau; prior to her appointment, female appointments at the director level had been limited to the Women's Bureau and the Children's Bureau.[32]

Mint Director

The Mint was the first place where Nellie encountered overt gender discrimination. The Treasury secretary during the majority of Nellie's tenure, Henry Morgenthau, Jr., was a competent administrator who worked closely with President Roosevelt on the economic aspects of the New Deal.[33] To those subordinates whom he selected, he delegated considerable authority and was generous with his support and recognition. However, he was also insecure personally, noted for his mercurial temper, and he deeply distrusted those Treasury bureau directors who were not "his" men.[34] Nellie preceded him to Treasury, she had a political power base that insulated her from Morgenthau, and—perhaps worst of all—she was a woman.[35] Morgenthau did his best to patronize Nellie and to exclude her from any decision or issue affecting the Mint in which he had personal interest.[36] Nellie soon learned to keep her head low during the weekly meetings with Morgenthau and his bureau directors; she took no part in the occasional banter between Morgenthau and the higher-status directors—Customs, Internal Revenue, the Secret Service, and the Coast Guard; she generally limited her involvement to reading her one-page weekly briefing.[37]

While Nellie's relationship with Morgenthau may have been unpleasant, Treasury's impact on internal bureau affairs was limited. Like most executive bureaus, the Mint enjoyed substantial independence from departmental supervision. While Nellie functioned under the general direction of the secretary, she was appointed by and served at the pleasure of the president. Nellie began her Mint career four years before the Brownlow Committee recommended the strengthening of the executive branch's chain of command and urged Congress to leave the administrative supervision of federal agencies to the president. One of her subordinates remembered that

> Mrs. Ross ran the Mint pretty much on her own. . . . She was governed by a set of statutes that Congress had passed. And as long as she followed these, there wasn't any . . . need for anybody to supervise her.[38]

Sexism may also have played a part in her appointment to the Mint. True, it was a groundbreaking selection for women, but the appointment may have seemed a safe way to reward Nellie's political labors.[39] As a result of the Depression, Mint operations in 1933 were at an all-time low. Within the first year of her tenure, however, the sleepy atmosphere at the Mint was shocked into seven-days-a-week, round-the-clock production in response to Roosevelt's new monetary policies and the increased demand for coins. In her second annual report, Nellie reported that total coinage produced had increased during her first year to 65.7 million pieces, an increase of more than 72 percent over 1933 totals—yet Mint staffing had increased only from 538 to 607, or an increase of less than 13 percent. Mint production continued its unprecedented expansion through the end of World War II, when Nellie found herself presiding over three mints, two assay offices, two bullion depositories, and almost 4,000 employees. Total production for 1945 was a record 4 billion coins.[40]

Nellie had succeeded as governor due to her sharp political instincts, her intelligence, and her public relations skills. At the Mint, however, she developed into a strong and popular administrator. Lacking business experience and management training, she based her leadership style on the organizational structure that she knew best, the family—she always referred to her

workforce as "the Mint Family." She was able to create a working environment in which her employees felt valued as individuals. She combined an
almost maternal empathy and warmth with the reserved authority of a deeply
revered father figure. The daughter of Nellie's former secretary, in describing Nellie's personality, commented that she had "an up-on-the-pedestal feeling about her."[41] A former assistant Mint director observed that "she was a
leader [revered and respected as if she were] the Queen of England."[42] Another Mint top-level manager remembered that

> she had great success in the Mint, because she had everybody behind her. . . .
> The first few days I was there, she asked me if I'd drive her to church for a
> funeral of one of the employees. She had a habit of burrowing in and getting
> a little information about each employee's family, so that she had something
> to talk about. And she knew each employee. That gave her a personal part of
> their lives. . . . When something happened, she was right on hand at the
> hospital, or at the home, helping them out, doing things.[43]

During her tenure, Nellie presided over the construction of a new mint in
San Francisco and the gold depositories at Fort Knox and West Point and the
doubling of the capacity at the Denver Mint. She instituted a series of recla-
mation processes—washing down workers' clothes, filtering water from
workers' showers, and sweeping down walls and floors—that resulted in sav-
ings of about $100,000 a year. Following World War II, she introduced a
Management Improvement Program, which anticipated the quality circles
movement of the 1980s. As a result of this program, mechanical and opera-
tional procedures were revolutionized and new types of equipment were invented and installed, resulting in an estimated reduction in the cost of coinage
production of more than 84 percent between 1946 and 1951.[44]

Later Years

After serving four five-year terms as Mint director, Nellie was more than
ready to retire in 1953. By late September, Nellie had sailed for Europe,
ready to indulge her passion for travel; she was to remain in Europe, primarily Spain, for five months. This was the first of several trips she made abroad,
including one around the world. Her last trip overseas was a two-month tour
of the Holy Land when she was ninety-four. When she was ninety-five, she
made her last trip to Wyoming to participate in the centennial celebration for
Yellowstone Park. Between her trips, Nellie continued to write occasional
articles or deliver speeches, although by now she was little remembered by
the American public.

In December 1977, Nellie died after a short illness at the age of 101. At 10 A.M. on December 21, 1977, after a brief ceremony in the Wyoming State Capitol, Nellie's body lay in state in the Rotunda, surrounded by a military honor guard. One former state governor, two former first ladies, and the state treasurer and secretary of state attended the funeral that afternoon, but less than fifty people attended the simple service. Nellie had, one old friend observed, simply outlived all her contemporaries.[45] And then finally, on a wintry but sunny afternoon, Nellie was laid to rest next to William and two of her sons in the small, peaceful Cheyenne cemetery, under the shadow of giant blue spruces that had been planted about the same time Nellie had come to Cheyenne as a bride.

Conclusion

The year before her death, Nellie had joined her fellow citizens in celebrating the nation's bicentennial. Nellie herself had been witness to half the nation's history; her life had spanned the administrations of twenty-one presidents. She had witnessed the civil rights movement through the eyes of a Southern woman whose mother's family had owned slaves. She remembered life before the automobile, she was already in her late twenties when the Wright brothers flew their plane at Kitty Hawk, and she lived to watch Neil Armstrong on television when he walked on the moon. She was born the same year that Alexander Graham Bell invented the telephone, yet she was still alive to see the dawn of the Information Age. She was steeped in Victorian values as a child, she watched women fight for the suffrage as a young woman, and she witnessed the Women's Liberation Movement from the sidelines as a senior citizen.

"I have no interest in women's lib," Nellie said bluntly when asked about it in the early 1970s.[46] Inevitably, Nellie's traditional upbringing and the emphasis her mother had placed on the importance of ladylike behavior and values caused her to reject what she considered to be the strident actions of feminist leaders toward the end of her life. Nevertheless, if one defines feminism as a belief in equal opportunity and advancement based on merit, not on sex, then Nellie was not only a feminine, but a *feminist* pioneer. She may have chosen a life of marriage and motherhood but, ironically, she ended up achieving the very modern objective of "having it all"—happy marriage, children, an active social life, and a distinguished career. Nellie managed to strike a balance between her personal and business lives that most American women in the first decade of the twenty-first century are still struggling to pull off themselves.

"The term 'new woman' does not fall pleasantly upon my ears," wrote Nellie in the late 1920s:

for I do not think the so-called "new woman" is as new as she seems. She is merely adjusting herself to the changing conditions of a new era. . . . What woman does want and all she wants, I think, is better to meet the responsibilities that are essentially hers as a woman and at the same time to have a chance to develop the faculties with which she as an individual has been endowed.[47]

Notes

The author acknowledges with gratitude the financial support of three travel grants that have supported her Nellie Tayloe Ross research: the Franklin Delano Roosevelt Library, the American Heritage Center of the University of Wyoming, and the Lola Homsher grant program of the Wyoming Historical Society.

1. N.T. Ross, "The Governor Lady," *Good Housekeeping* 85, no. 2 (August 1927): 30. This issue is the first of three, which presented Nellie's serialized story of her married life and her gubernatorial years.

2. The content for this chapter is drawn from the author's unpublished biography, *Governor Lady: The Life and Times of Nellie Tayloe Ross, 1876–1977*. The manuscript is expected to be submitted for publication by the end of 2004.

3. *New York Times*, December 21, 1977.

4. L. Faderman, *To Believe in Women* (Boston: Houghton Mifflin, 1999), 79–81.

5. E.N. Blair, "A Who's Who of Women in Washington," *Good Housekeeping* 102, no. 1 (1936): 39.

6. *Proceedings*, Democratic Convention 1928, 104–107, 236, 249–250.

7. Despite her priority of reducing expenditures, Nellie was unable while governor to balance the state budget. The overdraft became a reelection issue, with Nellie's Democratic administration and the Republican legislature both blaming the other side. For her part, Nellie pointed out that the legislature appropriated funds beyond the conservative request that she had submitted.

8. M.S. Hayden, "Heretic in Skirts Heads Mint; Returns Money to Congress." June 25, 1950, clipping, newspaper unknown, Nellie Tayloe Ross file, Douglas County Historical Society, Omaha, Nebraska. The year 1950, in which Nellie returned $1 million of her $4.8 million appropriation, marked the fourth straight year in which she returned a substantial sum to Congress.

9. Kenneth Failor interview, March 23–25, 2002, Scottsdale, Arizona. Kenneth Failor was both an official at the Mint and a close friend of Nellie's from the late 1920s until her death.

10. Edness Kimball Wilkins Papers, speech notes, "Ross, Nellie Tayloe—Historical Information" folder. Wyoming State Archives, Cheyenne.

11. Nellie gave birth to twins eight and one-half months after her marriage; the premature boys were frail, but both survived. Her third son, born in 1905, died at 10 months. The couple's youngest son was born in 1912.

12. Scheer, *Governor Lady*, draft Chapter 4.

13. Undated NTR narrative written ca. Coolidge inauguration, NTR Papers, Accession number 10526-97-10-07, "Correspondence, 1922–1953."

14. George Green Tayloe to Nellie Kreider Tayloe, October 8, 1924. Letter courtesy of Kaye Tayloe Collins.

15. Teapot Dome is a rock formation near Casper, Wyoming. It sits atop a tract of

public land containing oil reserves that were intended for the future use of the Navy. Instead, shortly after he was appointed secretary of the interior by President Harding, former Senator Albert B. Fall convinced the Navy Secretary to allow the reserves to be leased secretly to private companies. A series of investigations and congressional hearings concluded that Fall had accepted gifts and loans from the oil companies in exchange for the leases. He eventually went to prison, and several other Harding administration officials were tainted by the scandal. The affair was a primary reason that the Harding administration acquired a reputation for corruption and malfeasance.

16. "Women's 'Bigger Dent in Politics,'" *Literacy Digest* 83 (November 22, 1924): 17.

17. N.T. Ross, "The Governor Lady," *Good Housekeeping* 85, no. 3 (September 1927): 212.

18. Ibid.

19. "Message of Governor Nellie Tayloe Ross to the Eighteenth Wyoming Legislature," *Wyoming State Tribune*, January 15, 1925.

20. "The Eighteenth Session," *Casper Daily Tribune*, February 27, 1925, and "The Eighteenth Session," *Wyoming State Tribune*, February 24, 1925.

21. T.R. Dye, "State Legislative Politics," in *Politics in the American States: A Comparative Analysis*, ed. Jacob Herbert and K.N. Vines (Boston: Little, Brown, 1965), 196.

22. Eula W. Kendrick to Nellie Tayloe Ross, January 18, 1925. NTR Papers, Accession number 948-97-10-07, Box 1, "Correspondence, Professional, 1922–1926."

23. "Democrats Honor Woman Governor," *Washington Star*, undated clipping. NTR Papers, Accession number 10526-97-10-07, Box 7, Folder 3.

24. N.T. Ross, "The Governor Lady," *Good Housekeeping* 85, no. 4 (October 1927): 72.

25. Ross clipping file, Bureau of the Mint.

26. *Wyoming Eagle* editorial, November 19, 1926. Also, Tracy S. McCracken to Nellie's brothers, November 11, 1926. NTR Papers, Accession number 948-97-10-07, Box 1, "Correspondence, Professional, 1924–26."

27. For a discussion of these three basic gubernatorial responsibilities, see C.B. Ransone, Jr., *The American Governorship* (Westport, CT: Greenwood Press, 1982), 86–88.

28. One of Nellie's earliest writing contracts was to produce a three-month series on her life and governorship, serialized by *Good Housekeeping*. The series was the closest Nellie came to writing an autobiography. The series, entitled "The Governor Lady," ran in *Good Housekeeping* 85, nos. 2–4 (August–October 1927).

29. "Govern'r Ross Accepts 'Bryan Contract' on Leading Eastern Chautauqua Circuit," *Wyoming Eagle*, December 31, 1926.

30. NTR Papers, Accession number 948-97-10-07, Box 3, "Manuscripts ca. 1940" folder.

31. See Folders 976, "Lists of Persons Receiving [Patronage] Endorsements," and 989, "Patronage Correspondence, 1932–1933, Ross, Mrs. Nellie T.," from the Papers of the National Committee of the Democratic Party, 1928–1948, FDR Presidential Library, Hyde Park, New York. Nellie received over seventy-five endorsements for interior, the seventh highest number; Harold Ickes, FDR's selectee, ranked thirty-second in the number of endorsements for secretary of the interior.

32. The first woman to head a bureau was Mary Van Kleek in 1918; she briefly directed the Women in Industry Service, which was established to facilitate the employment of women during World War I. When Van Kleek resigned in 1919, Mary Anderson was appointed to replace her. The agency became the Women's Bureau in

1920. Anderson served as its director until 1944. The first director of the Children's Bureau, which was founded in 1912, was Julia Lathrop. The second director was Grace Abbott, who served from 1921 until 1934.

33. The Mint was a bureau within the Department of the Treasury, so that despite her direct relationship with Congress and the independence given to her by the Mint's organic legislation, Nellie technically reported to Secretary Morgenthau.

34. H. Morgenthau III, *Mostly Morgenthau: A Family History* (New York: Ticknor and Fields, 1991), 263–264 and 307; H. Morgenthau III, "One of Two of a Kind," *Fortune* 9, no. 5 (May 1934): 138; P.W. Ward, "Henry Morgenthau and His Friends," *The Nation* 141 (August 14, 1935): 182–184.

35. In *Mostly Morgenthau*, Henry Morgenthau, Jr.'s son referred to his father's sexism when he wrote about the "male chauvinist jokes exchanged on chits of paper" with which Roosevelt and Morgenthau amused themselves during cabinet meetings. He included an example in which Roosevelt and Morgenthau were making fun of Frances Perkins in the photograph section following p. 312.

36. Morgenthau was compulsive in his documentation of staff meetings, telephone conversations, and official documents, and in his informal notes. These items are all documented in over 900 voluminous "diaries," which are located at the FDR Presidential Library. Morgenthau dealt with Nellie only when he could not avoid it; his diaries document less than ten references to her, and only one unpleasant telephone conversation, during his entire eleven years as Treasury secretary. In one example from Diary 53, pp. 204–205, Morgenthau is conducting his daily meeting with his departmental staff (administrative assistants and assistant secretaries) on January 28, 1937. One of his assistants tells him that Nellie has been trying to schedule a meeting to discuss the location of a proposed new mint. After making a joke at Nellie's expense, Morgenthau states: "This is a little game that, if anybody is smart, they'd keep out, because it's between the President of the United States and myself. . . . [T]ell her she's welcome to go and see the president [without me]."

37. See the minutes of Morgenthau's weekly staff meetings, interspersed throughout the Morgenthau diaries.

38. Kenneth Failor interview.

39. "Happy Birthday, Nellie Tayloe Ross," *Coin World* (October 27, 1976); and "Many Firsts for First Female Mint Director," unattributed and undated clipping, both from the Nellie Tayloe Ross historical file, Bureau of the Mint, Washington, DC.

40. *Annual Report of the Director of the Mint* (Washington, DC: Government Printing Office, 1933–1945).

41. Ann Loomis Jesse interview, January 20, 2003, Denver, Colorado.

42. Frederick Tate telephone interview, August 15, 2002, Washington, DC.

43. Kenneth Failor interview.

44. *Annual Report of the Director of the Mint* (Washington, DC: Government Printing Office, 1951), 9–11.

45. "Mrs. Ross Buried Beside Husband," *Casper-Star Telegram*, December 22, 1977. Wyoming State Archives, Acquisition HB81-1, Box 10.

46. P. McAuley, "First Woman Governor at Party," *Casper Star-Tribune*, May 31, 1972.

47. NTR Papers, Accession number 948-97-10-07, Box 3, "Speeches by Nellie Tayloe Ross, ca. 1920–1953, #2."

Part II

Pioneers in the Upper Echelons
of the Federal Government

*As Aristotle knew, and as feminism argues, the more knowledge
of the particular facets of situations we can uncover and heed,
the more rational our ethical reflection becomes. . . . [We
must] take seriously an idea of administrative discretion
that is concrete, situational, experience-based, interactive,
and grounded in perception and feeling as well as in
rational analysis.*

(Stivers 2002, 146)

The life of Nellie Tayloe Ross—mother, wife and widow, governor, federal
executive—provides a natural bridge to Part II, in which our authors depict
the lives of two prominent federal executives: Frances Perkins and Patricia
Roberts Harris.

Introduction to Part II

Meredith Newman brings to life the rich legacy of Frances Perkins, first female member of the cabinet, the nation's fourth secretary of labor, and "the
architect and engineer of some of the most profound social changes in our
history." To hear Perkins's story is to "relive the history of machine politics,
settlement houses, the Great Depression, and presidential politics." Through
Newman's words, we come to know this remarkable woman who " 'sat below the salt' at Jane Addams's table" at Hull House in Chicago, married and
mothered, believed that "'there is a moral aspect to this human and yet economic relationship of employer and employee" and was included in the

inner circle of some of the most powerful men of her day, including Alfred Smith and Franklin Roosevelt. A paragraph does not do justice to either Madam Secretary Frances Perkins or her biographer, Meredith A. Newman. We invite you to immerse yourselves in her story.

In chapter 6, *Elizabeth Williams* portrays the life and times of Patricia Roberts Harris, civil rights advocate, educator, attorney, and the first African American woman to serve in the highest reaches of government, including U.S. ambassador to Luxembourg, secretary of the U.S. Department of Housing and Urban Development, and many other distinguished posts in government and academia. Former House Speaker Thomas P. "Tip" O'Neill "noted that Harris 'had overcome the double dose of discrimination that befell a black woman who sought a career in politics and the law. . . . Pat spent a lifetime overcoming barriers.' " And she did so proudly, whether as the transformative leader of *three* federal agencies or facing down a skeptical senator during her nomination hearing: "I am a black woman, the daughter of a Pullman car waiter. . . . I didn't start out as a member of a prestigious law firm but as a woman who needed a scholarship to go to school. If you think I have forgotten that you are wrong."

We have much to learn from the pride, power, and heart of these women. Their legacy to public service will not be denied. Prepare to be taught, by Perkins and Harris, and by their biographers.

5

Madam Secretary Frances Perkins

Meredith A. Newman

> *May we be wise enough while walking the path called service to the mountain called achievement to gather the wayside flowers of happiness.* (1902 class letter, Mount Holyoke Library)

In a telling remark before the House of Representatives in February 2002, Secretary of Labor Elaine L. Chao extolled the following words spoken by her predecessor some sixty years earlier: "One of the things we have tried to do is to become very realistic about requests for any increases in this coming year's budget. We know only too well that the great expenditures should be directly on the war effort." Secretary Chao is a direct beneficiary of the rich legacy of Frances Perkins, the nation's fourth secretary of labor and most often referred to as the first female member of the cabinet. But Secretary Chao is not alone in this regard.

Perkins has a hand in our daily lives. Former secretary of labor, Willard Wirtz, says it best: "Every man and woman who works at a living wage, under safe conditions, for reasonable hours, or who is protected by unemployment insurance or social security, is her debtor." She is credited with cementing the foundation of labor legislation and imprinting her administrative footprint on the Department of Labor. As the second-longest-serving cabinet member in U.S. history, her tenure as secretary of labor lasted throughout President Roosevelt's four terms, from 1933 until 1945. Minimum wage standards, the forty-hour week, child labor legislation, women's suffrage, industrial safety codes, workers' compensation, labor relations, social work, industrial home work, unemployment insurance, and Social Security have all evolved from her pioneering work. When she was once asked to appraise her place in history, Perkins modestly replied, "You might say that I happened to be a woman, born in my own time" (Severn 1976, 9).

But Perkins was far ahead of her time. Her general preference for preventive over remedial legislation was forward-looking. Her administrative style was similarly progressive. She was decades ahead of her time in her advocacy of the *conference* method to reach consensus over seemingly intractable problems. Her singular focus on the *human* nature of work predates the behavioralist school of management by several decades. Her philosophy that "man could control his own destiny—if the government could provide the conditions that made action and self-help possible" (Perkins, as cited in Thompson 1975, 118) is reminiscent of contemporary governmental reform. Her scrupulous attention to accurate and timely labor and economic statistics was a hallmark of her tenure both as industrial commissioner of New York and later as U.S. secretary of labor. Her steadfast belief in the inalienable rights of all workers was the touchstone of a long and illustrious public-service career. To tell her story is to relive the history of machine politics, settlement houses, the Great Depression, and presidential politics. As one of my former colleagues once said to me, "If you want to really learn about a subject, write a book about it!" I have reluctantly stopped reading about Frances Perkins in order to set down on paper the remarkable contributions of *Madam Secretary*.

The Early Years

Be ye steadfast.

In an uncharacteristic departure from her commitment to accuracy, Frances Perkins would declare her date of birth as 1882. In fact, she was born Fannie Caroline Perkins in Boston on April 10, 1880. Her New England lineage was traced to the first Perkins in Massachusetts Bay Colony who had come from England in the mid-seventeenth century. The Perkins family was among the early settlers of the Maine coast. The site of the ancestral home at New Castle, on the Damariscotta River, is still marked on maps as "Perkins Point" (Josephson and Josephson 1969, 104). Her father, Frederick W. Perkins, married Susie Ella Bean of Bethel, Maine, on September 20, 1877. In 1882 the family moved to Worcester, Massachusetts, where her father opened a retail and wholesale stationery business. A second child, Ethel Cynthia, was born in Worcester on December 15, 1884. The family lived comfortably. In later years, Perkins described her mother as a late sleeper who allowed her grandmother to run the household (Mohr 1979). Cynthia Otis Perkins exerted a profound influence over the young child: "I am extraordinarily the product of my grandmother" (Perkins, as cited in Martin 1976, 42).

After graduating from Worcester's Classical High School on June 20, 1898,

Perkins entered Mount Holyoke College, one of the leading women's colleges, where she majored in physics, biology, and chemistry. Her years at Mount Holyoke, from 1898 to 1902, were extremely happy. Her classmates proclaimed "Perk," as she was affectionately known, as "the girl who has done the most for her class" and elected her the permanent class president of 1902 (Martin 1976, 48). Among her extracurricular activities, she served on the prayer meeting committee and in June of her senior year she led the class prayer meeting with the theme "Be ye steadfast" (I Cor. 15:58), which became the class motto and appeared in the yearbook as *Beop Stapolfaste* (Mohr 1979, 16). Based on the philosophy of its founder, Mary T. Lyon, Holyoke's purpose was that its graduates "live for God and do something" (Cassuto 1985, 17). Perkins, who was a devout Episcopalian, was to take that philosophy to heart.

After graduation in June 1902, Perkins worked as a teacher in a number of different schools, including Bacon Academy in Colchester, Connecticut, and Monson Academy in Monson, Massachusetts. In the fall of 1904, she accepted a position teaching chemistry at Ferry Hall, a private school for girls in Lake Forest, near Chicago. The following year, in an assertion of her independence, she changed her name to Frances Perkins. She spent her free time volunteering at settlement houses, including Chicago Commons and Hull House. In 1906 she quit her teaching position at Lake Forest and became a full-time volunteer at Hull House. She stayed for six months where, as she later told a *New York Times* reporter, "[I] sat 'below the salt' at Jane Addams's table, helping case workers, leading clubs, and accompanying nurses 'back of the yards' " (*New York Times*, as cited in Streeter 1934, 2).

Her Hull House experience was to set the course of her life. She understood that her vocation lay not in teaching but in settlement work and social reform. "I had to do something," she explained later, "about unnecessary hazards to life, unnecessary poverty. It was sort of up to me . . . to do something about it" (Frances Perkins Oral History, Book I, as cited in Martin 1976, 64). Hull House was home to an extraordinary group of resident workers whose vitality and compassion would reshape the social reform landscape of the country. Principal among them were Jane Addams, Florence Kelley, Julia Lathrop, Grace Abbott, Alice Hamilton, Sophonisba Breckinridge, Harold Ickes, and Perkins. Many of these Hull House graduates were to hold significant positions of power on the national level during the New Deal, thereby translating the Hull House social philosophy into national legislation.

Reference to Charlotte Perkins Gilman, a distant relative of Frances Perkins, serves to illustrate the character of a Hull House resident. Gilman (1860–1935) was a noted feminist author and activist. The publication in 1898 of her *Women and Economics: A Study of the Economic Relation Between Men and Women as a Factor in Social Evolution* made her an international figure. At age thirty-five, Gilman went on a five-year speaking campaign, with Hull House her first stop. She rejected the "family values" of her day, finding the traditional home to be a prison for women. Women's access to work would be the "humanizing of women," the way to growth (Gaylor 1997, 339). Parenthetically, one can only speculate that Frances Perkins's apparent ambivalence toward "feminism" did not sit well with the elder Gilman. She apparently characterized Perkins as "more human than female" (Thompson 1975, 53). The results of Perkins's collective labors on behalf of women and children, however, speak for themselves.

In 1907, Perkins left Chicago to become executive secretary of the nascent Philadelphia Research and Protective Association at a salary of $40 per month. Her work focused on investigating the mistreatment of immigrants and black women in that city. These activities reflected the philosophy of her Hull House mentors. During her years in Philadelphia, Perkins attended the Wharton School of Finance and Commerce at the University of Pennsylvania. Here she met Simon Nelson Patten, one of the foremost economists and scholars of his day. His social and economic theories had a profound influence on Perkins (Thompson 1975). Patten encouraged Perkins to continue her postgraduate studies, and in 1909 he recommended her for a Russell Sage Foundation fellowship at the New York School of Philanthropy (later known as the New York School of Social Work) that would permit her to study at Columbia University for a master's degree. She earned a master's degree in economics and sociology from Columbia on June 10, 1910. Her master's thesis, entitled "A Study of Malnutrition in 107 Children from Public School 51," was based on her study of Hartley House, a settlement on the upper west side of Manhattan where she lived. Her thesis appeared in *Survey* in October 1910, her first published article in her field (Martin 1976).

New York City Consumers' League

> *A half-loaf girl: take what you can get now*
> *and try for more later.*

In 1910, with her master's degree in hand, Perkins became executive secretary of the New York City Consumers' League. Florence Kelley, of Hull House, was the executive secretary of the National Consumers' League and mentored her protégé. This position launched Perkins's career as an activist and social reformer that would lead to decades of government service at the state and national levels (Sternsher and Sealander 1990). In this position Perkins "made and directed investigations of factories, mercantile establishments, tenement homework manufacture, bakeries, laundries, etc." (Letter of February 27, 1934, from Miss Perkins's secretary as cited in Streeter 1934, 2). She became a recognized expert on sanitary regulations for cellar bakeries and fire prevention techniques in factories, and her detailed reports and testimony at public hearings resulted in new city regulations.

Perkins was known in the New York State capital, Albany, as a highly effective lobbyist for labor legislation. Her methods were unconventional at times. As an example, in order to persuade the Bloomingdale brothers on the merits of the "Fifty-Four Hour Bill,"[1] she talked to their rabbi—it was all part of lobbying to Perkins (Martin 1976, 92). Her campaign in 1912 for the passage of this bill proved successful. Despite the fact that several thousand female cannery workers were excluded from coverage, she reasoned that the vast majority of female workers (some 400,000 of whom worked in factories throughout the state) would benefit from its passage. The following year the law was broadened to include the canneries. This approach became a trait of Perkins. She was willing to make progress in incremental stages in order to push her reform agenda forward. Noting this characteristic, a friend described Perkins as "a half-loaf girl: take what you can get now and try for more later" (interview by George Martin with Agnes Leach, as cited in Martin 1976, 98).

Until she could afford a small apartment of her own, Perkins lived at Greenwich House, a settlement in the heart of Greenwich Village (Severn 1976). In 1911 she witnessed the tragic Triangle Shirtwaist Company fire there, the worst factory fire in New York's history, in which 146 workers (many of them women and children) died because of the lack of fire escapes. This tragedy became the catalyst for industrial reform across the state.

In May 1912, and with the Consumers' League's blessing, Perkins resigned as their executive secretary to accept a similar position with the New York Committee on Safety, where she worked until 1917. Perkins was to describe this appointment as the "biggest thing in my life" (*New York Times*, as cited in Thompson 1975, 42). The committee's purpose was to keep alive the public's interest in the Factory Investigating Commission (FIC) that had been established the year before (Martin 1976). The FIC was empowered to investigate the circumstances under which manufacturing was carried on in the state, with special attention to the health and safety of workers. It was hoped that the FIC would be instrumental in securing enactment of remedial legislation (Thompson 1975).

Perkins was loaned by the Committee on Safety to the FIC to direct its investigations. She arranged factory inspections for the commissioners throughout the state and brought in experts to advise on such subjects as building construction, fire prevention, and insurance (Martin 1976). By 1914, thirty-six of the FIC's recommendations had been enacted into law (Josephson and Josephson 1969). Many of these dealt with the registration of factories, standards of construction, fire prevention, sanitary regulations, workmen's compensation, and limits on work for women and children. These laws became models for study and legislation in other states, and marked "a change in American political attitudes and policies toward social responsibility" (Perkins 1946, 23).

"To get it off her mind," Perkins married economist Paul Caldwell Wilson in a private, Episcopal wedding ceremony at Grace Church in New York on September 26, 1913. Neither was young at the time of their marriage; she was thirty-three, and he was thirty-seven. Wilson was a native of Chicago and a graduate of Dartmouth and of the University of Chicago, and he had come to New York in 1905 to join the staff of the Bureau of Municipal Research as an expert on budgets.[2] A Progressive Republican, Wilson was appointed budget secretary to the mayor of New York in 1913. The fact that Perkins chose to retain her maiden name upon her marriage generated much debate. Her "critics, all her life, used it as a club to beat her" (Martin 1976, 128). Sometime in the spring of 1915, she bore a child who died in infancy. On December 30, 1916, she gave birth to a girl, who she named Susanna Winslow after a maternal ancestor.[3]

Perkins continued her professional activities as a mother who worked outside the home.[4] In 1917 she became executive director of the New York Council of Organizations for War Service. The following year, Perkins helped found the Maternity Center Association, becoming its executive secretary. She later became director of the American Child Hygiene Association. She was also a member of the National Safety Council and the Academy of Political Science (Streeter 1934).

In January 1919, New York governor Alfred Smith, for whom Perkins had campaigned, appointed Perkins to serve as one of five members of the New York State Industrial Commission, the reorganized state labor department. She was the first woman appointed to this position, and on the announcement of the governor's intention, the critics had a field day. Manufacturers complained that she was usurping a manufacturer's seat on the commission, labor officials complained that she was not a union member, and men complained that she was not a man! (Martin 1976). With a salary of $8,000 (the highest salary any woman had earned in state government), Perkins's charge was "to reform [the commission], to turn it inside out and get it to be a good department" (Smith, as cited in Martin 1976, 142)—no small feat. Perkins took charge of the Bureau of Mediation and Arbitration, reorganized the Factory Inspection Division, and went into the field to "settle" strikes (Felder 1996, 43).

In 1923, Smith appointed her to the newly created three-member Industrial Board, and on January 1, 1926, he named her chair.[5] The Industrial Board was a subdivision of the New York labor department, responsible for judicial and legislative affairs. It administered the state's workmen's compensation program. As chair of the Industrial Board, Perkins was successful in extending the compensation coverage beyond what had been previously allowed, as in the matter of giving death benefits to common-law wives. Indeed, the field of workmen's compensation was still relatively uncharted, and many of Perkins's rulings had the effect of creating new laws, once they were upheld in the courts (Josephson and Josephson 1969). The Industrial Board also dealt with the establishment and enforcement of safety codes for the state's industries.

By 1928 Perkins had become one of the governor's key labor advisers, rising from her position as chair of the Industrial Board to the position of chair of the Industrial Commission, a promotion that gave her outright responsibility for running the largest state department of labor in the country.

Industrial Commissioner of New York

There will be less death, misery, and poverty
because you are at the helm.

Perkins was sworn in as industrial commissioner on January 14, 1929, at an annual salary of $12,000, in charge of a staff of 1,700 employees, with offices in seven cities, and with more than fifty various boards, bureaus, and agencies. "Perkins reportedly worked her staff hard, but since she worked harder, they couldn't complain. On the contrary, her charisma was such that they felt inspired to commit themselves to the same holy charge that seemed to drive her on" (Mohr 1979, 99–100).

Alfred Smith's successor, Franklin Roosevelt, retained Perkins in that post during his two terms as governor from 1929 to 1933. In a (January 17, 1929) congratulatory letter to Perkins, Florence Kelley wrote: "There will be less death, misery, and poverty because you are at the helm. . . . I can see Mr. Roosevelt depending upon your wisdom more and more as his army of villains settle down to the business of bedeviling him" (Perkins Collection, Connecticut College, as cited in Thompson 1975, 92).

Perkins vowed that under her leadership, the labor department would be more than a regulatory agency. It would become a "service organization," a clearinghouse for impartial advice and information on all matters relating to labor. She held that the department had an educative role. The relationship between government and industry was henceforth to be one marked by cooperation. As noted earlier, she was an advocate of the conference method of handling industrial disputes, whereby she would bring together representatives of government, employers, workers, and other experts. This was one of the lessons she carried with her from Hull House. It was Jane Addams "who taught us to take all elements of the community into conference for the solution of any human problem" (Perkins 1943, 41). Perkins considered this technique as the representative democratic process in action (Perkins 1946). She had a profound distaste for government by decree. Commissioner Perkins believed that progress "made from the inside out" would be more lasting than if it were "superimposed by the government" (Streeter 1934, 17). The technique of the conference was also her signature method "of finding out what our common problems are, and discovering common approaches to their solution" (U.S. Department of Labor 1934).

Her administrative style is reflected in advice she received from her grandmother, that those in authority had a duty "to deal fairly, to do justly, to think nobly, to respect [their] fellow man, and to listen patiently" (Transcript of June 1957 lecture at Cornell University, Recording session no. 13, as cited in Thompson 1975, 16). Accordingly, her administrative style was both methodical and inclusive. For example, she commissioned a study of worker risks associated with fire hazards and explosives in the chemical industry. The committee included representatives from the state and federal government, chemical engineers, workers, employers, and the general public. She applied this method of research, inquiry, and consensus to countless aspects of labor, including worker strikes, safety, and compensation. It is revealing that one of her first official acts was the revitalization of the Labor Advisory Board, and the involvement of representatives of labor, employers, and the general public as "true public advisers" in the development of those policies that would ultimately affect them (Perkins 1946, 59).

She was also an early adherent to what was much later to become known as "Management by Walking Around" (or Theory Z)[6]: "I am not afraid to put my hand into the dirt of the department, to do the petty, unpleasant jobs when they must be done . . . and you must not be afraid to do the same thing" (*New York Times*, as cited in Streeter 1934, 18).

She was an advocate of compulsory unemployment insurance and worked tirelessly toward its adoption. She studied England's system during a visit there in the summer of 1931. She also lobbied for old-age assistance, believing that it was a matter of social justice to provide security for elderly citizens who could no longer work to support themselves (Thompson 1975). Another of her projects was the establishment of a Junior Employment Service within the department, to assist high school dropouts in finding jobs.

Feminist scholars writing today may find common ground with Perkins's characterization of the workplace: "The industrial world has been man's and its conceptions of comfort and convenience are based on man's physical structure, habits, and social status. The woman wage-earner enters a misfit world—we need laws to allow her to compete fairly with men" (Perkins, as cited in Streeter 1934, 21–22).

She was instrumental in the passage of the 1927 law and subsequent amendments that reduced the working week for women to forty-eight hours. The equal opportunity legislation since the 1960s echoes Perkins's earlier calls for gender equality. Her sentiments about women and careers are reminiscent of the arguments in support of family-friendly workplace policies today: "You know as well as I do that many fathers are closer to their children than mothers, and I do not see why, because a woman works either in politics or in any other field, her home life must suffer" (Perkins, as cited in Severn 1976, 86).

By any measure, her record as state industrial commissioner was truly impressive. It is all the more extraordinary when one considers that some nine months into her appointment, the stock market crash precipitated the Great Depression. As a result, during the majority of her tenure, her time was absorbed with the exigencies of unemployment relief. Perkins was about to transfer her considerable experience on the state level to a larger, national plane. She cared deeply about the department and would maintain an abiding interest in its activities all of her life.

U.S. Secretary of Labor

> *We are chiefly concerned with men and women in the*
> *process of living and working . . . to humanize the laws which*
> *affect them, is the purpose which must form the background of*
> *everything a department of labor does.*

Not a union man—this summed up the vocal opposition to the Roosevelt appointment of Frances Perkins as his secretary of labor in 1933. This office was considered a political plum that had usually gone to a member of organized labor. Moreover, there was the additional insult of her being a woman and the threat of feminizing the Department of Labor, making it an agency of social welfare influenced by "do-gooders" (Severn 1976, 108). Stating that the American Federation of Labor (AFL) would never become reconciled to a woman in that position, William Green (President of the AFL) was reported as saying that he "objected to her proposed appointment because 80 percent of labor was masculine, and with a woman at the head of both the Children's Bureau and of the Women's Bureau, the appointment would put the department almost completely under feminine control" (*New York Times*, as cited in Streeter 1934, 59). Perkins's response was to appoint him to her Labor Advisory Board! By all accounts, she was highly skilled in the art of politics and diplomacy and was effective at bringing all manner of people on board.

Many more publicly applauded her appointment. As reported in *The Nation*, "When I think of Frances Perkins's point of view and attitude, her humanity, wisdom, and statesmanship, it seems to me that she will be an angel at the Cabinet table in contrast with the sordidness and inhumanity of her predecessors" (Villard, as cited in Streeter 1934, 59). The *New York Times* reported that labor problems had very definitely become human problems, and "what better position should be held by a woman than as head of the Department of Labor" (*New York Times*, as cited in Abels 1974, 37). Others hailed her appointment as the beginning of a "New Deal" for women (Miller 1967, 37). Certainly, her credentials were impeccable.

"More pay, more comfort, and more security for the ordinary workers" (Perkins, as cited in Miller 1967, 1)—these were the watchwords of the incoming secretary of labor that were to leave an indelible imprint upon the department. They reflected the statutory purpose of the Department of Labor when it was created in 1913: "[T]o foster, promote, and develop the welfare of the wage earners of the United States, to improve their working conditions, and to advance their opportunities for employment" (Perkins 1943, n.p.). It should be noted that since its founding, the department's role in labor legislation was minimal. Perkins was to push the envelope on nationwide labor legislation throughout her tenure, redefining the role of the department in the process. She had laid out her reform agenda to President Roosevelt as a condition of her appointment. Her proposals included immediate federal aid to the states for direct unemployment relief, an extensive program of public works, the establishment by federal law of minimum wages, maximum hours, unemployment and old-age insurance, abolition of child labor, and the creation of a federal employment service (Perkins 1946). Her reform program thus forecast her greater involvement in promoting the general welfare than had previous secretaries of labor. If this represented the feminization of the department, so be it.

The background and interests of Perkins's predecessors were reflected in the department that she inherited. The first secretary of labor, William Bauchop Wilson, concerned himself with developing trade union relationships and settling labor disputes. He was succeeded in 1921 by James J. Davis who oriented the department "in such a way as to gain the confidence of the business community with which he was identified" (Fenno 1959, 74). He emphasized the immigration services aspect of the department, an emphasis continued by his successor, William Nuckles Doak, former vice-president of the Railway Trainmen's Union (Mohr 1979, 127). Doak served from 1930 to

1933. The Department of Labor was seemingly ripe for reform: "Up to 1933, the Department of Labor was a happy hunting-ground for superannuated labor union officials and the headquarters of some of the dirtiest deals in the history of the United States. . . . In a capital where there was a faint suggestion of bad drains in every government department, the Labor Department stank" (Carter 1934, 174). As the fourth secretary of labor, and the first with a college degree in lieu of a union membership card, Perkins proceeded to clean house.

A seismic shift occurred in the focus of the department when Perkins took the helm in 1933. William Doak was of the opinion that the department should be "run for the general benefit and not for the particular interest of organized or unorganized labor" (Martin 1976, 110). Critics, citing the department's organic act, argued that the purpose for which it had been founded was to help the worker, but they did not prevail. For her part, Perkins believed that the department had failed in its true function of looking after the interests of labor because her predecessors had concentrated on immigration problems to the detriment of the department's broader mandate. Perkins took up the mandate and charted a course correction. Inheriting a "meager little department" (Perkins and St. Sure 1965, 12) with a budget of only $3 million, the department would henceforth be an organization *for labor*. She believed deeply that there was a moral imperative for society, through the government, to enforce workers' rights because "all men are their brothers' keepers" (Martin 1976, 327).

The administrative philosophy of the department underwent a similar transformation. Up until this point, the department had mostly functioned as a regulatory agency, with "policing" functions and a culture of patronage prevailing. Consistent with Perkins's philosophy as industrial commissioner, the department of labor would henceforth be a *service* organization based on principles of merit. Perkins laid out her action plan for the department in her first book, *People at Work*, stating that the department "can develop a service of technical and economic information to help wage-earners in their bargaining. . . . Employers . . . should be able to turn to the Department . . . and get expert, intelligent direction . . . [and] it can be a source of information for the public" (Perkins 1935, 270–273).

She established a merit system by administrative order. Henceforth decisions on selection and advancement were to be based on qualifications rather than patronage. She staffed her bureaus with lawyers and administrators familiar with labor legislation, sociologists, economists, statisticians, and other experts. It is to Perkins's credit that many congressmen and union leaders "felt cheated." (Gilbert, as cited in Martin 1976, 298)

Perkins's personal approach to reform was manifest in the centrality of the human aspects of the work of the department and her insistence on the "humanness of things." The word "manpower" was inimical to her. "[T]he Labor Department is always dealing with men and women of flesh and bone. . . . We are chiefly concerned with men and women in the process of living and working . . . to humanize the laws which affect them, is the purpose which must form the background of everything a department of labor does" (Perkins 1943, 283).

This commitment to human values extended to the department's role in labor relations. "There is a moral aspect to this human and yet economic relationship of employer and employee" (Perkins 1943, 253). In this regard, the department was "to act as the stimulating and advising agency, the counselor rather than the ruler, to evoke . . . self-direction, self-government, and self-development" (Perkins, as cited in Severn 1976, 189).

Perkins was ever mindful of the educative function of the Department of Labor. She was a firm believer in the power of public opinion. "Though the people's will can be trusted it must first be informed. Democracy must have the facts" (Perkins 1943, 273). Her efforts at laying the legal groundwork were considerably strengthened by favorable public opinion. Characteristically, she would evaluate the likelihood of a bill's passage by the extent to which the country had been educated on its particular provisions.

In her reform and reorganization of the department, Perkins aimed at greater efficiency, an objective that encompassed factually sound policy proposals, good administrators for effective action, and goodwill between her department and another (Martin 1976). She advocated salaries comparable to those paid by private industry. In personnel matters, she stressed the "art" of public service rather than the "science" of personnel. She regarded government employment as a vocation, not merely as a way of making a living (Mohr 1979).

As the largest bureau in the department with some 1,700 employees, the Immigration Service was her immediate target for cutbacks. She consolidated the Immigration and Naturalization Services into a single bureau for greater efficiency. She abolished the infamous undercover squad. Henceforth, immigration laws would be enforced with "due regard to human values" (as cited in Severn 1976, 119). To institute her realignment of the department, she next set about strengthening the other five bureaus—Labor Statistics, Women, Children, Employment, and Conciliation Services. Within the first five years of her tenure, she would establish four new agencies in the Department: the Division of Labor Standards (which became the Bureau of Labor Standards), the Division of Public Contracts, the Federal Committee on Apprentice Training, and the U.S. Employment Service (Perkins et al. 1938). The latter was created in response to the passage of the Wagner Bill on June 6, 1933. Attention to job analysis was central to this service: "No longer will the old sign 'Men Wanted' be the lure of a horde of applicants who may or may not be especially qualified or even able to meet the demands of available jobs, but specific information concerning the work to be done and the degree of training or experience required will be provided in advance" (Perkins, as cited in Streeter 1934, 66).

The sheer level of activity of the secretary of labor in the first 100 days of her administration was marked by a sense of urgency. Within the first three weeks of her appointment, she testified before a congressional committee on the merits of the Civilian Conservation Corps as an emergency disaster relief measure. She was to create the National Reemployment Service to set up the machinery for recruiting 250,000 unemployed men for the corps.

It should be emphasized that, for the most part, the Roosevelt administration was drafting pioneering legislation from a "clean slate" in response to the unprecedented social and economic circumstances of the time. Debate on the Black Bill[7] serves to illustrate the groundbreaking nature of the labor legislation of this time. When President Roosevelt and Perkins came to Washington in 1933, this bill was already before the Congress. The bill was criticized on the grounds that it lacked flexibility and failed to accommodate necessary variations between industries. In a now classic reference to the dairy industry, Roosevelt understood that "there have to be hours adapted to the rhythm of the cow" (Perkins 1946, 194).[8] As Perkins reflected in 1965:

Today we have the tools with which to work. . . . In 1932 we did not have unemployment insurance; we had no old age insurance . . . we had no way at the federal level of regulating hours and wages. . . . The current administration started with equipment never available before in the United States. (Perkins and St. Sure 1965, 1–2)

This point is underscored by a comment made many years later by one of Perkins's students at Cornell, "But in the United States we have always had social security!" (Martin 1976, 484).

Perkins spearheaded the development of much of this federal legislation that we so readily take for granted. Interstate cooperation and cooperation between the state departments of labor and the federal department were key elements of Perkins's legislative strategy. Consistent with her signature conference approach, she organized the first annual national conference on labor legislation. She invited the governor of each state to appoint one delegate to represent that state and another delegate to represent the workers. She also invited experts on labor legislation. She presided over the first such conference in Washington, DC, in February of 1934, attended by delegates from forty-six states. She was to preside over every national conference "joyfully and indefatigably" (Andrews, as cited in Martin 1976, 425). Committees were organized around industrial health and safety, limitations of hours of work, child-labor standards, unemployment reserves, minimum wages, industrial home work, provision for old age, employment exchanges, workmen's compensation, and cooperation between federal government and state labor departments. Her stated goal was to evolve an *American* labor legislation policy, "a sound program of Nation-wide legislation, other than Federal legislation" (U.S. Department of Labor 1934, 2). A cooperative federal-state system has the twin benefits of permitting variations in state laws and "insures uniformity in respects in which uniformity is absolutely essential" (Perkins et al. 1935, 15). In her keynote address, she stated: "We have a duty to perform. We have a joint responsibility to the 40,000,000 wage earners of the United States for the development of a program of labor legislation and a policy which will be broad enough and flexible enough to meet the needs of these earners wherever they live" (U.S. Department of Labor 1934, 7).

Perkins applied the principles of the conference method in all manner of venues. The following anecdote that took place in August of 1933 in the steel center of Homestead, Pennsylvania, serves as an illustration. At a hearing in the local Hall of Burgesses on the rights of workers in the establishment of the National Recovery Administration (NRA) Steel Codes, several hundred disgruntled steelworkers had been denied access. Believing that it was the Platonic "duty of public officers . . . to listen patiently to all citizens" (Perkins 1946, 219), Perkins ushered these men into a nearby post office. Remembering that federal buildings in any locality are under the jurisdiction of the federal government, the meeting took place in a "long corridor lined with postal cages" (220) at the local post office! While Perkins was often criticized because she was not a "tough two-fisted man," the Steel Trust, for one, understood that her velvet gloves packed their own punch.

In mid-1934 Roosevelt appointed Perkins to head a cabinet-level Committee on Economic Security. The committee was tasked with drawing up the Social Security Act. Perkins became its chief architect. It is of interest that while Roosevelt did not like the word "social," semantics meant little to Perkins; and even though "it was really social," Roosevelt called it the Committee on Economic Security (Perkins 1962, 23). During this period, Perkins made over a hundred speeches in different parts of the country about Social Security for the purpose of educating the public (Perkins 1962). The funding issue had the potential to derail the committee's progress—their deadline of January 1, 1935, was at hand. In a characteristic gesture, Perkins invited the committee to her home in Washington, seated them around the dining room table with one bottle of scotch, locked the door, and said: "Gentlemen, that is all you get until this bill is drafted!" (Interview with Alice Cook, as cited in

Abels 1974, 49). The act established unemployment insurance, provided for old-age pensions, and provided "security for dependent and crippled children, mothers, and indigent disabled and the blind" (Perkins, as cited in Dudley 1994, 163). Not surprisingly, the cornerstone of the act was a plan of cooperative federal-state action. According to Perkins, the act represents a "cooperative venture participated in by both the Federal and State Governments, preserving the benefits of local administration and national leadership" (166). It is noteworthy that the committee's discussions included plans for health insurance, but "health insurance was then, as now, a difficult question. Powerful elements of the medical profession were up in arms over the idea of any kind of government-endorsed system" (Perkins 1946, 289).

Another project that she conceived and promoted was the adherence of the United States to the International Labor Organization (ILO)—a permanent organization to promote improvement in conditions of labor. On August 20, 1934, the United States joined the ILO. Over the years, Perkins worked steadily to strengthen the ILO and the country's contribution to it (Martin 1976).

The Fair Labor Standards Act of 1938 was the last of Roosevelt's New Deal measures. Perkins supervised the preparation of this law and shepherded it through the legislative process. The act would put a floor under wages and a ceiling over hours and effectively outlaw child labor in factories. In congressional testimony prior to its passage, there was a discussion on the subject of different wages for men and women. Representative George A. Schneider from Wisconsin asked if there should be a "differential." Perkins replied: "I think wage is an economic factor, and it should be the same no matter who does the work" (*Fair Labor Standards Act of 1937*. Hearings, 75th Cong., 1st sess., June 2, 1937, 190, as cited in Miller 1967, 139). Reflecting on the passage of the act, Perkins later said: "Everybody claimed credit for it. . . . I cannot remember whether the President and I claimed credit, but we always thought we had done it" (Perkins 1946, 265–266).

At several points in her career, she was called upon to explain the legal limits of her job in order to dispel misconceptions of her powers. The "famous case" of the drive to impeach her was one such occasion. Resolution 67 was presented to the House, on January 24, 1939, by Rep. J. Parnell Thomas, a New Jersey Republican. The Committee on the Judiciary was directed to investigate her official conduct (along with James L. Houghteling, the commissioner of the Immigration and Naturalization Service, and Gerard D. Reilly, the Department of Labor solicitor) to determine whether Perkins and her two colleagues "have been guilty of any crimes and misdemeanors," specifically that they had "entered into a conspiracy to refuse to enforce the deportation laws of the United States . . . and to defraud the United States by not deporting one Harry Bridges [an Australian] (Resolution 67, 76th Cong., 1st sess., *Congressional Record*, vol. 84 [1939]: 711). In her testimony, Perkins stated: "As Secretary of Labor I have no general commission or power to remove an alien merely because I believe him to be 'undesirable,' or because he is believed to be, or is in fact, a labor agitator" (3743). The committee unanimously recommended that Resolution 67 "not pass" (3285).

After Roosevelt's death, Perkins served briefly under President Truman, stepping down as secretary of labor in 1945 after twelve years on the job. In a characteristic gesture, she personally shook hands in farewell with each of the 1,800 employees of the department. Of her administration, it was said that the Department of Labor under Perkins was as different as the "old shack sandwiched between a rooming house and a garage on F street . . . to the new marble Labor Department building down by the Washington monument (Carter as cited in Miller 1967, 59).[9] For her part, in response to a letter she received upon her resignation, she replied: "I came to work for God, F.D.R., and the millions of forgotten, plain, common working men (Letter of June 7, 1945, to Felix Frankfurter, Frances Perkins Papers, Columbia, as cited in Martin 1976, 375).

Return to Academia

Be not afraid. It is I.

For a short time, Perkins retired to a private life of writing. Her second book, *The Roosevelt I Knew*, was published in 1946. Parenthetically, Perkins's unfinished manuscript and papers on Alfred Smith became the basis for *Al Smith: Hero of the Cities* by Josephson and Josephson (1969).

Her retirement from public service was short-lived. On September 12, 1946, President Truman appointed her as one of three commissioners of the U.S. Civil Service Commission at an annual salary of $15,000. Upon her resignation from the commission on April 11, 1953, she started working as a visiting professor at the University of Illinois. In 1956, she went to Austria to lecture at the Salzburg Seminar in American Studies. The following year, at the age of seventy-seven, she began a new job, as professor at Cornell University's School of Industrial and Labor Relations.

She was to spend eight years at Cornell. In the spring of 1960, the twenty-seven members of the Telluride Association at Cornell, all men, and considered the intellectual elite of the university, invited her to be a guest in residence in their house on campus. The invitation was unprecedented in that no woman had ever lived in the house. She apparently thrived on the intellectual and social stimulation there.

Despite her advancing age, she retained her sharp wit and sense of show-manship. Speakers' lecterns are typically sized to fit (tall) men. On one occasion she walked up to a lectern, heard the applause following her introduction, but could not see—or be seen. There was a pause. Then the startled audience heard a powerful voice: "Be not afraid. It is I." While the audience roared, the lectern was replaced (Perkins, informal conversation with Dr. Arch Troelstrup, as cited in Mohr 1979, 293).

Reflections on Her Public Service Career

The technique of administration in a democracy is not easy.

It is not an exaggeration to say that the nation's fourth secretary of labor is the epitome of excellence in public service, an inspiration to those who have had the privilege of meeting her, either in person or in print. As an administrator, she was pragmatic, honest, compassionate, dedicated, energetic, dutiful, loyal, politically astute, trustworthy, and courageous. She was also a master of complex policy details. In her Oral History, Perkins recounts the following anecdote. When asked how Al Smith "knew so much and where he got his information that made him such a strong advocate for all this labor and social legislation," the response was that he "read a book. . . . He knew Frances Perkins and she was a book" (Perkins's Oral History, Book I, as cited in Cassuto 1985, 46).

Above all, she had an inner strength, derived from her deeply held religious beliefs and her social consciousness. Her moral fiber was the unifying thread that tied her many programs together. Her staff recalls the "holy charge" that would drive her ever forward. Perkins articulated the values of her administrative ethic as follows: "The technique of administration in a democracy is not easy. . . . The statute law and the natural law, the law of God, must be somehow or other blended together, and fairness and decency and patience must prevail" (Perkins 1939, 6). She was to repeat this message some nine years later. In a series of three lectures entitled "The Christian in the World" delivered to the parishioners of St. Thomas Episcopal Church in New York, Perkins said that bureaucrats ought to be aware of God's laws and be eager to apply them. Her success in implementing her beliefs was arguably her most extraordinary quality.

Another of Perkins's redeeming qualities was her ability to thrive in her male-dominated administrative and political world. She allied herself with some of the most powerful men of her day, Alfred Smith and Franklin Roosevelt principal among them. She was included in the inner circles of both men. Despite these alliances and her own authority as commissioner and secretary, derogatory references to her gender were ubiquitous and unrelenting. Her "Ma Perkins" moniker was frequently attached to news media reports about her clothing. For example, *Time* reported that "her drab clothing looked as though it had been designed by the Bureau of Standards." Others retorted: "If [only] she wasn't a woman! And if she would just take her hat off." (Her tricorn hat became her trademark.) Still others quipped: "This feminine stowaway would surely sink this ship of state" (Tucker 1934, 16); [She has been called] "'woozy in the head' . . . although she would make an excellent housewife, she did not know as much about economics 'as a Hottentot does about moral law'" (*Time*, as cited in Miller 1967, 60). She has been disparagingly referred to as the "Perfect Secretary"—"though she said she wanted to be a 'Secretary for Labor,' she has ended being another secretary *for* Mr. Roosevelt" (P.W. Ward in the *Nation*, as cited in Miller 1967, 60). Even one of her fellow Hull House alums, Secretary of Interior Harold Ickes, reportedly complained about Perkins's incessant talking and referred to her as "Madame Queen" (Ickes, as cited in Abels 1974, 44).

There were also those who made "chivalrous and very awkward gestures" (Mohr 1979, 94). For example, Hugh Johnson, the administrator of Title I of the National Industrial Recovery Act, praised Perkins as "the best man in the Cabinet" (Perkins 1946, 204). In delivering an address on the occasion of Perkins's appointment as industrial commissioner, New York State Supreme Court Justice Bernard Shientag stated that "she had not been appointed because she was a woman, but rather in spite of that fact" (*New York Times*, as cited in Thompson 1975, 91). A final reference to her gender may be the most compelling. During Perkins's eighth year as secretary of labor, *Fortune* magazine published an article prefaced by the following: "If [she] had done no more than take the oath of office on March 5, 1933 . . . she would have earned fame as the nation's first woman cabinet officer. Actually her experiences in office have created their own fame . . . overshadowing the mere circumstance of gender" (Hamill, as cited in Thompson 1975, 1).

It is characteristic that Perkins actively continued her work at Cornell University until two weeks before she died. She passed away in New York on May 14, 1965, at the age of eighty-five, the architect and engineer of some of the most profound social changes in our history (Felder 1996). Her accomplishments had become a part of the fabric of American social reform by the time of her death. The eulogy by Supreme Court Justice Arthur Goldberg personalized her legacy: "The nation has lost one of its first citizens. . . . Under her wise and inspiring leadership, the department of labor came of age" (as cited in Severn 1976, 243).

Perkins has been the recipient of numerous post-humous awards and honors. The U.S. Postal Service created a fifteen-cent stamp in April of 1980 with her image. That same year, the U.S. Department of Labor in Washington, DC, dedicated their headquarters building as the Frances Perkins Federal Building. She has been inducted into the National Women's Hall of Fame and the Labor Hall of Fame. Very few cabinet officers have had such an impact sixty years after they have left office.

Notes

1. The "fifty-four-hour bill" prohibited women of any age and boys under eighteen from working in factories more than fifty-four hours a week (Martin 1976, 77).

2. For a detailed account of the Bureau of Municipal Research and of settlement houses, see Stivers (2000).

3. In 1934, Susanna graduated from the Brearley School and was accepted at Bryn Mawr College. She married socialite David Meredith Hare on March 12, 1938, but the marriage ended in divorce. In 1953 she married artist Calvert Coggeshall, and the following year they had a son.

4. During the 1920s, her husband suffered increasingly from depression and unemployment. From 1930 until his death on December 31, 1952, he spent most of his time in institutions.

5. Between 1920 and 1922 (when Alfred Smith was reelected governor), Perkins served as executive secretary of a new organization, the New York Council on Immigrant Education. In character, Perkins became the workhorse of this organization, setting policy and implementing programs (Martin 1976, 170).

6. See Ouchi (1981).

7. The Black Bill proposed a limitation of thirty hours a week for all persons working in interstate commerce. The intent was to reduce unemployment by dividing the existing jobs among more workers (Martin 1976, 260).

8. Perkins spearheaded an amendment to the Black Bill, but it did not pass. The National Industrial Recovery Act was subsequently passed in June 1933.

9. The Department of Labor was originally housed at 1712 "G" Street, in a nine-story, boxlike building constructed during World War I, before moving to a new building at Fourteenth Street and Constitution Avenue, NW in January 1935.

References

Abels, Margaret D. 1974. "Frances Perkins and Eleanor Roosevelt: Two Women in Reform America." MA thesis, State University College of New York at Buffalo, August.

Carter, J. Franklin. 1934. *The New Dealers*. New York: Simon and Schuster.

Cassuto, Thalia. 1985. "Frances Perkins: Establishing the Links Between New Deal Social Welfare Legislation and National Consumers' League Social Welfare Policies." MA thesis, Sarah Lawrence College, December.

Dudley, William. 1994. *The Great Depression. Opposing Viewpoints*. San Diego: Greenhaven Press.

Felder, Deborah G. 1996. *The 100 Most Influential Women of All Time. A Ranking Past and Present*. New York: Citadel Press.

Fenno, Richard F., Jr. 1959. *The President's Cabinet: An Analysis in the Period from Wilson to Eisenhower*. Cambridge, MA: Harvard University Press.

Gaylor, Annie Laurie, ed. 1997. *Women Without Superstition. "No Gods—No Masters." The Collected Writings of Women Freethinkers of the Nineteenth and Twentieth Centuries*. Madison, WI: Freedom from Religion Foundation.

Josephson, Matthew, and Hanna Josephson. 1969. *Al Smith: Hero of the Cities. A Political Portrait Drawing on the Papers of Frances Perkins*. Boston: Houghton Mifflin.

Martin, George. 1976. *Madam Secretary: Frances Perkins*. Boston: Houghton Mifflin.

Miller, Jeanne Kurth. 1967. "Frances Perkins: First Woman Cabinet Member." MA thesis, Central Missouri State College, August.

Mohr, Lillian Holmen. 1979. *Frances Perkins: "The Woman in FDR's Cabinet!"* Great Barrington, MA: North River Press.

Ouchi, William G. 1981. *Theory Z: How American Management Can Meet the Japanese Challenge*. Reading, MA: Addison-Wesley.

Perkins, Frances. 1935. *People at Work*. New York: John Day.

―――. 1939. "The International Labor Organization as an Agency of Democracy." Address before the Democratic Women's Luncheon Club of Philadelphia, March 27.

―――. 1943. "Three Decades. A History of the Department of Labor." *American Federationist* 50 (3): 20–23.

―――. 1946. *The Roosevelt I Knew*. New York: Harper Colophon.

―――. 1962. "The Roots of Social Security." Remarks of Address to the General Staff Meeting of the Social Security Administration, Baltimore, Maryland, October 23.

Perkins, Frances, and Joseph Paul St. Sure. 1965. *Two Views of American Labor*. Los Angeles: University of California.

Perkins, Frances et al. 1935. *Report to the President on the Committee on Economic Security*. Washington, DC: Government Printing Office.

―――. 1938. *The Federal Government Today. A Survey of Recent Innovations and Renovations*. New York: American Council on Public Affairs.

Severn, Bill. 1976. *Frances Perkins. A Member of the Cabinet*. New York: Hawthorne Books.

Sternsher, Bernard, and Judith Sealander. 1990. *Women of Valor. The Struggle Against the Great Depression As Told in Their Own Life Stories*. Chicago: Ivan R. Dee.

Stivers, Camilla. 2000. *Bureau Men, Settlement Women: Constructing Public Administration in the Progressive Era*. Lawrence: University Press of Kansas.

Streeter, Doris Irene. 1934. "The Public Career of Frances Perkins." MA thesis, University of Colorado.

Thompson, Cathy Rosann. 1975. "The Pre-New Deal Career of Frances Perkins 1880–1932." MA thesis, Florida Atlantic University, Boca Raton, August.

Tucker, Ray. 1934. "Fearless Frances." *Colliers*, July 28, 16.

U.S. Department of Labor. 1934. *Proceedings of the National Conferences on Labor Legislation, 1934 to 1955*. Washington, DC, February 14 and 15.

6

Patricia Roberts Harris

A Pioneer Champion of Civil Rights and Social Justice

Elizabeth G. Williams

A Pioneering Lifetime

Patricia Roberts Harris was a superachiever driven in her professional life by an ambition for excellence, a brilliant intellect, and a passion to make a difference for social justice for blacks, for women, and for the disadvantaged. Through persistence, tremendous energy, sheer determination, and hard work she gained not only political power, but also emerged as a respected colleague of American presidents and congressional leaders. Patricia Harris is frequently remembered as a tough, abrasive, assertive, no-nonsense administrator; an educator; and a dedicated career public administrator. She was often labeled arrogant, sharp-tongued, contentious, and harsh by critics, subordinates, associates, and the media. But even critics agree that personal integrity powered her unwavering commitment to improving the quality of life, civil rights, and educational opportunity for blacks, women, the poor, and those in America's inner cities.

In only sixty years (by today's standard, a life cut short) Patricia Roberts Harris grew from being the daughter of a small-town railroad dining-car porter to a high-profile cabinet executive. In her amazing lifetime, Patricia Harris was a civil rights advocate, educator, and attorney. She was appointed ambassador to Luxembourg, cabinet secretary of U.S. Housing and Urban Development (HUD), and cabinet secretary of the then single-largest U.S. government agency, the Department of Health, Education, and Welfare (HEW). She was also a board member of Fortune 100 corporations and even a mayoral candidate in our nation's capital.

What makes these achievements and her life of service even more out-standing is that she accomplished much of this in an era when racial dis-crimination and "separate-but-equal" segregation was the law of our land, prior to the school desegregation rulings of *Brown v. Board of Education* (1954, 1955) or the enactment of the 1964 Civil Rights Act. Twenty years before the 1964 act prohibiting racial and sexual discrimination passed, Patricia Harris was participating in desegregation sit-ins. As vice-chair of Howard University's student chapter of the National Association for the Advancement of Colored People (NAACP), she was in the forefront in desegregation sit-ins, protesting "white-only" public accommodations in Washington, DC, as early as 1943. This was more than a decade before the Reverend Dr. Martin Luther King, Jr. would lead the 1955 Montgomery, Alabama, city bus boycott, bringing the American civil rights movement into national attention.

Former U.S. House Speaker Thomas P. "Tip" O'Neill noted Harris "had overcome the double dose of discrimination that befell a black woman who sought a career in politics and the law beginning in the late 1940s. Pat spent a lifetime overcoming barriers" (Pianin 1985, D1). As an African-American woman, Patricia Harris opened many doors, accomplishing many firsts in spite of facing racial and sexual discrimination not only from whites—but also from black men.

> One thing about us Black women is, we are at the very bottom of the totem pole. I have had to contend with discrimination by White men, White women, and Black men. I have had Black men tell me, "Oh, you really should have this job but we can't put a woman in this job." (Brinkley 1982, 3)

Shortly after being confirmed secretary of HUD she said: "I feel I've knocked down yet another barrier and it's all right to be first as long as you're not the only [one]. I try to use being first as a way of being the first of many" (DeWitt 1977, H6). To date, too few outstanding women and minorities have followed her lead into the highest levels of national public service. But the legacy of Patricia Harris remains alive and well today, inspiring and training women and people of color for public-service leadership in the twenty-first century.

From Unassuming Roots in Mattoon, Illinois

Patricia Roberts was born May 31, 1924, the only daughter and first of two children to "Bert" Fitzgerald Roberts, a railroad dining car porter and his wife, Hildren, in Mattoon, Illinois. "Her [mother's] ancestors were Negro slaves who had moved from Virginia to Illinois, where they bought their freedom through work [nearly fifty years before the U.S. Civil War]" ("Patricia Roberts Harris"). In the 1920s Mattoon was a small prairie town three hours from Chicago, which had a population of 15,000 with fewer than 200 blacks.

By the time Patricia was six, her parents had separated and her mother sent her and her two-year-old brother, Malcolm ("Mickey"), to live with a great-aunt while she went to work as an actuarial clerk for the black-owned Victory Mutual Life Insurance Company. Eight years later, Hildren packed up the two children and moved the family to Chicago where Patricia graduated from high school. In interviews, Hildren said the family was "relatively poor" but they were not on welfare and "things weren't backward by any means" (DeWitt 1977, H6). The household had books and a strong focus on hard work, the importance of education, self-improvement, and achieving success. Patricia learned to admire her mother, who loved cooking and playing the piano. Hildren was a very capable and strong-minded woman—these were qualities Patricia would also come to be admired for as an adult.

But Hildren was cold, distant, and emotionally withdrawn from her daughter. According to Patricia's life-long adult friend, the late Dr. Jeanne Noble:

> Harris' mother strongly preferred her son [Malcom] to her daughter. She didn't even bother pretending. Pat, I believe, was greatly influenced by her relationship with her mother, in never being able to experience her mother's love. [She] wanted a withholding mother to love her, even at the end of her [own] life! ("Personal Dimension" 1998, 4)

Harris described her mother:

> [She was] a tiny, beautiful, extraordinarily beautiful woman. She can wrap a package or repair an iron with equal skill. She expected me to be reading at a very early age, she expected A's, not A minuses. (DeWitt 1977, H6)

Undergraduate Years at Howard University

Patricia Roberts was an excellent, hard-working high school student. She graduated with highest honors from Chicago's Englewood High School with scholarship offers to six different universities. Intending to become a linguist, she chose Howard University—according to her mother, because she "wanted more competition from a larger student body" (DeWitt 1977, H6). Fellow Howard freshman and sorority sister Jeanne Noble remembered:

Photo 6.1 *From left to right:* **Mrs. Hildren Roberts, Judge William B. Harris** (*background*), **President Jimmy Carter, and HEW Secretary Patricia Roberts** (*foreground*). **August 1979 inside the White House.** (Carter Presidential Library. Photo courtesy of Ms. Fran Phillips-Calhoun.)

Pat wore a huge head of hair, she was skinny, indifferently dressed [and] not thought to be attractive. [She was] a very unpretentious coed. Soon [she was] referred to as the brilliant, plain girl from Chicago. ("Personal Dimension" 1998, 2)

Delta Sigma Theta

Jeanne Noble and Patricia Roberts were "line sisters" together at Howard seeking to become members of the Delta Sigma Theta Sorority (Delta). Today Delta is an international sorority of over 200,000 primarily African-American college-educated women, dedicated to promoting academic excellence and service. Founded in 1913 by twenty Howard University co-eds, it worked for women's suffrage prior to the passage of the Nineteenth Amendment in 1920. Noble recalls: "[Patricia was] a frightened sorority initiate with a black and white panda under her arm, trying to avoid sorority hazing and with a look of fright in her eyes. She was absolutely terrified of the Big Sisters" ("Personal Dimension" 1998, 2).

This frightened initiate would later organize the first Delta Sigma Theta national headquarters office in Washington, DC, and become its first Capitol Hill civil rights lobbyist in the late 1940s. At Delta's biannual national conventions the sorority now recognizes women of outstanding public achievement with the Patricia Roberts Harris Medallion for Public Service.

Early Civil Rights Activism from Roots at Howard University

Patricia Harris's life-long commitment to the advancement of civil rights and social justice through nonviolent, orderly protest blossomed while she was an undergraduate at Howard University. By 1943 she became vice-chair of the campus chapter of the NAACP. She participated in frequent desegregation sit-ins protesting "white-only" public accommodations at Washington cafeterias and drugstore lunch counters. She led the April 1943 sit-in at the Little Palace Cafeteria at 14th and U Street near the campus. The sit-in resulted in the integration of the cafeteria, which had previously refused to serve Howard students. She later picketed the Thompson Restaurant, which is located only a few blocks from the White House (Pianin 1982c, A8). Former *Chicago Defender* editor Louis Martin recalled:

She [Harris] spent several years badgering congressmen about civil rights. She was a feature in protest marches because she was the youngest thing around, a pretty girl and smart. [She was petite, slender, had a lightly freckled butter-cream complexion and reddish-blonde hair.] When black newspapermen came to Washington, you were always told to get ahold of Pat. She was a source of knowledge. She learned not to be intimidated by big shots long ago. (DeWitt 1977, H6)

Patricia Roberts would go on to become chair of the District of Columbia's NAACP political education committee, chair of the Washington Urban League's welfare committee, vice-chair of the national capital area American Civil Liberties Union (ACLU) chapter, and a board member of the national ACLU.

Summa Cum Laude in Only Three Years

Although perhaps only plain in appearance as an undergraduate, Patricia was brilliant academically. According to Noble, "Harris was so advanced in every subject that the professors made her their assistant in most classes. This meant both teaching and grading papers" ("Personal Dimension" 1998, 1, 2). She held research assistantships throughout her undergraduate years at Howard from 1943 to 1945. Patricia Roberts graduated summa cum laude, after only three years, and was elected to Phi Beta Kappa. After graduation in 1945, she briefly returned home to Chicago, completed two years of graduate work in industrial relations at the University of Chicago, and worked as program director for the local YWCA.

Patricia Roberts Settles in Washington, DC

After two years in Chicago, she returned to what would become her permanent home, Washington, DC, to launch the first of many successful political careers. She resumed graduate work in industrial relations at American University, while working from 1949 to 1953 as the assistant director of the American Council on Human Rights. It was midway through her tenure as executive director of Delta Sigma Theta from 1953 to 1959 that her life, political future, and career would be forever changed through her marriage to William Beasley Harris.

A Life-Long Partnership in Marriage and Achievement

Patricia Roberts had met William Beasley Harris, a practicing attorney and member of the Howard University Law School faculty, in 1953 while she was assistant director of the American Council on Human Rights. Neither had initially made much of an impression on the other. In fact, years later when Sadie Yancey, dean of women at Howard University, insisted to Patricia,

"There's a fellow up here you should marry," she replied, "I already know him and he doesn't pay me a bit of attention" (DeWitt 1977, H6).

William Harris had come from his childhood home in Philadelphia to Washington, DC, in the early 1950s. Nine years older than Patricia, he was a "tall, courtly man with a soft voice and reserved manner" (Pianin 1982c, A8). Five months after their "reintroduction," Patricia Roberts and William (Bill) Harris were married on September 1, 1955. In the course of their twenty-nine year marriage, Bill would become a major factor in encouraging, supporting, and fostering his wife's professional career and political ambition.

Patricia later became frustrated and disillusioned in her academic career by limited opportunities. In the 1950s black faculty members' careers were primarily limited to historically black colleges and universities. Bill encouraged her to act on her passions in civil rights and social justice by attending law school. Later, Bill closed his own private law practice and accepted a position with the State Department, so he could accompany her to Luxembourg. He became an administrative law judge with the Federal Power Commission in 1979, and finished his career from 1974 to 1984 as a judge with the Maritime Commission. Throughout Bill's professional lifetime he, like Patricia, was extremely active in civic affairs, especially dealing with urban issues, civil rights, and welfare concerns.

Personal friends commented on the "warm and friendly [side of Patricia], her love of family and devotion to Bill" ("Personal Dimension" 1998, 2). Jeanne Noble said:

> Bill was bright, accomplished, handsome and he adored the very ground she [Pat] walked on. I still remember the adoring look in Bill's eyes. There was love there which compensated for her mother's lack of affection. ("Personal Dimension" 1998, 3)

Bill admired his wife, her abilities, and accomplishments:

> She's a marvelous person. All these years, she's never played games. She's a lovely person, who's ultimately fair. If I was to be tried, I'd want her for my lawyer. (DeWitt 1977, H6)

This is high praise not only from an admiring husband, but from an attorney and judge. A staunch champion and advocate of his wife against personal criticism, Bill stated: "Sometimes people have run into her sharp mind and tongue . . . but never get a chance to see there is humor and joy attached. One of my weaknesses is I've always liked very smart women, because the returns are always better, despite what you may have to go through" (Pianin 1982c, A8).

Photo 6.2 **Patricia and Bill Harris at home.** (Patricia Roberts Harris Collection, Moorland-Spingarn Research Center, Howard University. Used by permission.)

When Patricia became ill with terminal breast cancer in 1984, Bill became her devoted, primary caregiver and constant companion until he died of a stroke at age seventy, just five months before she succumbed to cancer. According to close friend Sharon Pratt, in the final days of Harris's illness, she asked her "Is there nothing that can bring you joy? Pratt said Harris thought for a long moment or two and then replied, 'Bill Harris'" (Pianin 1985, 2).

George Washington University Law School

With Bill's encouragement, and while intending to join him in private law practice after graduation, Patricia entered George Washington Law School. Once again her brilliant intellect and strong work ethic drove her to excellence. She held research assistantships, was associate editor of the *George Washington University Law Review*, and graduated first in her class of ninety-four in 1960. Her interests in politics, civil rights, and public law continued to flourish at George Washington. Years later in a 1982 interview following her unsuccessful mayoral candidacy, Harris would comment:

> I wanted to be mayor in order to do what needs to be done. I wasn't burning to be mayor. . . . There are few things I've burned [i.e., longed] to do in my life. I really wanted to be a lawyer. . . . I have not been a woman of burning ambition, but a woman who wanted to serve and lead a satisfying life. (Rimer 1982, B3)

After graduation, instead of immediately entering private practice with Bill, she accepted a position as trial attorney in the appeals and research section of the Criminal Division of the Department of Justice. During this time she also chaired the DC Law Revision Commission. Less than a year after graduation she was appointed to the Howard Law faculty and admitted to practice law before the U.S. Supreme Court. During her year at Justice, she met and became friends with the new U.S. attorney general, Robert F. Kennedy—brother of the president of the United States. This friendship would later open many doors of opportunity for public service.

Howard University Law School Faculty Years

In 1961, Patricia Harris was appointed associate dean of students and lecturer of law at Howard University Law School, where she would rise through the academic ranks to full professor. She taught courses in constitutional law, government regulation, and torts. Harris greatly enjoyed teaching law. "As a law instructor at Howard, I teach students to seek the relevant, so they can usually move with some degree of rapidity and security to almost any job. . . . Students would be equipped for managerial functions" ("Patricia Roberts Harris" 1965, 190).

Former law students of Harris's gathered to remember her on the tenth anniversary of the Patricia Roberts Harris Public Affairs Program at Howard University. Former student and then Howard professor J. Clay Smith recalled her:

[She was] rather distant but polite, and helpful, very helpful, an extremely apt, intelligent person, a no-nonsense person and a real taskmaster. I remember being struck by her directness as she asked questions and attempted to penetrate our minds, to make us think. She, I believe, was trying to free us . . . by her rigor, to free our minds so we could be the best people in the world. ("Patricia Roberts Harris as Educator" 1998, 1, 2)

Former student Carolyn D. Jordan remembered Harris:

[She was a] woman of enormous energy, doggedness, integrity and character. Her moral compassion and conviction was an inspiration to us all. Her standards of excellence, her keen intellect, and her unyielding courage guided us toward exemplary service. ("Patricia Roberts Harris as Educator" 1998, 3)

As professor and dean of students at Howard Law School, Harris mentored many young women. According to attorney Joan Ann Burt, who first met Dean Harris while she was a freshman law student, Harris instilled the value "that you must open doors for others—give back, as I have tried to do, to young people coming behind me" ("Patricia Roberts Harris in Law and Public Service" 1998, 1).

During the Kennedy Administration

National Women's Committee for Civil Rights

Harris's friend, Attorney General Robert F. Kennedy, brought her excellent work to the attention of his brother, the president. In July 1963, President John F. Kennedy appointed Harris as co-chair (with Mrs. Mildred Mcafee Horton) of the National Women's Committee for Civil Rights. The committee was an umbrella organization intended to coordinate nearly 100 national women's groups in pursuing civil rights, peaceful desegregation, and most important [according to Harris] to establish avenues of communication between the races ("Patricia Roberts Harris" 1965, 190). The most lasting impact of the committee's efforts was support and lobbying by women's groups for the inclusion of both race and sex as protected classes in the 1964 Civil Rights Act.

During the Johnson Administration

A Rising National Star in the Democratic Party

Patricia Harris was a life-long Democrat who served her political party in many national leadership capacities. In 1964 she was a campaign worker for

Lyndon Johnson and the first-ever member of the Electoral College from the District of Columbia. It was the first presidential election in which the residents of the District participated. Harris came into national prominence and political visibility when she seconded the presidential nomination of Lyndon B. Johnson at the 1964 Democratic National Convention in Atlantic City. In subsequent years she would assume the powerful party position of chair of the Rules and Credential Committee for the 1972 Democratic National Convention and in 1973 be named a member-at-large of the Democratic National Committee.

Racial Conflict Rocks the 1964 Democratic National Convention

The 1964 Democratic National Convention was held the last week of August in Atlantic City, New Jersey. There was racial conflict among its members and party elite over whether black delegates from the Mississippi Democratic Freedom Party or the all-white Mississippi delegation would be recognized. Just the month before, on Independence Day, President Johnson had signed the 1964 Civil Rights Act into law. It made racial discrimination in housing, jobs, public accommodations (and voting) illegal. Conservative, southern, predominately white Democrats, members of Congress, and governors in the Deep South were furious with their president over signing the law.

Mississippi Freedom Party Delegates. In June 1964 the Mississippi Freedom Party held a convention to select delegates to the Democratic National Convention to challenge the all-white delegation previously chosen by the white voters of the state's regular Democratic party. They nominated sixty-four black and four white delegates who arrived in Atlantic City to contest the seating of the "white" delegation controlled by Governor Paul Johnson and U.S. Senator James O. Eastland (Kling 1964, 13). President Johnson and his convention operatives were embarrassed. They were anxious to publicly portray a unified Democratic party in the convention's media coverage. A special five-member committee was quickly appointed to attempt to quietly resolve the issue through compromise.

The Alabama Alternate Delegation. Simultaneously, the Alabama delegation very publicly and disruptively refused to sign a loyalty oath pledging to support the party's likely nominee—President Johnson. Although a southerner from Texas, the president was viewed by many deep southerners as a traitor to his party's ideals for having championed and signed the highly resented 1964 Civil Rights Act into law. The Alabama delegates were refused credentials and recognition, resulting in their being officially barred from participation. However, most were able to sneak in past the sergeant at arms using day-old credential passes and assume their seats in defiance of the rules (Kling 1964, 13). Many of the party's southern governors, including those from Mississippi, Louisiana, Georgia, and Alabama, boycotted the proceedings. Mississippi's governor Paul Johnson and Louisiana's governor John J. McKeithen told their delegates to stand by the embattled white Alabama delegation and "demonstrate their feelings about the treatment given our neighboring states by words and actions, including departure if necessary from the convention itself" (Kling 1964, 1). Eugene ("Bull") Connor was Alabama's National Committee member. Today, he is most remembered as the Birmingham, Alabama, police chief who had ordered that dogs, water cannons, and fire hoses be used against Dr. King and Southern Christian Leadership Conference voting rights demonstrators in May 1963. As a member of the alternate Alabama delegation, Connor declared:

> I've said twenty-five times I won't sign that loyalty oath, and I don't change my mind. And I won't walk out. If I walk out, it's on me, but if they throw me out, it's on them. (Kling 1964, 13)

Seconding the Presidential Nomination of Lyndon B. Johnson

In this convention of chaos, racial conflict, and an environment of overt racism, it is extraordinary that Patricia Roberts Harris—an outspoken and highly accomplished black woman, and life-long champion of civil rights—would second the presidential nomination of Lyndon Johnson. Reflecting on the 1964 convention speech, she said, "I must say that was a great experience. One doesn't talk to millions of people very often and I must say that I had a sense this was significant great fun" ("Luxembourg and the UN" 1969, 15). Below are excerpts from her, remarks that were in her typical brief, plain-spoken, blunt, and directly to the point style.

> As a woman of Negro ancestry, I have felt the overwhelming effect of his [President Johnson's] role in extending and making real the historic promise of the American dream for the deprived and the disadvantaged. For the first time in our history, we who labor under the double handicap of race and sex, see at hand a time when interest and ability, not sex or race, are the criteria by which individuals are judged, and permitted to make their contribution to our society. The appointment of women to positions of responsibility and leadership in our national government, without condescension, without diminution of the high standards required for these

positions; the leadership to secure the enactment of a Civil Rights Bill which prohibits discrimination in employment on grounds of race or sex; programs to eliminate the eroding, degrading effects of poverty upon families are but a few of the activities of the remarkable American whose nomination I second. . . . This country cannot afford either overt or subtle appeals to prejudice and hostility. We cannot risk the coming of a day when the United States turns to the world a face distorted by injustice condoned. (Harris 1964, 77–78)

Patricia Roberts Harris's remarks in August 1964 continue to ring true and carry as much urgency today, forty years after she addressed the convention.

Madam Ambassador

Despite a divisive, contentious nominating convention, Johnson would go on to a landslide victory, winning election as president of the United States in his own right. President Johnson had pledged he would appoint fifty women to high-level government positions within his administration. On May 19, 1965, he nominated Patricia Harris to be U.S. ambassador to Luxembourg when, according to the *Washington Post*, "he couldn't persuade her to work for him in the White House" (Pianin 1982c, A8). Patricia Harris was the first woman of color to ever serve as U.S. ambassador. Commenting on her nomination, Harris said: "I feel deeply proud and grateful the President chose me to knock down this barrier, but also a little sad about being the first Negro woman because it implies we were not considered before" ("Patricia Roberts Harris" 1965, 190).

The U.S. Senate immediately and unanimously approved Harris's nomination as ambassador. Bill closed his private law practice in Washington, and accepted a position as special counsel on European Affairs with the State Department so the Harrises could spend 1965 to 1967 in Luxembourg together.

Patricia Harris described her responsibilities:

An ambassador does almost the same thing as any head of any office, who has a combination administrative and public relations responsibility. I supervised the staff that reported to the United States on things of interest in the country. In addition the ambassador is the person responsible for maintaining the relationship between the President of the United States and the head of the government in which the embassy is [located]. So I spend a good deal of time coming to know and talking to the officers of the government of Luxembourg. ("Luxembourg and the UN" 1969, 15)

Photo 6.3 **Madam Ambassador Patricia Roberts Harris** *(far left)* **in a Luxembourg classroom, 1966. Judge William B. Harris is on the far right.** (Patricia Roberts Harris Collection, Moorland-Spingarn Research Center, Howard University. Used by permission.)

The first formal reception Harris hosted at the embassy for a visiting dignitary was for Roy Wilkins, national director of the NAACP. Harris stated, "I just wanted certain people to know how I still feel about civil rights. I didn't want anybody to think that I'd divorced myself from the problems at home simply because I was a few thousand miles away" ("Luxembourg and the UN" 1969, 16).

Delegate to the General Assembly of the United Nations

Upon her return from Luxembourg, President Johnson appointed Harris to another office—as a delegate to the General Assembly of the United Nations in New York. As a UN delegate, Harris worked on two major projects, each of which resulted in important covenants or declarations. As a member of the Committee on Humanitarian Social Questions she worked to guarantee citizens the right to vote and to an impartial judicial process. Both were ultimately included in the Covenant on Human Rights.

She also worked on the commission to study global political, economic, and social discrimination against women. The Declaration to End All Discrimination Against Women ultimately resulted from the committee's research and efforts. It has now been ratified by more than 140 countries (although not the United States). The declaration states: "Discrimination against women, denying or limiting as it does their equality of rights with men, is fundamentally unjust and constitutes an offense against human dignity" ("Luxembourg and the UN" 1969, 17).

Madam Cabinet Secretary: The Carter Years

Patricia Roberts Harris is most frequently remembered for her service as a presidential cabinet secretary in the Carter administration. In 1976 President Carter nominated her to become secretary of Housing and Urban Development. After thirty months and much success in that capacity, President Carter nominated her to a second cabinet position during the summer of 1979. On August 3, 1979, she was sworn in as secretary of the then-largest U.S. government agency, the Department of Health, Education, and Welfare. After Congress created the separate Department of Education in 1980, Harris remained as secretary of Health and Human Services (HHS) until the end of the Carter administration in 1981.

In each position, Harris was the first black woman to serve and continues to this day to be the only female to have served in three cabinet secretary positions. At both agencies, Harris is remembered for her very effective, but at times abrasive, management style. At both HUD and later HEW Harris

implemented her commitment to appoint minorities and women to significant government positions of responsibility. In her thirty months at HUD,
half of her appointees were women and more than one-quarter were people
of color. As HEW secretary, more than two-thirds of her appointees were
women and racial minorities.

Transforming Housing and Urban Development

Senator, I am one of them. (Harris 1977a)

The greatest single impact of Harris's cabinet years is her transformation
of HUD. However, Senate confirmation of her appointment as secretary
was very controversial. At her nomination hearing before the Senate Banking, Housing and Urban Affairs Committee on January 10, 1977, its chair,
Senator William Proxmire (R-WI), claimed: "HUD is in a shambles, it has
neglected a major responsibility for publicly assisted housing construction for low-income families" (Krause 1977a, A1). Further, Proxmire would
categorize HUD's 1976 performance as "an incredibly pathetic 41,000
[housing starts] although Congress had authorized 600,000" (Krause 1977a,
A4).

Proxmire challenged how Harris, a former ambassador to Luxembourg
and partner in the prestigious Washington law firm of Fried, Frank, Harris,
Shriver, and Kampelman since 1969 could be "someone sympathetic to the
problems of the poor" (Krause 1977a, A1). Harris sternly erupted, putting
the senator in his place, with what has become perhaps her most famous
quote:

> Senator, I am one of them. You do not understand who I am. I am a black
> woman, the daughter of a Pullman car waiter. I am a black woman who
> even eight years ago could not buy a house in parts of the District. I didn't
> start out as a member of a prestigious law firm but as a woman who needed
> a scholarship to go to school. If you think I have forgotten that, you are
> wrong. (Harris 1977a, 2)

Harris was confirmed secretary of HUD on January 20, 1977. When she
assumed leadership at HUD, it had an annual budget of $11 billion and a
staff of 17,000 employees. As HUD secretary, she created the United States'
first coherent National Public Housing Policy. During her tenure at HUD,
Harris transformed the agency from an ineffective extension of the housing
construction industry to an effective advocate for low- and moderate-income
urban housing for the poor.

Urban Development Action Grants

The cornerstone of the National Housing Policy was the Urban Development Action Grant (UDAG) program developed by Harris. In two years, HUD provided a total of 400 HUD innovative action grants to private investors and businesses to develop inner-city businesses in blighted neighborhoods. Some $400 million in grants was awarded to 320 cities based on the criteria of having "a marked impact on economic development and neighborhood stabilization" (Harris 1977b). To receive the grants, cities were required to secure additional private matching funds and pledge other municipal public dollars to leverage the resources for maximum result.

In speeches before the National Housing Conference and the National League of Cities, Harris vowed that she and HUD would become advocates for the poor and for inner cities. "[She called for a] new urban partnership involving government, business and the neighborhoods as equals in the process of revitalizing American cities. We must affirm, as a nation, that a decent home is a right and that adequate shelter is a basic commodity equivalent to food and clothing in the spectrum of human needs" (Krause 1977b, A6).

Harris pushed to divert UDAG funds to poorer, older inner cities. She promulgated rules that rewarded urban areas for spending three-quarters of their grants on improving infrastructure in low-income urban neighborhoods. These often included building sewers, improving sanitation, lighting, and roads; as well as constructing parks and developing community areas in impoverished inner cities. In spite of large budget reductions in 1981, UDAG grants had proven so successful in only two years that they were continued into the Reagan administration.

At HUD, Harris became known as a "hard-edged, spirited, and unusually effective member of the Carter administration, loyal to the president but a tiger in fighting to protect her own turf" (Pianin 1982b, A1). Harris would comment in response to criticism at the time of her 1982 mayoral campaign: "If I were male and white, I would be known as the very firm, strong manager, who communicates clearly and precisely. The fact that I am what others would call an uppity black female means that what is positive in a white male is seen as off-putting and arrogant in me" (Pianin 1982a, B1).

The Office of Independent Living for the Disabled

In 1977, Secretary Harris spoke at the White House Conference on Handicapped Individuals. She pledged 5 percent of all newly constructed federally subsidized house and apartment construction would be designated and designed to accommodate the disabled. Long before the 1990 Americans with

Disabilities Act would bring access to the disabled in buildings onto the public policy agenda, Harris created the HUD Office of Independent Living for the Disabled. In her subsequent HEW confirmation hearings, Harris would state: "Not only did we [HUD] establish the Office of Independent Living, but we moved to make everyone cognizant of the needs of the handicapped in every aspect of the administration of HUD. . . . I think as I look back in later years on the things that I was responsible for at HUD, that I will get the greatest satisfaction from the movement toward implementation of real benefits for the handicapped" (Pianin 1982b, A10).

Harris Proved Her Cabinet Effectiveness at HUD

Harris implemented Management by Objectives, delegating considerable line, program, and personnel authority to her top assistants. "During her two years at HUD, 12 minority group members and/or women were named to top area manager jobs that previously had been all male and all white" (Causey 1979, B2). While she was secretary, subsidized housing starts quadrupled. In 1976, prior to Harris's becoming HUD secretary, only 41,623 federal subsidized housing units were begun. In 1977, 101,800 were started and the following year that increased to 175,100 units of low- and moderate-income federally subsidized housing (Pianin 1982b, A10). She quickly mastered the federal budget appropriation process. Harris was known to fiercely defend her programs from Office of Management and Budget cuts. Stuart Eizenstat, President Carter's chief domestic adviser, says:

> She did the job as well as any Cabinet officer. She was by no means afraid of presenting her views bluntly to the President. . . . She had a lot of battles over spending and she sure won more than she lost. (Pianin 1982b, A10).

Under her leadership, HUD became a functioning champion of housing for the poor and the disabled. It was also transformed into a vehicle for inner-city economic development. Harris won high praise from former opponents who had doubted or opposed her nomination as HUD secretary. Former opponents-turned-supporters included the U.S. Council of Mayors, the National League of Cities, and many of the senators—including Proxmire who had once challenged her credentials.

Criticism from Black Civil Rights Activists

> *I did not have wide eyes over the civil rights movement of the 1960s because that was what I had pushed for during the 1940s and 1950s.* (Harris, as quoted in Pianin 1982c, A8)

Occasionally in her professional career Patricia Roberts Harris faced harsh criticism from black activists who charged her with being "bourgeois," distant to other blacks, elitist, and uninvolved in the civil rights struggles of the 1950s and 1960s. According to close friends, she viewed these charges as unfair criticism:

> I was on the next step of the movement, which was the civil liberties concerns—the effective use of power concerns. I didn't have to sit-in because there was somebody else sitting in by then. When I sat-in . . . there was nobody else to do it. (Pianin 1982c, A8)

Of criticism from 1960s activists Harris has said "They weren't on the front lines [of early demonstrations], they were there when it was safe, when the television cameras were there. I was there when there were no television cameras" (Williams 1985, A10).

A one-time Harris critic-turned-eventual political supporter, D.C. school board member R. Calvin Lockridge recalled: "I fought her being named to the Cabinet, because I thought that she wasn't black enough. I felt she did not relate to the black community" (Gilliam 1985, D3).

Harris's critics argued that her home District of Columbia did not benefit much from her very successful UDAG program. It received only two grants for a combined total of $3.3 million. Typical to her blunt, sharp-tongued style, Harris replied, "This city cannot write grant applications, cannot put together a program in terms of the clear standards that are set forward" (Pianin 1982b, A10). After being confirmed secretary of HUD, she would say, "People don't understand that I really care about what happens to black people in this country. Blacks still have limited horizons and it still makes me mad" (DeWitt 1977, H6).

Assuming the Leadership of HEW

The Department of Health, Education and Welfare was created in 1953. By 1979 it had become the single largest U.S. government agency with more than 158,000 employees. It was responsible for more than 300 different programs. The 1979 HEW budget of $182 billion was more than fifteen times that of HUD's. HEW's budget was "the third largest budget in the world, outranked only by those of the U.S. government and the [former] Soviet Union. Its spending roughly equal[ed] that of all fifty states combined" (Harris 1979b). HEW administered social service, health, education, and income assistance programs for retirees, middle-class, and poor Americans. Included in its program responsibilities is the single largest federal government expenditure, Social Security. It also administers Medicare, the second most expensive U.S. government program, which cost $29.3 billion in 1979. It provides health care primarily for senior citizens and some disabled Americans. Other HEW program responsibilities included the then $21.7 billion Medicaid health care program for the poor.

It was an agency in bureaucratic, organizational, and leadership crisis when President Carter nominated then HUD Secretary Harris to lead HEW in 1979. President Carter had just summarily fired his previous HEW secretary, Joseph Califano. Senator Herman E. Talmadge (D-GA), a member of one of HEW's oversight committees, referred to the agency as "an organizational nightmare, the most ungovernable agency in the United States. [This resulted in] an extreme lack of [congressional] confidence in the operation, the programs and policies of HEW . . . [leaving a] vacuum in the leadership" (Harris 1979a). President Carter had proposed and advocated splitting the education program responsibilities of HEW off the giant bureaucratic agency. He planned, and in 1980 subsequently did create, the independent Department of Education as a separate cabinet-level agency. Califano had resisted this change, at times being covertly opposed in the media to the president's efforts. Califano was known for an abrasive, tough managerial style that led to "personality conflicts" between him and high-level White House staffers, including the press secretary and budget director. One of his highly visible, public interagency budget squabbles had been with Harris while she was at HUD. His zealous pursuit of efforts to enforce desegregation proposals against the University of North Carolina system further angered the administration. Although Harris was also known for a tough, no-nonsense, at times harsh or abrasive managerial style, she was, unlike Califano, unwaveringly loyal to the president, his policies, and programs.

Harris had impressed former congressional critics with her highly effective managerial capability at HUD. Her confirmation process to become secretary of HEW contrasted starkly with the conflict-filled hearings two years earlier. Four senators from the 1977 HUD confirmation committee were then members of the Committee on Labor and Human Resources at her HEW confirmation. The atmosphere was friendly and deferential; all prior combativeness and skepticism had been overcome. Committee chair Senator Harrison A. Williams, Jr. (D-NJ), a member of the former contentious Banking, Housing Committee hearings, opened the HEW hearing with high praise for her accomplishments at HUD. In her characteristically brief to-the-point statement, Harris said:

> I am pleased to see old friends from the Banking Committee, including you, Mr. Chairman. . . . I hope you and your colleagues in the Senate will

find it possible to advise and consent to my being appointed, to provide me the opportunity to continue to serve the people of the Nation who most need the help of their Government. No issues of our time are more important than those involving the way in which a rich, democratic society deals with the young, the poor, the handicapped, the infirm and the aged. No one in this country should lack the opportunity to realize his or her potential or to live with dignity. That has been my concern during the last 30 months that I have served as the Secretary of Housing and Urban Development. That has been the major concern during all my life. And if confirmed, that will continue to be my concern as the Secretary of Health, Education, and Welfare. Thank you. (Harris 1979a)

In the presence of President Jimmy Carter, Patricia Roberts Harris was sworn in as the 13th U.S. secretary of HEW by Supreme Court Justice Thurgood Marshall on August 3, 1979. At the ceremony President Carter said he "had selected Harris because she has 'superb management capabilities [and is] bold, strong and outspoken'" (Bredemeier 1979, A1).

HEW School Desegregation Cases in a Political Minefield

Within days of becoming HEW secretary, Harris and her top assistant, Randolph Kinder, began the top-down process of bringing diversity to the agency's personnel, similar to what they had previously implemented at HUD. They replaced the "white male syndrome" that existed at HEW with women and minorities often excluded from lists of candidates for top jobs. "Personnel runs this place, and we are going to make sure that all qualified candidates are considered, not just white males" (Causey 1979, B2).

School Desegregation Enforcement

As soon as Harris took the helm at HEW she was confronted with a backlog of highly visible and controversial civil rights school desegregation issues. One extremely high-profile case would involve the public school system in her childhood home of Chicago. School desegregation cases against the states of Texas, Maryland, Alabama, and North Carolina as well as in the Democratic political strongholds of New York City and Chicago had been lingering. HEW's efforts to negotiate satisfactory plans for racial desegregation in these systems had failed or stalemated. It was up to Harris to determine whether and how much federal education aid would be withheld from states or cities because of these continuing civil rights violations.

At that time President Carter was about to launch his unsuccessful 1980

124

Photo 6.4 **Secretary Patricia Roberts Harris being administered the oath of office as Secretary of Health, Education, and Welfare. August 3, 1979.** *From left to right:* **President Jimmy Carter, Patricia Roberts Harris, Judge William B. Harris, and U.S. Supreme Court Justice Thurgood Marshall.** (Carter Presidential Library. Photo courtesy of Ms. Fran Phillips-Calhoun.)

reelection campaign. He would need continued good political relations and active support from Democratic governors and mayors in most of the states and cities involved in the disputes. The president needed Harris to handle the desegregation cases diplomatically, carefully, and without alienating potential Democratic support, especially mayors and governors. Civil rights advocates also had their critical eye on what would be Harris's first major decision at HEW.

The Chicago case was the most highly visible lingering conflict. Under her predecessor Califano, Chicago had been notified it would lose $20 million elementary and secondary federal public school funding as a result of historical racial segregation. The city had kept schools racially segregated by gerrymandering zoning lines and manipulating enrollments. It used substandard portable classrooms to overcrowd minority students into traditionally black schools rather than transfer them to half-empty "white" suburban schools. HEW investigations found fewer than 1 in 25 of the districts' 500 schools was racially desegregated. The School Board perpetuated this racial separation by assigning teachers to schools in discriminatory ways—black teachers to all-black schools. In last efforts to forestall losing federal education dollars, Chicago mayor Jane Bryne proposed an "Access to Excellence" plan for public school desegregation. Secretary Harris rejected the proposal as too little, too late. In August 1979, she ordered HEW to refer the case to the Department of Justice for criminal prosecution. HEW proposed mandatory busing orders which, if the city failed to comply, could cost them up to $100 million in federal education monies from the Chicago school system. A month later, Harris prepared to deny between $2 and $4 million to Chicago schools.

After Chicago rejected an HEW feasibility study proposal to desegregate Chicago schools through busing 114,000 students, Harris gave Chicago less than one month to propose a satisfactory alternative. Harris announced her decision on October 18, 1979. "I have concluded that compliance cannot be secured by voluntary means, and I cannot in good conscience agree to further delay in the guise of negotiation. Therefore, the department [of HEW] is today initiating the process of referring this matter to the Department of Justice for appropriate action" (Associated Press 1979b, A11). Thus began one of the largest school desegregation court cases in American history.

By mid May 1980, the Department of Justice and Assistant Attorney General Drews S. Day III had become involved in "exploratory meetings and negotiations" with Chicago. Chicago school desegregation plans for high schools were also being challenged in the court systems. In August 1979, the Federal District Court struck down as unconstitutional "desegregation quotas" proposed by the Chicago Lawyers Committee for Civil Rights Under the Law.

The decision would be upheld by the Federal District Court of Appeals a year later (July 1980) and the U.S. Supreme Court would subsequently hear the case. While court actions continued, the Department of Justice pursued negotiations with the Chicago system into the end of the Carter administration.

Other Complicating Politically Volatile Desegregation Cases

President Carter carried Texas in the 1976 elections, but its Republican governor would oppose his reelection in 1980. Because it had thirty-two votes in the Electoral College, Carter desperately needed Texas for a successful reelection. The Texas school desegregation case was even worse than Chicago's. HEW investigations found pervasive racial discrimination in Texas ranging from the public schools to the university systems. Many colleges remained either all-black or all-white. Potentially, Texas could be facing a cutoff of millions of dollars in federal education funding.

The situation was similar in Maryland, which faced a potential cutoff of $60 million in federal education dollars. Other higher education school desegregation investigations were proceeding to similar findings in seven more states (Alabama, Delaware, Kentucky, Missouri, Ohio, South Carolina, and West Virginia). Asked in a 1980 interview whether she would refer more of these cases to Justice for prosecution, she replied: "Let me say with all my heart that I hope I don't have to do so. But if the cases reach the point that the Chicago case did and we are unable to deal with them through negotiations and if I am convinced of this, I will take whatever steps are necessary, including referral to Justice" (Reynolds 1980, Sec. 1, 4).

Harris handled these situations with deliberate care, referring only the Chicago case to the Department of Justice prior to the splitting off of the Department of Education in 1980. In later years she would acknowledge that a shortcoming of her administration of HEW was the slippage of civil rights enforcement, a charge that would haunt her in her unsuccessful campaign for mayor of the District of Columbia in 1982.

Other Accomplishments at HEW

One of Harris's greatest successes at HEW was her administrative ability not only to protect and maintain her department from budget cuts but to secure large budget increases. By 1980, public, political, and financial support for social programs was dwindling. But Harris was able to get an amazing $25 billion increase, for a total 1981 HHS budget of $225 billion. She also reached out to presidents of women's colleges to include their representatives in the HEW policymaking process. She made special efforts to provide them access to education grants and government services by establishing a special assistant to be her liaison to the Women's College Coalition. While at HEW Harris also put a major policy focus on improving rural, poor and minority health care and education. She was a champion of the president's national health care coverage proposals. She remained publicly loyal to the president, and discreetly silent about her disagreement with his Medicaid restrictions that prohibited funding abortion for poor women.

The Mayoral Campaign of 1982

> *I am ready to be a mayor with answers and actions*
> *—not alibis and apologies.* (Harris 1982)

In January 1981, Republican Ronald Reagan was sworn-in as the fortieth U.S. president. Patricia Harris returned briefly to private life and teaching law as a full professor at Howard University, her alma mater. But she would not be away from politics long. On April 3, 1982, she announced her candidacy for mayor of the District of Columbia, saying:

> Today, less than eight years after home rule, we look to our local govern-ment and ask what has gone wrong. Instead of answers we get alibis . . . the mayor says he is not responsible for the failures of his government. If he is not responsible, who is? It's time that we put someone in charge of this city's government who won't be afraid to be in charge. I am ready to be a mayor with answers and actions—not alibis and apologies. The central question is, which candidate will bring the most effective leadership to this city. I believe I am that candidate. . . . No other candidate has more experi-ence in leading and managing organizations, both large and small. I know that I can do the job that so sorely needs to be done to put Washington, DC on the right track again. (Williams 1982, A1, A12)

The campaign of Mayor Marion Barry for re-election was nasty, charac-terized by personal attacks, and full of social class warfare. Harris, Barry argued, was out of touch with the city, having been "away holding presti-gious jobs in government at a time when others like Barry were in the front lines of the civil rights movement" (Williams 1982, A12). Repeatedly the Barry campaign argued Harris was "bourgeois." She would respond: "That is a very sad, sad thing coming out of the black community. . . . It says that a person who has educated herself, who has proved successful at getting jobs done . . . a person who has been able to be a spokesperson for continuing concerns for justice, is somehow unacceptable to the black community" (Brinkley 1982, 2).

Harris demonstrated great skill at raising campaign contributions during the first month. By June she took the lead in early polls by as much as 11 points. When she became the unexpected front-runner in a field of nine candidates, she also became a much easier target of many more and harsher character and personality attacks. Barry said, "Harris has never balanced a budget, many of the programs Harris administered at HUD would have functioned smoothly even if Mickey Mouse had been Secretary" (Pianin 1982a, B5).

Harris lost that 1982 mayoral election, in large part, because she was a lesser campaigner. She frequently avoided candidate forums which she considered a waste of time. She argued: "Three minutes, as one forum offered me, to tell what I would do as mayor of the District of Columbia is very troubling to me. It becomes theater, it does not become dialogue" (Pianin 1982a, B5).

Instead, she relied on small-group social gatherings and complex detailed budgetary arguments in opinion pieces she wrote in the *Washington Post* (Harris 1981, A19). After the election she would say:

> I do not enjoy the core process [of campaigning] which is saying to people: "Vote for me because you just touched me." I like people to think. The idea that you want people to feel, not think, runs counter to my basic beliefs about democracy—that people ought to think. I worry about people who vote for me because they shook my hand. The question should be "Who can do the best job?" (Rimer 1982, B1)

Although Harris had the votes of nearly all the black middle and upper class, she would finish a surprisingly distant second to Barry's 59 percent in the September 14, 1982, Democratic primary. Weeks after the defeat Harris had no regrets.

> It was worth doing. We set the choice and set it clearly. We proved that the solutions are out there. We offered proposals. The people chose not to adopt them. I wanted to be mayor in order to do what needs to be done, I wasn't burning to be mayor. (Rimer 1982, B3)

In retrospect in 1998, Dr. Bobby W. Austing, Harris's speech writer in her mayoral campaign, commented:

> I think of [Harris] as a formidable Sister. I was scared to death of her when I first met her. . . . She was both moral and ethical at a time when I'm not sure government knew how to define those terms. In her, however, one

found this strong sense of public service. . . . She was the epitome of the democratic process in America, representing all that was good and best about the society. ("Patricia Roberts Harris in Law and Public Service" 1998, 1–2)

Breast Cancer: The First Unconquerable Adversary

After her campaign for mayor, Harris would return to teaching law, this time as a full-time professor at George Washington University Law Center. But her greatest challenge would lie ahead—an unsuccessful year-and-a-half-long battle with breast cancer. Despite aggressive treatments for more than a year—and the constant nurturing care of her husband, Bill, for most of that time—on March 23, 1985, at age 60 Patricia Roberts Harris died at George Washington University Hospital.

At her funeral services in the Washington Cathedral, hundreds of mourners from the highest levels of political power to those she had worked with at HUD, HEW, and HHS, Delta sisters, life-long friends, law partners, former students, and her mother were present to pay tribute to her remarkable life. There were seven eulogies. Tributes came from the very pinnacle of U.S. government power, including President Carter, top congressional leaders, cabinet officials, and national civil rights activists. President Carter remembered: "She was sometimes abrasive, even explosive, when circumstances warranted such action. [She was] a tough, honest, strong administrator with a low threshold of outrage over injustices" (Pianin 1985, 1).

The Living Legacy of Patricia Roberts Harris Continues

Life-long friend Sharon Pratt, treasurer of the Democratic National Committee and manager of Patricia Harris's 1982 mayoral campaign, summed it up eloquently: "When you think of a woman, a black woman born in 1924 in Mattoon, Ill., who moved to such heights and achieved such incredible firsts, made such extraordinary contributions to the nation, and paved the way for so many women, particularly black women, then you can understand that hers was not an easy row to hoe. She leaves an incredible legacy" (Williams 1985, A10).

The Patricia Roberts Harris Public Affairs Program

Shortly before her death in 1985 Harris made a bequest to Howard University. It has grown, with the help of foundation grants, into the Patricia Roberts Harris Public Affairs Program. Established in October 1987, the program is housed in the Ralph J. Bunche International Affairs Center. In 1993 generous grants from the W.K. Kellogg Foundation and the Henry M. Jackson Foundation totaling $325,000 permitted the program to significantly expand and establish the now prestigious Patricia Roberts Harris Public Affairs Fellows Program. The program is under the leadership of Ambassador Horace G. Dawson, Jr., Ph.D., who describes it here: "[It is designed to] complement the University's course offerings in areas related to public policy, and to encourage students to consider careers in public service. The program sponsors a high profile national lecture series, public service internships and career development for outstanding Howard University students in international and domestic affairs in selected government offices, private voluntary organizations" (Dawson 2000, 1–2).

In 1998, the program celebrated its tenth anniversary by hosting symposia speakers including Harris's former colleagues, friends, and students to consider her remarkable legacy as an educator and as an administrator in public service. Former Harris law student Inspector General Vernon Gill of the District of Columbia, believes: "Were she [Harris] here today, I think she would be pleased to know that the spark she lit through her service in education, business, public policy, diplomacy and law burns on" ("Patricia Roberts Harris as Educator" 1998, 3).

The Moorland-Spingarn Research Center

Harris also left her papers, political artifacts, and memorabilia to Howard University. Today her collection, which includes materials from the 1950s to her death in 1985, are housed at the Moorland-Spingarn Research Center. Included in Harris's collection are personal letters, scrapbooks, photos, committee hearings, news clippings, travel souvenirs, diplomas, awards, and even videotapes highlighting her career.

U.S. Postal Stamp, Black Heritage Series

In 1990 Ms. Fran Phillips-Calhoun, a fellow Delta sister and Howard alumna, was the first scholar to help open and study the Harris's collection.

> Pat Harris was my childhood hero, a truly great woman who deserves recognition for all that she did and all that she meant to so many. ("Patricia Roberts Harris: The Champion . . . " 1998, 1)
>
> I first remember Patricia Harris from 1976, when Carter appointed her to his cabinet. I was in fifth grade in elementary school, we held mock Presidential elections for Carter, I became intrigued by politics and law. Her most significant work with the biggest community impact was at HUD. (Phillips-Calhoun interview 2003)

Harris's legacy and reputation at Howard University and within Delta Sigma Theta inspired Fran to begin a journey to seek recognition for Harris's public service. With the endorsement of President Carter, Phillips-Calhoun would launch a five-year campaign to convince the U.S. Postal Service to print a commemorative postal stamp in the Black Heritage Series in honor of Patricia Harris. Calhoun gathered support from Delta sisters at their 1998 National Convention and established a Web site for petition signatures. Later she commissioned an artist "to render a postage stamp image of Pat Harris and used it as a lobbying tool to brand the idea" (Phillips-Calhoun interview 2003). She lobbied the Postal Citizens Advisory Committee and congressional committee members, obtained support from U.S. Senators Ted Kennedy (D-MA), and Robert Dole (R-KS), cabinet officers, and the Congressional Black Caucus. She circulated signature petitions among co-workers, women's groups, Delta Sigma Theta, and African-American groups. More than 30,000 supporters signed petitions. Some 10,000 education packets were sent to public school teachers to spread the inspiration of Patricia Harris's legacy to the young.

In October 1999, the U.S. Post Office announced that Patricia Roberts Harris would be honored with a commemorative postage stamp. She was the twenty-third American and only the seventh woman to have a commemorative stamp in the Black Heritage Series issued in her honor. "Dignitaries from around the nation assembled in Howard University's Cramton Auditorium, on Thursday, January 27, 2000, to pay tribute to Patricia Roberts Harris and to witness the dedication of a U.S. postage stamp in her honor by the United States Postal Service" (Dawson 2000, 1–2).

Epilogue

> *If my life has any meaning at all, it is that those who start out as outcasts can wind up as being part of the system.* (Harris 1977)

At her 1977 Senate confirmation hearings to become HUD Secretary, Harris stated:

> I have been a defender of women, of minorities, of those who are the outcasts of this society, throughout my life. By being part of the system one does not forget what it meant to be outside it, I shall never forget it (Harris 1977a).
>
> I've spent my life working to end segregation. The first years of my life I was unable to travel because of segregation. I was unable to do what I wanted to do because I was black and female. . . . It has been a lifetime of getting over barriers. (Rimer 1982, B3)

I can do a lot of things that seem very difficult when I look back on them, because I care—really care—about what happens to people. And one of the things I have said for years is, I want to make sure that no black child ever has to go through what I went through. I don't think anybody in an affluent society should have to be crippled by lack of money or lack of power. . . . I still get angry at the injustice of the system, even though the injustice may go pass me and reach somebody else. (Brinkley 1982, 2)

Stuart E. Eizenstat, former chief domestic advisor for the Carter White House, remembers Harris:

[She was] a role model for African Americans and for women through out the country. On her own, with perseverance and genuine sense of self, she worked her way to the top. Each post and each job and each assignment was singly impressive. But when taken as a whole, we can understand the tremendous impact she had on not only the community but our country and the world. ("Patricia Roberts Harris in Law and Public Service" 1998, 3)

Washington Post columnist Dorothy Gilliam reflecting on Harris's life, writes: "What she [Harris] would probably want to see for all of us, black and white, is that we try to judge each other not on our outward trappings, mannerisms or even associations, but on our individual commitment to justice and equality" (Gilliam 1985, D3).

Acknowledgments

Special thanks and appreciation to Ms. Fran Phillips-Calhoun of Atlanta who is currently writing a young persons' biography of Secretary Harris's life. Fran has significantly contributed to the quality and content of this work by providing research assistance, materials, networking contacts, encouragement, and photographs of the career and life of Patricia Roberts Harris.

This chapter is dedicated to the memory of a beloved friend and colleague, Dr. Barbara Roth. Her brief life and careers as a social worker, then teacher, advanced social justice and civil rights locally.

Special thanks for her assistance, persistence, and generosity go to Ms. Joellen ElBashir, Curator of the Patricia Roberts Harris Collection at the Moorland-Spingarn Research Center at Howard University, Washington DC.

Sincere appreciation for their various assistance, encouragement, support, and many suggestions are given to Dr. David A. Jones, Mr. John R. Bloom, my tireless editors Wendy Haynes and Claire Felbinger, and to Elizabeth Granda of M.E. Sharpe who always responded promptly to requests, frequently making very helpful suggestions.

Dr. Thomas Battle, the current director of the Moorland-Spingarn Research Center, and Ms. Joellen ElBashir, its curator, have graciously assisted in providing materials, including networking and photographs for this work.

Appreciation is also given to the very efficient staff of the Prints and Photographs Division of the Library of Congress for their research assistance in locating 1977 HUD photographs.

References

Associated Press. 1977. "Harris Pledges to Designate 5% of Housing for Disabled." *Washington Post*, May 28, Sec. D8.

Associated Press. 1979a. "Plan for Busing Pupils in Chicago Rejected by HEW as Inadequate." *Washington Post*, September 22, Sec. A3.

Associated Press. 1979b. "Harris Seeks U.S. Suit in the Desegregation of Chicago Schools." *Washington Post*, October 19, Sec. A11.

Bredemeier, Kenneth. 1979. "Harris Sworn In at HEW." *Washington Post*, August 4, Sec. 1, 1, 4.

Brinkley, Sidney. 1982. "An Interview with Patricia Harris." *BLACKLIGHT online* 3, September 6, 1–5.

Causey, Mike. 1979. "Harris Keeping Eye on Superjob Choices." In the Federal Diary, *Washington Post*, September 18, Sec. B2.

Dawson, Horace G. 2000. "The Legacy of Patricia Roberts Harris at Howard University." *HUArchieveNet: The Electronic Journal MSRC-Howard University* (May): 1–2; available at: www.howard.edu/rjb/PRharris/.

Delta Sigma Theta Sorority Official Website: www.deltasigmatheta.org (2002).

DeWitt, Karen. 1977. "Patricia Harris: The Cerebral Angers of a Superachiever." *Washington Post*, April 10, Sec. H1, 6.

"First Day Cover Store: U.S. FDC: 33 cent Patricia Roberts Harris PSA Black Heritage Series." U.S. Postal Service: www.unicover.com/EAICAVDP.HTM (May 23, 2003).

Gilliam, Dorothy. 1985. "You Define Yourself." *Washington Post*, March 28, Sec. D3.

Harris, Patricia Roberts. 1964. "Seconding of Presidential Nomination of the Hon. Lyndon B. Johnson." *Official Report of the Proceedings of the 1964 Democratic National Convention*, 77–78. Atlantic City, NJ: Democratic National Committee.

———. 1977a. *Testimony before the U.S. Senate Banking, Housing and Urban Affairs Committee*, 95th Cong., 1st sess., January 10.

———. 1977b. *Testimony before the U.S. Senate Banking, Housing and Urban Affairs Committee*, 95th Cong., 1st sess., April 19.

———. 1979a. *Testimony before the U.S. Senate Labor and Human Resources Committee*, 96th Cong., 1st sess., April 26.

———. 1979b. *Testimony before the U.S. Senate Labor and Human Resources Committee*, 96th Cong., 1st sess., July 28.

———. 1981. "D.C. Budget: Let the People In On It." *Washington Post*, August 13, Sec. A19.

"Judge William B. Harris, 70, Active in Civic Affairs (obituary)." 1984. *Washington Post*, November 7, Sec. B8.

Kling, William. 1964. "Delegates Stay as Convention Backs Ban." *Chicago Tribune*, August 25, Sec. 1, 1, 13.

Krause, Charles A. 1977a. "HUD Nominee, Sen. Proxmire Clash." *Washington Post,* January 11, Sec. A1, 4.

———. 1977b. "Harris Pledges Housing Aid to Cities." *Washington Post*, March 8, Sec. A6.

"Luxembourg and the UN: Patricia Harris at Work." 1969. In *Black Americans in Government*, 15–17. Jamaica: Buckingham Learning Corporation (photocopied materials courtesy Fran Phillips-Calhoun).

"Patricia Roberts Harris." 1965. *Current Biography Yearbook.* New York: H.W. Wilson, 188–190.

"Patricia Roberts Harris as an Educator." 1998. *Tenth Anniversary Patricia Roberts Harris Program Report.* Ralph J. Bunche International Affairs Center, Howard University.

"Patricia Roberts Harris in Law and Public Service." 1998. *Tenth Anniversary Patricia Roberts Harris Program Report.* Ralph J. Bunche International Affairs Center, Howard University.

"Patricia Roberts Harris: The Champion Who Couldn't Hear 'No' " 1998. *Tenth Anniversary Patricia Roberts Harris Program Report.* Ralph J. Bunche International Affairs Center, Howard University.

"Patricia Roberts Harris: The Personal Dimension." 1998. *Tenth Anniversary Patricia Roberts Harris Program Report.* Ralph J. Bunche International Affairs Center, Howard University.

Phillips-Calhoun, Fran. 2003. Interview with author, June 3.

Pianin, Eric. 1982a. "Harris—Is She Tough or Arrogant?" *Washington Post*, June 6, Sec. B1, 5.

———. 1982b. "The Harris Record." *Washington Post*, July 25, Sec. A1, 10.

———. 1982c. "Pat Harris: Striving To Be a Champion." *Washington Post*, September 7, Sec. A1, 8.

———. 1985. "Carter, O'Neill Eulogize Pat Harris." *Washington Post*, March 28, Sec. D1 final edition, 1–2.

Reynolds, Barbara. 1980. "Q & A. HEW Chief Pushes Aid to Rural Poor." *Washington Post*, 28 June, Sec. 1, 1, 4.

Rimer, Sara. 1982. "Patricia Harris After Defeat: 'No Pain. It Was Worth Doing.'" *Washington Post*, October 10, Sec. B1, 3.

Williams, Juan. 1982. "Harris Begins Campaign with Attack on Barry." *Washington Post*, April 4, Sec. A1, 12.

———. 1985. "Patricia R. Harris Dies at 60: Career Distinguished by Many Firsts." *Washington Post*. March 24, Sec. A1, 10.

Part III

Into the Twenty-First Century:
More Women of Courage and Substance

> *Finally, we need a form of competence in public administration*
> *that moves beyond the myth of the heroic male professional*
> *who sacrifices "selfish" family concerns in single-minded*
> *fashion to his career. . . . [T]he legitimate public administrator*
> *will be a whole person, one who is understood to have*
> *developed in and to be a continuing member of a family.*
>
> (Stivers 2002, 131)

Each of our outstanding women in public administration faced difficult choices and overcame barriers of thought and custom that were peculiar to her era. And few more so than the two women in Part III: Naomi Lynn and Maxine Kurtz. Their lives inspire in us the sure belief that we as a society will, indeed, come to embrace and celebrate "whole" persons in service to the public.

To our regret and enduring sense of loss, few of us had the privilege of reveling in the presence of the remarkable women portrayed in the first seven chapters of this book. Fortunately, the next two women still live among us. We want you to appreciate, as do their biographers, their fine contributions to the art and science of public administration.

Introduction to Part III

In the next chapter, *Linda Richter* paints an unabashedly admiring portrait of the contemporary life of Naomi B. Lynn, university dean, chancellor, and president; loving mother, wife, and parent to many; the first Hispanic and second female president of the American Society for Public Administration;

and a woman beloved by her colleagues and friends. Richter's narrative il-lustrates the truth in her observation that "Naomi's life canvas is full of color and exquisite detail." Because of Lynn's leadership in higher education ad-ministration, states, federal advisory bodies—and even the United Nations—seek her counsel. And although "people continue to warn women about trying to have it all, . . . no one told Naomi!" We are fortunate to have still present and contributing in our midst such women as Naomi Lynn, and the subject of the final chapter, Maxine Kurtz.

Van Johnston captures the essence of the contributions of Maxine Kurtz, innovator, civil rights activist, urban planner, attorney—a professional ad-ministrator who would not be constrained by the "invisible cage of mindless conformity to the status quo." Students of urban planning—be they scholars or local administrators—have Kurtz to thank for her keen sense of the inter-play of economics, transportation planning, utility infrastructure, zoning or-dinances, and the other elements that comprise modern-day comprehensive land use planning. She demonstrated consistently the ability to see beyond dualities, or as Camilla Stivers put it, "to accept the inseparability of politics and administration, facts and values, policies and procedures, theory and practice" (Stivers 2000, 135). Kurtz's story is still unfolding, but here is the most recent edition of a life well-lived in the interest of the public good, whether the arena be urban planning, civil service reform, the Supreme Court, or the classroom.

Read, enjoy, and learn from their stories.

7

Naomi B. Lynn

Painting a Rich Canvas

Linda K. Richter

Introduction

Women who fill this volume have surmounted barriers and excelled in the field of public administration. Some are honored for their cutting-edge research. Still others such as Laverne Burchfield were talented women who cared more about getting the job done than who got the credit. Only after their deaths do readers learn of their contributions. The men around them enjoyed the titles, prestige, and glory that these women made possible. Other women included here did not shun the limelight, but seized leadership roles in departments and agencies of government, in their professional associations, and in academia.

Naomi Lynn has done it all. The sheer breadth of her professional and administrative life, the quality of her teaching and many superb publications, the quantity and quality of her civic and partisan involvement amaze those who know her. She cannot be neatly confined to a single category.

Her accomplishments illustrate the richness of a career combining academic research and teaching with extensive practitioner experience. She merits inclusion in this volume not only because of her versatility and talent in public administration, but also because of her fidelity to the highest standards of the profession.

She was a chancellor of the University of Illinois, president of one university, and acting president of another. When she became the dean of the College of Public and Urban Affairs at Georgia State University, she was the first female academic dean in the university's history. She was the first Hispanic and the second female president of the American Society for Public Administration and the only female department head at Kansas State University's Department of Political Science. She combined these roles with being a wife for forty-nine years, the mother of four talented daughters, and the grand-mother of nine reputedly perfect grandchildren.

The Historical Context

Women born in the 1930s, as was Naomi Lynn, faced a society in transition from fixed gender-based roles with considerable societal criticism for devi-ance from those roles to a nation on the brink of World War II. That war demonstrated for all time the ability of women to do almost any work. Yet, after the war, the roles defined by society for women reverted to prewar confines as the troops returned.

Naomi married in 1954 shortly after finishing her B.A. in political science at Maryville College, a small conservative school in Tennessee. Her career exemplified the nontraditional student whose graduate education and career were launched after marriage and starting a family. Naomi struggled to make the role of wife and mother and the life of academic and administrative leader mesh into a satisfying experience for herself and those around her.

Yet, Naomi was fortunate in having an attitude toward life and talents both domestic and professional that allowed her to enjoy each stage and role even as she prepared for the next. While she recognized what Betty Friedan (1964) would refer to as the depression faced by many educated women confined to homemaking, Lynn enjoyed child rearing and many other do-mestic roles. But that did not stop her from being quite active in her commu-nity and working on her master's degree.

The metaphor of the canvas captures Lynn's life so much more elegantly than "multitasking," "mommy track" or "working mother." Mary Catherine Bateson, the daughter of Margaret Mead, writes in *Composing a Life* (1989) that too often women are counseled to make tough either-or choices about which track in life to follow. Do they want to be homemakers and mothers? Do they want professional careers? Which career ladder do they want? Strad-dling both, they are warned, will cost marriage or career or both.

Bateson challenges the notion of life as a set of career ladders from which one must choose. She argues for seeing life as a canvas on which one paints one's life. In such a metaphor, any single ladder no matter how high looks boring. With life seen as a canvas, diversions from one career path are seen not as obstacles to a single goal but as elements that make the picture more interesting, richer, and more complex.

In her later writings with Cornelia Flora, Lynn researched the politically circumscribed lives of new mothers (Flora and Lynn 1973; Lynn and Flora

1974b), but she knew she must invest in her own life so that she could pursue a fulfilling home life while preparing for a career in public administration. Lynn believed that too many women postponed their own intellectual growth and opportunities until those dreams were forgotten. She wanted family and career without compromising either. Naomi never saw life as an either-or choice, but as a challenge to integrate what mattered in the most beautiful way possible.

The Kansas Years, 1968–1984

Naomi and Bob Lynn had four small daughters when she started her master's degree in political science at the University of Illinois. She loved her studies, was active in the community, and even found time to bake bread and entertain as the department head's wife.

When Bob became Dean of Business at Kansas State University (KSU) in 1968, they moved to Manhattan, Kansas. KSU did not have a graduate program in political science, so Naomi Lynn "commuted" 170 miles roundtrip to the University of Kansas (KU) where she would receive her doctorate in little more than two years. Characteristically, when she ran into tough methodology courses that stymied and discouraged others, she hired tutors to coach her in math and statistics. What she needed to know she would always set out to learn rather than avoid. Others have commented that this trait was central to her success (Schirding 2003).

Even as she was commuting to KU, she was encouraging others to continue their education, to invest in their dreams. To those who were hesitant because of small children and busy husbands, she would respond by pointing out her four little girls and her husband, the dean. Dutifully, a new contingent of Lynn conscripts marched off for their GEDs, their B.A.s, or their Ph.D.s. Examples abound, but one later headed KSU's affirmative action program; another became a professor of political science. Her record at KU was both a blessing and a curse for those who followed in her wake. The KU political science department assumed a long commute could be easily managed because Naomi had made it look so easy. With those she mentored, Naomi celebrated every step and soothed every setback. She made everyone feel they could do the extraordinary.

She continued this pattern of mentoring in concrete and helpful ways all her life. She cajoled those around her into going to business meetings, volunteering for new responsibilities, and becoming known for delivering results. People around Naomi never lacked for opportunities, but they did crave sleep. Mentoring ranked high among the many facets of her personality and proved to be an important source of her strength and competitiveness for future positions. Naomi wove a web of friends that she nurtured and who in turn nurtured her. Nearly everyone who speaks of her—whether as academic peer, employee, friend, or a fine mix of all three—refers to her as a mentor and a role model.

The Lynns invested in their family by hiring live-in quality help during those years of balancing multiple roles. Naomi said that for many years, the help at home made more than she did as an instructor at KSU. But they regarded the decision to spend their limited resources on home help as essential to their family's welfare and their own careers. Whenever Naomi got a raise, the woman who cared for the home received the same percentage raise. They both had an incentive for Naomi to succeed. The Lynns splurged on wonderful caring help and hospitality toward others, but they saved on old cars, few vacations, and comfortable but unpretentious homes.

Naomi had other advantages, as well. She was reared in a traditional close-knit Puerto Rican family, which placed an extraordinary emphasis on education and public service. One sister died very young and her children hold an important place in the Lynn family. Her other sister, Ruth, like Naomi, is an exceptional woman. At one time, they were perhaps the only "sister act" in university presidencies, when Ruth was president of San Antonio Community College and Naomi was president of Sangamon State University. Later, Ruth would be chancellor of the Houston Community College system while Naomi was chancellor of the University of Illinois at Springfield.

Another major advantage Naomi had was that she married a talented, endlessly energetic, and very secure man, who also combined cooking, home-making, and nurturing with academic administration and scholarly publications as naturally as she did. For forty-nine years, they have woven their careers, their marriage, and their friends and family into a rich and warm collaborative effort.

Her family and ever-widening friendship circle forged an important support for her aspirations, but she also overcame many hurdles. She specialized at KU in international relations and public administration. Her dissertation on J. William Fulbright, *The Fulbright Premise,* was published quickly following her degree. Swamped by teaching at Kansas State as a temporary instructor, she opted to share the credit for the book with Arthur McClure, who located the publisher, handled the editing, index, and other details (Lynn and McClure 1973). For Naomi, sharing credit and moving forward has been a win-win approach all her life. A look at her resume includes examples of collaboration with numerous talented individuals who, like her, were at key points in building their careers. Others, like Aaron Wildavsky, already one of the best known individuals in political science and public administration, would collaborate with her on the study of the state of the discipline (1990).

By 1972, Naomi had a doctorate, had her book under contract, and was teaching full time as an instructor in political science at KSU, when a tenure-track position opened up in her area of specialization. The department liked Naomi, but they already "had her," because her husband was the dean of Business Administration. Where would she be going? So they looked outside the university and all around her. At last, they settled on a young man who had not yet completed his doctorate and had no teaching experience. Fortunately for KSU and Naomi, the man broke his contract at the last moment and has never been heard of since.

The department, terrified of losing the tenure line, hired Naomi with the expectation that they would search again the next year. When she came up for reappointment one of her colleagues recommended against it, saying she was very nice, but would never be one who could mix it up with the big guys—the political scientists at the national level. Her then department head told her the story some years later when Naomi was elected to the National Council of the American Political Science Association.

This anecdote does highlight what life was like on campuses in the years before affirmative action. Even a year or two later, a woman of her caliber could not be so easily passed over for a less-qualified male, certainly not at KSU. The university vice-president, John Chalmers, appointed the newly hired assistant professor to form a committee to draft KSU's first affirmative action plan. This they did. Naomi never dodged politically controversial tasks, but this clearly was a challenge for a new hire.

It was also a serendipitous break for KSU. One of her early students wrote to the political science department in the spring of 2003 when she learned this chapter was being written. She had been thrilled and excited to be in a department with a female political science professor—a rarity in the discipline in those days. She also remembered what a sensation the new course was that Lynn and Bill Richter had designed: "Sex and Politics." This course predated almost all gender politics courses in the country and would hasten the development of a women's studies program in which Naomi would teach until she became department head in 1982.

Naomi was a speedy and voracious reader who quickly sought out linkages with others across campus, becoming a source of information and advice to many beyond political science and public administration. She read and critiqued the work of others and gave sage advice on publishing books. She helped organize the Women's Studies Program and was active in encouraging new courses and developing solid administrative support in those early years.

Professor Emeritus Carol Oukrop, who directed the School of Journalism and Mass Communications for many years, recalls how Naomi in the early 1970s showed her alarming statistics on how few women were seeking advanced degrees in journalism (Oukrop 2002). Lynn's prodding led Carol to teach a "Women in Journalism" course, join the Women's Studies faculty, and embark on a life of research and leadership on gender issues in journalism.

Over and over again at KSU, at professional meetings, even during the American Society for Public Administration (ASPA) panel at which this volume was launched, women would tell how Naomi interested them in public-sector research on women, on careers for women in the civil service, and how she galvanized support for their bids for official positions in the leading political science and public administration professional organizations. Coaching was second nature for Naomi, so perhaps it should not have been surprising to walk into her office one afternoon and find her on the phone counting the minutes between contractions and encouraging her daughter during the birth of her first grandchild!

At KSU, Naomi Lynn proved to be an immensely successful teacher, a prolific researcher, and one of the leading professors not only in political science, but on the entire campus. She advanced to full professor eight years after her appointment to a tenure-track position and was the department head within ten years. During this time she developed the master's degree in public administration (MPA) program at KSU, was president of the Kansas ASPA chapter, and assumed numerous roles in the national ASPA and other organizations.

She endeared herself to the political science faculty and subsequent department heads by two changes she made in departmental business. The evaluation process had suffered from a reputation for secrecy and favoritism. The process itself bred rumors, caused low morale, and put additional pressure on the department head. Naomi opened the process up at a time when this was very unusual on campus. She created a rotating advisory evaluation committee composed of individuals from each rank. Everyone could serve. Everyone had an accurate understanding of what everyone else was doing. Moreover, everyone had an incentive to be fair, as someone would one day be looking over their credentials. Demystifying the evaluation process resulted in a huge improvement in morale and encouraged much greater productivity.

Another decision was to increase the number of social events for students and faculty, to celebrate each new book and publication, and to do it all with potluck participation. She knew only too well the pressures on spouses (usually women) of department heads and deans. Her potlucks became an opportunity for increased faculty-student contact.

Naomi's civic contacts also benefited the department. She was quick to involve alums and others from the community in the support of the department. Thus, the department was launched on the road to computerization and enjoyed a far larger number of scholarships than most other departments in the university. These were skills she had seen used by the Business College and she would apply them not only to the department but to all subsequent positions she would hold.

In the spring of 1984, Naomi Lynn told a stunned faculty that she had accepted a position as dean of the College of Public and Urban Affairs at Georgia State University. In only two years as department head at KSU, she had done so much. It seemed impossible she would be leaving. The reaction both cheered and hurt her. A few of her best friends felt abandoned by her decision. Naomi felt real grief at their inability to recognize what an opportunity and challenge it would be for her. Most, though saddened, wished her well and celebrated her success. It was at that time she told this writer that real friends are not just there for you when you are down; real friends also share your joy.

The Georgia Years, 1984–1991

In her years at Georgia State, Lynn demonstrated an ability to take the leadership qualities honed in a small town and transfer them to a major city. She was dean of a college of several very different departments, including public administration, hotel and restaurant management, and criminal justice. She moved from a large suburban home to a luxury condo in the city. Her husband, Bob, planned to retire, but was immediately persuaded to become dean of business at Atlanta University, so once more the deans became sounding boards and helpmates in one another's careers.

The children were grown and married, but the adjustment to Atlanta was tricky. For one thing, Naomi didn't drive. In theory she knew how, but no one had seen her do it more than a mile at a time. Bob and other "chauffeurs" from Manhattan, Kansas, days were not available. Naomi made a deal with her secretary. In exchange for a ride to work and back, the secretary had the use of the dean's reserved parking stall. Once again, she took a win-win approach to problem solving.

During her years as dean, Naomi led the college's expansion, opened new opportunities for minorities and women, and forged linkages with the Atlanta political and economic leadership that served the college well. She courted new hires to the public administration program who would strengthen it and assure continued accreditation.

During her first year in Atlanta, she became the president of ASPA. It was also during her first year that she would encourage many women's groups to support and attend the third UN Decade for Women conference in Nairobi, Kenya. The highlight of her years in Atlanta was the 1988 conference on Women and the Constitution. She took the lead in organizing the event.

Naomi, in her own quiet way, continually surprised others and even herself. She had begun to consider a university presidency.

The Illinois Years, 1991–2003

Naomi Lynn became president of Sangamon State University in Springfield, Illinois, in 1991. As she arrived July 15 at the beautiful estate provided for the university president, the gardener joked: "Our first woman president and my paycheck disappears." The university was mired in problems both with the legislature, which had not appropriated the funds for the fiscal year beginning July 1, and the campus, which had become embroiled in hostile labor-management relations. Unlike the other university administrations for which she had worked, Sangamon had strong union ties.

Naomi had been a fact finder in Kansas, a weak union state, and she had taught public administration long enough to know the basics of public unionizing do's and don'ts, but it was a tough start. She was also a political scientist, a factor that she credits with helping her understand the dynamics of political organizations (Pokorski 2001a, 1).

She would once again utilize the skills and habits, the integrity and fairness that had served her well in other posts. Under her leadership, which was the longest in the history of Sangamon State and the University of Illinois at Springfield: "Lynn will go down in the record books as the Springfield President/Chancellor whose tenure was least troubled by conflict and controversy" (Pokorski 2001a, 1).

She also had to parlay her strong Democratic Party credentials into giving her some breathing space to proceed. At the same time, she immediately became involved, as did Bob, in myriad important civic causes in the city. They were, for example, co-chairs of the Springfield United Way campaign. The responsibilities were numerous as were the awards for their enthusiastic implementation. In 1998 *Springfield Magazine* named her one of the seven most influential people in Springfield, and in 2000 she was featured on the cover of the magazine.

Still, her research and consulting continued. Her old friends remained and new ones multiplied. Her activity in her professional groups never faltered. When asked to name the most daunting challenge she faced during her years as a university president, she answered that it was the difficult transition of Sangamon State University (a primarily upper graduate and graduate institution) into the University of Illinois system. In the process, she became its first chancellor. Institutional change and a new administrative culture required delicacy, patience, and every bit of tact and diplomacy she could muster (Pokorski 2001b, 1).

By the year 2000, Naomi had planned to retire. Bob had been in semiretirement during her presidency though he continued to write and consult, and actively kept the grandchildren and the home front well organized. In April 2000, her retirement reception attracted over 800 people, described by one spokesperson as "Lynn's closest friends" (Pokorski 2001b, 1). Countless others sent flowers and their regards. At that event, she was told that a Naomi B. Lynn Distinguished Capitol Scholar program had been established to support talented undergraduate students—a group she had encouraged when Sangamon State made the transition to a four-year institution (Reynolds 2000, 1).

But perhaps the most touching event of that year was the surprise gift of $1.25 million to the university to endow the Naomi B. Lynn Chair of Lincoln Studies. It was given by Eric and Val Vaden, two sons of friends and colleagues since the KSU period. They were teenagers when their mother died. The Lynns took the whole family under their wing, though by this time, Naomi was dean in Atlanta. The Lynns' friendship and support never wavered. The young men, who went on to successful careers, talked of how much she had meant to them both before and after their loss. To them, she exemplified the qualities of caring, integrity, and leadership that Lincoln had displayed. But most of all, they simply loved her and knew that by supporting higher education, they could honor her in the way she would most appreciate. As the press announcement noted: "The establishment of the Naomi B. Lynn Distinguished Chair of Lincoln Studies is a tribute to the Chancellor whose vision guided the University of Illinois at Springfield [UIS] through a decade of great achievement" (UIS, 2001). Val and Eric Vaden attributed the scholarship to "the greatness of Abraham Lincoln, the greatness of the University of Illinois and the greatness of Naomi Lynn" (UIS 2001).

When the search for Naomi's replacement failed, she agreed to the University of Illinois president's request that she remain for another year. "She has our deepest gratitude not only for adapting her plans, but working as if it was her first year on the job" (Pokorski 2001, 1). The headline in the *State Journal Register* said it all: "Stepping Out in Style After Decade of Success" (Pokorski 2001b, 1). University of Illinois President James Stukel put it more wistfully: "She will be impossible to replace" (Reynolds 2000, 1).

By 2001, the Lynns were at last retired . . . or so they thought. But the call came for Naomi to consider being an acting president of Lincoln Land Community College. Naomi had intended to spend part of her retirement doing some consulting to other presidencies and this presented an opportunity to work with a totally different institution for six months.

Now, in 2003, Naomi Lynn is supposedly retired with a home in Springfield and one in Florida. In her "retirement," she heads an ASPA subcommittee on fundraising and serves on a search committee for the National Academy of Public Administration. Community and family activities abound. In August 2004, she and Robert will celebrate their fiftieth wedding anniversary and the family and careers they have forged.

The Difference She Has Made

Naomi Lynn's life canvas is full of color and exquisite detail. One has only to look at the many fields of study she has affected and the thousands she has influenced. While one can scarcely close the chapter on her career with any certainty, readers can reflect on a rather amazing life.

Public Administration

Naomi Lynn's contributions to public administration, through both her activism and her scholarship, will endure. As noted before, she founded Kansas State's MPA program, was president of the Kansas chapter of ASPA, served on numerous boards and committees of national ASPA, and on the Executive Council of the Section on Public Administration of the American Political Science Association.

In 1985 she became national ASPA president. During her tenure, she sought tirelessly to grow the organization and its many specialty sections, and to enlarge its financial base. She also greatly increased the diversity of the organization, particularly recruiting women and minorities.

She served on the editorial boards of *Public Administration Review*, *Public Administration Quarterly*, and *Review of Public Personnel Administration*. Elected a fellow of the National Academy of Public Administration, she has been a trustee since 1996. She also was elected president of the National Association of Schools of Public Affairs and Administration.

Her many scholarly publications have focused on the federal civil service. One of her most important publications came in 1979 shortly after the passage of the Civil Service Reform Act of 1978. That act was the most important piece of federal civil service legislation since the 1883 Pendleton Act, which set up the Civil Service. With Richard Vaden, Lynn set out to measure attitudes and the impact of the seminal act. Their ambitious study, "Bureaucratic Response to Civil Service Reform," was published in the *Public Administration Review.* It was widely quoted and praised, setting the benchmark for subsequent studies of the federal civil service (1979a, 333–343).

She also wrote widely on the roles and contributions of women in public life and on the barriers to effective participation of women in elective and appointive public-sector careers. Her specific research has illumined but never obscured her study of the discipline as a whole. For example, in 1990, she co-edited with Aaron Wildavsky an impressive and widely cited book—*Public Administration: The State of the Discipline.*

Political Science

There is some overlap in her work for political science and public adminis-tration, though much of her research went to the heart of the field's subdisci-plines. Her book, *The Fulbright Premise*, has already been noted. In 1973, a paper co-authored with David Brady was given an award for the best paper at the American Political Science Association annual meeting. "Switched-Seat Congressional Districts: Their Effect on Party Voting and Public Policy" would later be published in the *American Journal of Political Science* (Brady and Lynn 1973, 528–543). She authored numerous studies on public person-nel as they intersected issues of management, the civil service, and opportu-nities for women (Vaden and Lynn 1979, 22–25; Lynn and Vaden 1979b, 66–71; Lynn and Vaden 1979c, 209–215).

She sought to open the profession and its offices and committees to women and minorities, by urging them to seek out the unglamorous roles in the dis-cipline, to be active in the various caucuses, and generally to make the pro-fessional associations dependent on their talent. Typically, she led by example and was a leader particularly in the women's caucuses of the American Po-litical Science Association and the Midwest Political Science Association. She served on the editorial boards of *The Journal of Politics*, *Women and Politics*, *Political Science and Society*, and *American City and County.*

Women's Studies

Her advocacy, committee work, networking, and many publications strength-ened the women's studies field. One of the most useful of her many publica-tions was a collaboration with Ann Matasar and Marie Rosenberg-Dishman, *A Resource Guide to Women's Studies* (1974). She was one of the founders of the KSU women's studies program in which she taught and worked for years on the KSU Status of Women Commission. She attended and reported on the first UN International Women's Year Conference in Mexico. When the United Nations decided to hold three more such conferences, she was involved in promoting and writing about each of them and their nongovern-mental organization equivalents. She would be in Denmark, Nairobi, and later in 1995 in Beijing.

Characteristically, once she started attending these remarkable conferences she insisted on going to all of them. Naomi is thorough and always prepared.

Two instances from the 1985 Nairobi conference stand out. She convinced several of the delegates to also include a safari in addition to the conference. She made all the arrangements for the tour company and the game parks. Most packed jeans for the safari but Naomi, with a thoroughness that would have awed Dr. Livingston, had not only several safari outfits complete with boots and hat, but also a five-gallon water can she toted everywhere. Naomi, in fact, had no ordinary casual clothes, so when she walked to the pool it was in swimsuit, safari hat and boots—an unforgettable memory. Unfortunately, this was pre-Internet so there is no way to create the Web site this traveler deserved. She also managed to throw a large surprise birthday party complete with guests from all over the world and a lovely cake in the midst of the Kenyan bush!

Her studies with Cornelia Flora were among the first to document empirically the societal barriers to the female sense of efficacy and involvement in politics. Several have been widely cited (Flora and Lynn 1973, 91–103; Lynn and Flora 1974a, 227–248; Lynn and Flora 1977, 139–149). These works demonstrated how gender and societal opportunity structure make the inclusion of women and their promotion problematic. At the time, the factors described were ones both public and private bureaucracies were slow to appreciate.

In 1988 as briefly noted earlier, she organized the program of the Women and the Constitution Conference, which celebrated 200 years of the Constitution but also highlighted the failure of the Constitution to guarantee equal rights to women. This conference was one of the largest bicentennial events in the country and attracted not only several first ladies, but also Supreme Court Justice Sandra Day O'Connor, then the first and only female Supreme Court justice. Leaders in government, academic scholars, and even satirist Erma Bombeck made the conference an unforgettable experience for all who attended. Later Naomi edited the book, *Women, Politics, and the Constitution,* based on key conference presentations (1990).

Once at UIS, Lynn developed the Women's Center on Campus and continued the pattern of organizing women and encouraging them to follow their dreams. The center later established a Naomi B. Lynn annual award for service to women.

A Citizen Leader

Naomi Lynn's leadership has benefited not only the thousands who have known her as a teacher, mentor, friend, and through her scholarship, but also the administrators who have worked with her in the many institutions she has served. She is a gifted leader in higher education administration who has been sought out as a consultant to local and state governments in Kansas,

Georgia, and Illinois. She has also served on federal advisory bodies and as a UN consultant to Thailand.

Lynn led more than a dozen not-for-profit groups including the United Way and Leadership Atlanta. She also took the lead in developing "The Springfield Project," patterned after former President Jimmy Carter's community service program in Atlanta. The Springfield Project Board established an annual community service award in her name.

Illustrative but not exhaustive of her leadership roles have been the positions she held in university governance and the numerous honors and awards she has received. The latter include the Naomi B. Lynn Chair of Lincoln Studies, the Illinois Woman of Achievement Award, the Elizabeth Cady Stanton Award, the Outstanding Community Leader Award, and the Administrator of the Year Award. Her elections to the presidency of ASPA, NASPAA, and other high leadership positions testify to her efforts and commitment to the public sector and the public interest. The awards and honors she received demonstrate her role as an example of excellence. She has also been tireless in exposing bureaucracy bashing, and encouraging talented role models in government. Lynn examined structural and psychological barriers to careers in the public service and studied issues of morale and inclusiveness.

Lynn believes that effective leadership shares credit, nurtures talent, and provides opportunities for others to succeed. When approached about Lynn's influence, virtually everyone mentioned these qualities. Her executive assistant at UIS summed her impact up quite nicely: "She was a role model, a wonderful boss, my good friend. It was a blessing to know her. She pushed me to try new things. I am so glad she has remained in Springfield for she will always be my friend" (Schirding 2003).

At conferences at home and abroad, Naomi is a magnet for people. She loves dining with people at some tourist trap at the end of a long cab ride. But she convinces people to go for meals simply because they enjoy her company. She has a spontaneous sense of humor, but when it comes to the many speeches she committed to give, she leaves nothing to chance. Thus, she is notorious for stealing jokes and writing them in her little programmer. "Heard any good jokes, Naomi?" prompts her to read a few out loud from her stash of winners!

Conclusion

Naomi has held twenty-four positions related to public administration. All under her leadership were linked to raising the prestige of the profession, the quality of scholarship, and the commitment to equal opportunity. No resume, no collection of anecdotes does justice to this woman, but what many in public administration appreciate is her consistent commitment to public service. She gives lie to the notion of the faceless bureaucrat by her own example and by the lives of those she has touched.

The canvas of her life is not complete, but it is already stunning in its complexity and beauty. People continue to warn women about trying to have it all, but fortunately, no one told Naomi!

This brief account of an extraordinary woman in public administration illustrates the potential for one person to make an incredible difference in the lives around her, her community, and her profession. Her success was not built on money or superhuman strength and ability. It was built on enthusiasm, integrity, hard work, and a willingness to share a vision of the public good that would motivate the best in her and others. Her approach to life was not built on the failures of others, but on enhancing the success of those around her.

A Personal Note

If this chapter seems unduly adulatory, it reflects not only a bias of one who has known Naomi for more than three decades, but also the fact that when invited to speak of Naomi's possible weaknesses and flaws or of those who may have opposed or resented her, no one could think of anything or anyone. Given the many honors, the length of her marriage, and the devotion of her family and friends, there just may not be a dark underside to the life of this irrepressible woman.

References

Bateson, Mary Catherine. 1989. *Composing a Life*. New York: Atlantic Monthly Press.
Brady, David, and Naomi B. Lynn. 1973. "Switched-Seat Congressional Districts: Their Effect on Party Voting and Public Policy." *American Journal of Political Science* 17, no. 3 (August): 528–543.
Flora, C.B., and Naomi B. Lynn. 1973. "Motherhood and Political Participation: A Changing Sense of Self." *Journal of Military and Political Sociology* (March): 91–103.
Friedan, Betty. 1964. *The Feminine Mystique*. New York: Dell.
Lynn, Naomi. 1990. *Women, Politics, and the Constitution*. New York: Harrington Park Press.
———. 2001–2003. Telephone interviews with author.
Lynn, Naomi B., and C.B. Flora. 1974a. "The Implications of Motherhood for Political Participation." In *Pronatalism: The Myth of Mom and Apple Pie*, ed. Ellen Peck and Judith Senderowitz, 227–248. New York: Crowell, 1974.
———. 1974b. "Women and Political Socialization: Considerations of the Impact of Motherhood." In *Women in Politics*, ed. Jane Jaquette, 37–53. New York: Wiley.

————. 1977. "Societal Punishment Aspects of Female Political Participation: 1972 National Convention Delegates." In *A Portrait of Marginality: The Political Behavior of the American Woman*, ed. Marianne Githens and Jewel Prestage, 139–149. New York: David McKay.

Lynn, Naomi B., Ann Matasar, and Marie Rosenberg-Dishman. 1974. *A Resource Guide to Women's Studies*. Morristown, NJ: General Learning Press.

Lynn, Naomi B., and Arthur F. McClure. 1973. *The Fulbright Premise*. Lewisburg, PA: Bucknell University Press.

Lynn, Naomi B., and Richard E. Vaden. 1979a. "Bureaucratic Response to Civil Service Reform." *Public Administration Review* 39, no. 4 (July/August): 333–343.

————. 1979b. "Public Administrators: Some Determinants of Job Satisfaction." *Bureaucrat* 8, no. 2 (Summer): 66–71.

————. 1979c. "Toward a Non-Sexist Personnel Opportunity Structure: The Federal Executive Bureaucracy." *Public Personnel Management* 8, no. 4 (July/August): 209–215.

Lynn, Naomi B., and Aaron B. Wildavsky. 1990. *Public Administration: The State of the Discipline*. Chatham, NJ: Chatham House.

Oukrop, Carol. 2002. Interview with author, May 8.

Pokorski, Doug. 2001a. "Hello to Ringeisen, and Thanks to Lynn." *State Journal Register*, March 11, editorial page.

————. 2001b. "Stepping Out in Style After Decade of Success." *State Journal Register*, March 11, 1.

Reynolds, John. 2000. "Scholarship Named After Chancellor of UIS." *State Journal Register* April 8, 1.

Schirding, Emily. 2003. Interview with author, July 15.

University of Illinois at Springfield (UIS). 2001. Press release, February 1.

Vaden, Richard E., and Naomi B. Lynn. 1979. "The Administrative Person: Will Women Bring a Differing Morality to Management?" *Michigan Business Review* 31, no. 2 (March): 22–25.

8

Maxine Kurtz

Knocking Down Bars of the Invisible Cage

Van R. Johnston

Maxine Kurtz was never concerned about being a woman in a man's world. She devoted her life to using the tools of government as a way of sharing the American dream with those who were excluded. She became an innovator, civil rights activist, and role model—not through the exercise of power, but rather through her enthusiasm and the persuasiveness of her example.

Who is Maxine Kurtz? She persuaded officials of Denver and its suburbs to enter into an agreement whereby Denver would share its water in return for suburban controls on sanitation, zoning, and building. She led a decade-long program that produced an innovative zoning ordinance for Denver that became a national model. She pioneered economic analyses of metropolitan areas and applications of the results to forecasting of population and of capital improvement needs. She was the technical director of a Model Cities program that for several years was the lead program for the U.S. Department of Housing and Urban Development (HUD) and the U.S. Department of Health, Education, and Welfare (HEW). She was an advocate for a rational basis for setting pay for civil service employees while at the same time opposing schemes that made no sense when applied in the real world.

She believed that public administrators had the responsibility of sharing what they learned so that others benefit from and, indeed, could improve upon her innovations. She testified before congressional committees on a variety of subjects, taught at the graduate level at two universities, and lectured at many others. For many years, she was a member of the Colorado Advisory Committee to the U.S. Commission on Civil Rights and was its chair for the statutory maximum two terms. She was an advocate of using ordinary language instead of jargon in the drafting of regulations and ordinances, and of basing public actions on a clearly defined foundation in the law.

She became a member of the American Society for Public Administration (ASPA) in 1947. Beginning in 1979, she served on the National Council of the society, including membership on the policy issues committee and the finance committee, and represented ASPA at the National Science Foundation's Project Knowledge 2000, Forum No. II.[1] She was a longtime member of the ASPA personnel section and for a time served as its chair. She also served as a member of the *Public Administration Review* editorial board, and was a frequent contributor of articles for the *Public Administration Times*. In 1984, she received the Donald C. Stone award for distinguished service to the society.

Throughout her career, Maxine Kurtz refused to be deterred by obstacles that would have defeated others of her era. Time and again, she advocated—and demonstrated—an approach characterized by knocking down bars of the invisible cage of mindless conformity to the status quo. This is her story.

The Early Years

Both of Maxine's parents were pioneers in their professions. Her mother, Beatrice Kurtz, attended Hunter College and Cooper Union, taking whatever courses were available that related to her work as staff member of the famous Henry Street Settlement House of New York City.[2] Later, she became head of the Talmud Torah in Minneapolis, a settlement house for Jewish people. These institutions were the precursors of the field of social work. Her father, Jack Kurtz, received the first degree awarded in the United States in what came to be known as the profession of optometry. He devoted his life to his practice and to activities to gain professional recognition of this field. Both parents put considerable emphasis on education for Maxine and her brother, Shulom. Both parents also were passionate supporters of civil rights and did not hesitate to attack abuses of freedom of speech wherever they encountered such actions.

The Challenge

As a sophomore at the University of Minnesota, Maxine encountered a book that was to shape her life. That book was Robert S. Lynd's *Knowledge for What? The Place of Social Science in American Culture*. In a chapter entitled "Some Outrageous Hypotheses," Lynd issued this challenge:

It is assumed that wherever our current culture is found to cramp or to distort the quest of considerable numbers of persons for satisfaction of basic cravings of human personality, there lies a responsibility for social science. In such cases, the first charge upon social science appears to be to ask: Does the trouble lie in the way we operate our culture, i.e., is it only a matter of relatively small internal changes within the going [sic] set of institutions; or is the trouble inherent in the kind of culture we have? If the latter, then the questions have to be faced: What alternative kinds of cultural situations would satisfy more directly and amply the cravings that are now starved? What specific research is needed to test out these alternatives? And, if a given alternative, when tested, seems sensible and desirable "in theory but not in present practice," what techniques and what stages of change would be needed in order to get us from here to there?[3]

Up to this point, Maxine had struggled to gain her goals within the existing structure. After reading Lynd's book, she concluded that society could do with some change itself. No longer would she accept unreasonable situations that she felt existed merely because of the restraints of the invisible cage of mindless conformity with the status quo. She decided to model her life on a "muckraker" named Ida Tarbell who successfully attacked the abuses of the Standard Oil Company. That decision included forgoing marriage in favor of a career.

During the next four years, Maxine intermittently tested the notion of knocking down bars of the invisible cage in various situations. More often than not, she was successful.

The Commitment: Developing the Needed Skills

Her first commitment to a life choice of this approach in local government administration occurred in 1944, when she decided to accept a Sloan Fellowship at the University of Denver to earn her master's degree in government management. She resigned her position as a personnel technician at the Minnesota State Civil Service Commission, cut her close ties to Minneapolis, and set forth on a new life and a new career in Denver.

The University of Denver would not compromise its standards for awarding fellowships despite being in the middle of World War II. Accordingly, it accepted only five applicants. The fellows received stipends for a program that required twenty graduate credits per quarter, half academic and half applied.

Academic training included fifteen credit hours in governmental accounting, auditing, and budgeting. Other academic courses covered such subjects as state and local government, personnel, and public finance. An independent readings program allowed each fellow to pursue a relevant subject of personal interest. She chose economics. The terms of the program included a prohibition against grading other than pass-fail because Sloan felt that in the real world, work is done by groups. Assignments became collegial indeed, as faculty members dropped in to participate in the group assignments.

Applied fieldwork ranged from drafting a legislative manual for newly elected members of the Colorado General Assembly to analyzing budget requests from departments of the State of Wyoming. (The elected official responsible for this analysis was a petroleum wildcatter—an occupation that did not equip him to analyze budget requests.)

Coincidentally, the head of the government management program had been a staff member of the National Resources Planning Board for the Rocky Mountain Region, and now was the Colorado state planning director. A faculty member had been the Denver planning director. The director of the Tri-County Regional Planning Commission was authorized to take any government management classes he desired. Small wonder that Maxine's interest in urban planning was piqued. As the program progressed, she decided to change her career from personnel management to urban planning. As her master's thesis, she developed a recreation plan for the three counties surrounding Denver.

When she finished her thesis, she accepted a position as a research assistant for the Tri-County Regional Planning Commission. Her duties were oriented toward enabling the suburban Denver cities and counties to manage the population explosion that followed the end of World War II. This included successful lobbying of numerous enabling acts through the Colorado General Assembly. Common wisdom was that at least three biennial sessions were needed to have a bill enacted into law. Close attention to detail enabled Kurtz to have all but one of her legislative agendas enacted by the end of the first session in which it was proposed; the one exception was blocked by the refusal of a cosponsoring organization to accept a reasonable compromise. The prime sponsors dropped the cosponsoring organization the next session, and the bill was enacted almost immediately. This immersion in lobbying set the stage for later lobbying activities before the U.S. Congress. After the laws were enacted, she spent a major portion of her time working with all types of local governments to take advantage of their new powers.

For Kurtz, the apparent obstacles—the bars—to achieving ends in the public interest presented challenges to be met with integrity and professionalism. Others might be daunted by invisible barriers to success, but Kurtz saw opportunities.

Bar #1: Governmental Chaos

Denver suburban governments could proceed only so far without the participation of the central city. Ben Stapleton had been mayor of Denver for twenty of the preceding twenty-four years. He was in his mid-seventies when Maxine was working for the Tri-County Planning Commission, and he adamantly refused to have anything to do with suburban officials. Late in 1946, he was asked how he would deal with the problems resulting from the massive influx of population at the end of the world war; he replied: "If those people would just go back where they came from, we wouldn't have any problems here."[4]

In contrast, 34-year-old Quigg Newton ran on a platform that included metropolitan area cooperation and urban planning. Following his election, he asked Kurtz to join his administration to set up a program to achieve these goals. The former planning commission members perceived that the election of Newton was a vote of no confidence in them so they resigned. Kurtz reported to work on September 1, 1947, and found that she was in charge of an agency that had four employees and no defined authority or mission.

The Problem

She was not alone in this situation. George Kelly, a long-time city hall observer, wrote:

> Once behind his big mahogany desk, Quigg was hit head on by the enormity of his task. He started from scratch, not only because he was a novice, but because his predecessor bequeathed nothing resembling a mayoralty blueprint.
>
> Stapleton, renowned as an administrator, unfortunately kept his knowledge of the job locked within himself. When he departed city hall, Ben left behind near-empty filing cabinets and little else.
>
> Newton looked back on this baptismal period as the most trying of his career as mayor. He frankly admitted that he and his associates were groping much of the time, fumbling some of the time, and praying all the time.[5]

Missing Records

City administrators were frustrated trying to find or reconstruct records. Kurtz and other agency heads had to meet frequently to ask: "Does anyone know where the records on subject x are located?" Maxine held weekly meetings of division heads and their counterparts in the public utilities and in other governmental jurisdictions to review applications for the creation of new land subdivisions. These meetings quickly became a major tool for the *ad hoc* coordination of city activities. Detailed records of what constituted the old city plan, for example, did not surface for nearly a decade.

Role of the Charter Convention

To add to the confusion, Denver voters at the mayoral election of 1947 had also authorized a charter convention to update the 1902 city charter. Like others in the administration, Maxine agreed to defer the organization of her agency until the new charter was passed. Meanwhile, when she discovered that the new city officials did not know where the current city limits were, she assigned her two draftsmen to produce maps for them so that city services could be provided, ranging from street cleaning to police protection. Everywhere they looked, they seemed to find that the apparent organization of city administration was scrambled. Nothing was easy or simple.

Due to the state tax calendar, Denver officials had to submit their budgets before the election on the proposed new charter. The mayor opted to reorganize the city government and base the 1948 budget on the provisions of that document. He guessed wrong; the new charter failed to pass by a narrow margin.[6] Weeks were devoted to returning the city structure to its organization as provided in the existing charter and redoing the entire budgeting process.

Planning Office Role Established

Finally, one year after Maxine was appointed to head the planning function in the city, an ordinance was enacted creating the planning office within the office of the mayor and detailing its duties and responsibilities. By this time, the staff had increased in size, and was coping with immediate problems relating to a massive public construction program and regulations to guide the development of privately owned land. An expert in construction planning had been named as planning director, and Maxine's preference was accepted when she was named head of the research and special projects division of the planning office. At least the planning function had been unscrambled.

Bar #2: Urban Highway Design

The second major test of Kurtz's philosophy of knocking down the bars of the invisible cage came when the city had to develop a new street plan.

The Problem

The U.S. Bureau of Public Roads had mandated the percentage of increase that should be used in projecting future traffic volumes. As Kurtz recalls, that formula provided that traffic on freeways would increase by 2.8 times, on limited-access surface roads by 2.2 times, and on major streets by 1.8 times. Maxine objected because that did not make sense. Metropolitan Denver was inundated by new housing construction to meet the needs of the booming in-migration, and a "one size fits all" set of projected traffic increases was ridiculous, she insisted. She documented the problem by referring to two parallel highways. One was developed along its entire length. The other abutted vacant farmland, but that farmland was vanishing as builders were purchasing it, subdividing it, and constructing tract housing on it at an unprecedented rate. It just made good sense that the future traffic volume increase on the second highway would be greater than the increase on the first highway.

Another Problem

State and regional federal officials would not accept any other projections than those mandated by the formula.

The Solution

Gene Simm, the assistant city traffic engineer, was assigned to work with Kurtz to develop a detailed explanation of exactly how the alternative approach would work. Finally, Denver's famous traffic engineer Henry Barnes took Kurtz's alternate proposal back to the research division of the bureau in Washington, DC. The research staff responded that the formulas were intended to apply only to the interstate highway system outside urban areas, and accepted the Denver proposal immediately, saying it was potentially the greatest advance in urban traffic engineering in decades. When applied, the first of the parallel highways was projected to increase 1.8 times; the second was projected to increase by 7.0 times. Annual traffic counts on these two thoroughfares showed that the projections were "right on the nose." Today's university civil engineering curricula include this concept; it is known as the "gravity model."

The same concept of using the land-use plan for the metropolitan area as the basis for projecting traffic volumes eventually came to be used in other studies including the relative future demand for Denver water by service area, planning for future needs for recreation, capital budgeting for fire protection, and estimating the costs and benefits of new annexations.[7]

Bar #3: No Comprehensive Plan for Rezoning

Too many cities had great future plans tucked away on shelves, while "practical" people ignored them in favor of hunches or custom. Denver led the way in making comprehensive city plans a working tool for the integrated development of the city.

What appeared initially to be a minor zoning case exploded into a city crisis. A decade of Kurtz's professional life was spent developing a solution.

The Problem

A judge in a Denver district court case ruled that if almost all properties in a two-block area were used for purposes inconsistent with the zoning ordinance, the provisions could not be enforced. Owners of hundreds of building sites throughout the city had been authorized to use their land for purposes not allowed by the original zoning map adopted in 1925. An investigation revealed that no one knew where all those hundreds of building sites were. The city had to develop a completely new zoning ordinance and map. There was no other viable solution.

Kurtz, as head of the research division of the planning office, and George Nez, the newly appointed assistant planning director, became a team to lead the project. While Kurtz emphasized the office activities and Nez oversaw the field work, most of the conceptualization was a joint effort.

Step #1 in Solution: An Economic Survey to Determine Land Use Needs

The first challenge was to determine how much land would be needed for each type of land use over the next two decades (1950–1970), and what had to be the characteristics of that land. For instance, large industries needed land assemblages, access to rail, highway, and air transportation; available capacity of utilities such as water, domestic sewerage, power, and communications; and nearby supporting enterprises such as financial institutions and university-based research capabilities. This was before business computers and videoconferencing were available. Housing for employees and cultural amenities were also featured in the profile.

Being a pragmatist, Kurtz figured that the best way to collect this information was to survey employers in the four-county Denver metropolitan area. The mayor initially resisted the idea, especially when he saw the questionnaire that called for information from which one could have determined both their current operations and their future market plans. But the employers agreed to cooperate; their only two conditions were that their individual replies would be held confidential, and that the city would issue a summary report that they could use in their business planning.

In addition to statistics about land needs, the data collected allowed population projection at a relatively refined scale. For instance, an economy based primarily on technology and "brain-based" enterprises such as research laboratories would generate a relatively young, well-educated workforce. In turn, that meant that the population profile would include many children, and the parents would be more interested in single-family housing than in apartments, and in public schools and active recreation rather than formal gardens and historic preservation.

The conclusion of the study was that the limiting factor on growth of the metropolitan area would be the availability of municipal water supplies.[8] The economic analysis became a self-fulfilling prophecy. The only major development inconsistent with the analysis was the location of the Martin-Marietta missile development and testing facility in the foothills west of Denver, which was based on defense considerations, rather than economic considerations.

Step #2 in Solution: Noncumulative Permitted Land Uses

In many ways, the proposed Denver zoning ordinance and map were revolutionary documents. For instance, zoning ordinances of the 1920s era existed for the purpose of protecting single-family residences from the noxious influences of everything from billboards to rendering plants. Kurtz knew that, but she also realized that in the society of the 1950s, more was needed. If the projected economic base was to be achieved, industrial sites had to be protected against encroachment from dwellings. This completely switched the rationale for zoning ordinances to a philosophy that every lawful use is the highest and best use in an appropriate location.

Traditional cumulative lists of permitted uses were abandoned in favor of focused descriptions of what was permitted in each zone. In some instances, uses were permitted if they could meet certain performance standards such as the amount of noise or traffic generated.

No longer would the higher population densities of apartments and rooming houses be used as buffers between single-unit dwellings and businesses. It made no sense, Kurtz and Nez maintained, to increase the number of people exposed to adverse effects, which was the result of that line of thinking. If buffer zones were needed, those zones would be designated as such. Appropriate buffers in this situation could be a zone for landscaped employee parking lots or small office buildings.

A primary purpose of a comprehensive plan was to improve the quality of life, and since the 1920s when zoning first became widespread, the uniform enabling acts provided that the zoning should be done in compliance with a comprehensive plan. Denver led the second generation of zoning ordinances in applying that criterion.

Step #3 in Solution: Limit Regulations of Land Use to Minimum Requirements

Regulations for construction of buildings and other improvements were subjected to a similar scrutiny. Why require a side yard if a building had no doors or windows on that side? Why regulate the shape of a building in order to control density? Instead, use the ratio between land area and floor space, and let the architects decide on the shape of the building. These are a sampling of the kinds of innovative thinking this process involved.

Step #4 in Solution: Defining Responsibilities

Over time, the legislative responsibilities had been delegated from the City Council to the Board of Adjustment-Zoning, and then from the Board of Adjustment-Zoning to the secretary of the board. The ordinance contained no standards to govern the decisions of either the Board of Adjustment-Zoning or the secretary. Enforcement was the responsibility of the building department; but that agency was too involved with enforcement of the building code to pay attention to the zoning ordinance requirements.

The proposed ordinance contained provisions that paralleled traditional American government concepts. The legislative responsibility would be returned to the City Council. The enforcement (executive) responsibility would be vested in a new agency to be known as the Department of Zoning Administration. The quasijudicial responsibility of dealing with variances and exceptions would continue to be vested in the Board of Adjustment-Zoning, but it would have to hold hearings, make findings, and issue formal decisions. No so-called use variances could be authorized. They were part of the legislative responsibility of the City Council.

Step #5 in Solution: Public Education

Some of the ideas included in the Denver proposed ordinance were adapted from proposals in other cities, but the important point was that none of those proposed ordinances had been enacted. In Denver, citizen advisory committees totaling more than 100 people reviewed the proposed ordinance, line by line. Hearings in each of the city's public high schools provided a parallel review of the proposed zoning map.

The mayor and City Council members had agreed not to intrude in the drafting process. The planning board persuaded them that they would have plenty of time to consider the finished proposal. Meanwhile, there was no reason for them to take public positions on issues that might never appear before them.

Step #6 in Solution: Enacting the Proposed Zoning Ordinance

In due course, the mayor and council did receive a proposed ordinance, and held their own hearings. However, they had agreed in advance to make no amendments to the draft ordinance. The staff had gone to extraordinary lengths to ensure that properties similarly situated would be treated the same, and also to ensure that property owners' rights to use the existing zoning would be protected until the new zoning ordinance and map were enacted into law. City officials were as good as their word; the zoning ordinance and map were enacted without amendment. Later, minor map adjustments were enacted, mostly for instances where property owners had built in accordance with the original ordinance and map.

Nez and Kurtz became the Department of Zoning Administration. They reviewed all building permit applications for compliance with the new zoning ordinance and map, while at the same time recruiting and training a staff for that department.

Step #7 in Solution: Defending New Zoning Ordinance in Courts

Then the inevitable legal challenges arose, and Kurtz was informally assigned to be a member of the city's defense team. The best known case was *Denver Buick v. City and County of Denver.*[9] Kurtz was supposed to be one of several experts testifying on behalf of the city, but the judge would not permit any of those other experts to testify, ruling that they had nothing relevant to present. When Kurtz was offered as an expert witness, however, he announced that "I want to hear what this witness has to say." A month later, Kurtz finally finished her testimony. The judge's action in barring some of the expert witnesses also meant that certain essential information was not in the record. The State Supreme Court, on appeal, followed the lower court's lead.

This case was notorious because a divided State Supreme Court (five opinions from seven justices) declared off-street parking requirements to be unconstitutional. That declaration was met with nationwide condemnation, both from appellate courts in other states and from authors publishing in law journals. Overlooked in the national uproar was the fact that the Colorado Supreme Court, at that time one of the most conservative courts in the nation when property rights were involved, upheld the right of a city comprehensively to rezone.

A secondary result of the entire process of the *Denver Buick* trials was that Kurtz decided to enroll in the University of Denver College of Law. Initially, she wanted to take just those courses related to her work. By the time that process was completed, she lacked only fifteen credits to earn a law degree, so she decided to complete her studies. In 1962, she received her doctor of jurisprudence degree, was elected to the Order of St. Ives (a legal honorary society recognizing high academic achievement), and passed the Colorado bar examination, placing in the top 10 percent of the more than 100 candidates taking the exam.

Meanwhile, Kurtz continued serving as a member of the legal team and an expert witness in several other zoning cases. The most significant of these, the *Frankel* case,[10] held for the first time that a zoning ordinance and map existed for the purpose of carrying out a comprehensive plan, and that an amendment to that ordinance could be made only on one of two grounds: (1) to correct a mistake, or (2) to adjust to a change in the comprehensive plan.

In the following years, many other cities adopted new zoning ordinances and maps, more-or-less modeled on the Denver ordinance. Maxine told this author that within five years after the Denver ordinance became effective in 1960, private land development interests were complaining that the Denver ordinance was primitive and out of date. She commented that "I've always enjoyed being a problem solver. I'm the one who is knocking down the bars of the invisible cage by hacking out a new path through the forest; others have the responsibility of widening and paving that path into a highway."

Transitional Activities

In the early 1960s, Kurtz returned to long-range planning, participating in studies needed to provide a foundation for a new comprehensive plan targeting 1980. On a part-time basis, she also taught at the University of Denver College of Law, initiating new classes dealing with municipal law and administrative law. Here again, she was innovating new educational techniques in a college that was traditional. Instead of examinations, she selected real issues confronting governmental jurisdictions in Colorado, and had each of her students prepare a legal opinion identifying options for solving that problem and justifying a recommendation as to the best course to follow. In the administrative law course, she invited outstanding legal practitioners in a variety of administrative law specialties to present "off the record" accounts of their experiences in trying or adjudicating cases. The university continued these teaching techniques after the courses had been integrated into the regular curriculum.

Maxine did not know it at the time, but this period was a lull between two career-changing events. The first had been the 1960 court decision sustaining the new zoning ordinance and map. The second was the June 1965 flood that did hundreds of millions of dollars of damage to the valley of the South Platte River, a major south-to-north waterway that bisected the city. Water experts dubbed it a "thousand-year flood."

Improving the Quality of Urban Life Using Management Techniques

Nationally, the last half of the 1960s was a period of social upheaval, following the assassination of President John F. Kennedy. In 1968 alone, the nation was rocked by the Vietnam War, the assassinations of Robert F. Kennedy and Martin Luther King, Jr., the Kent State massacre, the Chicago police riot during the Democratic Party national convention, and race riots in more than 100 American cities. The list seemed endless.[11]

Origin of the Demonstration Cities Act

Apparently, Congress was disillusioned by the act creating the War on Poverty. In 1966, it enacted a statute entitled in part: "The Demonstration Cities Act,"[12] generally designed to create in a limited number of cities experimental programs to improve the quality of urban life. This act had several unique features that shaped how the city programs were to be designed:

1. The program was supposed to be run by the mayor and city council, with widespread citizen participation.
2. Many goals were listed, ending with a catchall phrase: "To improve the quality of urban life."
3. City governments were to coordinate the efforts of federal, state, local public, and private groups.
4. The program was to be planned and executed in accordance with the principles of the "management by objective" system. The sequencing of events also included the principles of PPBS (Planning, Programming, Budgeting System). [These are spelled out here for the reader, but the terms were not actually used, only the acronym.]

In practice, the complex project management system known as Program Evaluation and Review Technique (PERT) charting also was essential.

These management techniques had been developed primarily by the private sector. The Ford Foundation funded the so-called 5–5–5 project to encourage the transfer of these management techniques to the public sector.[13]

Decades later, Camilla Stivers had this to say about such requirements: "A succession of management reforms made their way into the practice of public administration from profit-making business. Management by objectives, PPBS . . . zero based budgeting, and a 'passion for excellence' came and went, all hailed as the key to more effective public administration, all failing to make any significant alteration in administrative practices."[14] Kurtz generally concurs with that observation, as well as with this conclusion: "We need to accept the inseparability of politics and administration, facts and values, policies and procedures, theory and practice, instead of struggling fruitlessly toward a nonexistent conceptual or methodological holy grail that will finally make it possible for us to reach ultimate truth."[15] Maxine added that in her work with the Model Cities program, apparently it was easier for nonconformist practitioners of "people-oriented" professions such as social psychology, community psychiatry, law, medicine, group social work, the clergy, anthropology, and law enforcement to accommodate to the dualities expressed than it was for many classically trained public administrators.

Denver's Original Expectations

Denver Mayor Thomas G. Currigan perceived the Demonstration Cities Act to be a way of funding the recovery of the Platte River valley. He lobbied hard for the passage of the proposal, and once it was enacted, lost no time in detailing staff to prepare an application for funding. His first application committee was composed of his administrative assistant Lee F. Johnson, the city's federal liaison officer (grants officer) Kenneth Dybevik, and Maxine Kurtz, whom he borrowed from the planning office. Johnson, a Colorado native, had been head of the U.S. Public Housing Administration under President Franklin D. Roosevelt, and subsequently had become the highly respected congressional lobbyist for the National Association of Housing and Redevelopment Officials (NAHRO).

The Demonstration Cities Act was so broadly drawn that every activist group thought it should be entitled to benefit from the perceived bountiful funding. Currigan soon had stacks of applications from disparate groups, and was not sure what to do with them. After careful study, the application committee concluded that was not the way to develop a program. What was needed was to develop a city program, and then to seek qualified sponsors. The mayor then added his cabinet members plus selected executives of other agencies, governments, and major associations of service providers to the committee charged with developing the application.

Identifying the Problems

The group decided to find out what the problems of the poverty area were by asking the residents, drawing on such groups as the neighborhood action councils of the War on Poverty program and tenant councils of public housing projects. The poverty area included much of the land devastated by the Platte River flood. Committee members for the first (but not the last) time reacted to the replies by saying, "We had never realized that problem existed."

Kurtz then worked with individual committee members in their respective areas of expertise to respond to the outline of the application contents specified by the HUD. Denver was one of the first cities to submit its application. Congressional politics delayed the decision by HUD as to which cities would be named to participate in the program. By this time the name of the national program had been changed to the Model Cities program.

The Early Start

Many in the group who worked on preparation of the application became impatient with the delay in designation and funding. They were young, energetic, committed men who felt they really did not have to wait for designation and funding—some of their projects required no additional funding at all. The problem confronting the mayor, Johnson, and Kurtz was that the application called for a coordinated attack on the problems. As months went by, frustration grew. Finally, the mayor decided to start the Denver Model City program without waiting for designation or federal funding. He named Kurtz to be the technical director of the Denver Model City program, and Johnson to be his personal representative.

Training the "Establishment"

Organizations designated to sponsor projects were asked to name the staff director for each, and those men and women were given an intensive orientation both on the program itself, and on the multicultural character of the residents of the Model Cities neighborhood. These included blacks, Hispanics, Asians, Slavs, and "Okies" (migrants who moved west during the Dust Bowl days of the 1930s, who settled on acreage in Denver and ultimately gained title to their home sites through adverse possession). "Adverse possession" roughly means occupying land someone else owns, without that occupancy being challenged. These sites lacked urban utilities, in addition to other problems.

Recruiting the Militants

Several months after Denver started its program, HUD designated Denver to be one of the participants in the Model Cities program. The next challenge Kurtz faced was to persuade such militant minority groups as the Black Panthers, the Crusade for Justice (Chicano), and the American Indian Movement to participate in the Denver program. Kurtz met with the combined representatives of these groups during a December blizzard, telling them in effect that this was the program to bring about institutional reform. She added that it was their program, and if they chose not to participate, that was okay. After she left the meeting, the participants tried to figure out what her angle was. They could not find any, so they decided to participate until they did find that angle. Their search was in vain; they participated during the entire program. Some of the militants were removed from their national organizations because they were not militant enough. Over 100 cities burned during race riots in this period. Denver was not one of them. A federal evaluator of the Denver program told Kurtz that the militants were not co-opted by the "establishment"; they were co-opted by the program.

A Division of Responsibilities

As the Denver Model City program moved from the planning stage to implementation, Kurtz was named to a national council of directors of Model Cities programs to advise HUD on policies intended to guide local Model Cities executives. The Denver program expanded to such an extent that Kurtz and Johnson decided to divide primary responsibilities: Kurtz would handle liaison with federal representatives, resident relations, and administration of the office. Johnson would be responsible for liaison work with the private sector and "establishment" representatives, and would be the mayor's representative. These were not airtight assignments; the two collaborated or represented each other as needed.

Did it make any difference that Kurtz was a woman? Upon reflection, Kurtz thought the answer was "not much." The principal effect, she thought, was that when dealing with militant minorities, she did not present a challenge to their manhood. What role did the mandated management systems play in administration of the Denver program? Again, the answer was "not much." She explained that use of those highly structured systems was dreamed up by people who knew little or nothing about the lifestyles of the low-income residents. Above all, most residents led relatively unstructured lives. Mandated work schedules were some invention of the "establishment" in their view. When Kurtz insisted that deadlines had to be met, they were, but the process was anything but orderly. Statistics were meaningless in the poverty culture. Residents proceeded directly from identification of a problem to a solution. The staff could fill in the intermediate steps.

Problems of Evaluation

What were the benefits of this program? Kurtz noted that irreconcilable expectations of what a given project should achieve limited the ability to evaluate the results. She cited an exchange where an executive of HEW suggested to resident representatives that the way to measure success of a program to reduce infant mortality was to find out how many infants died before the program started, and how many died when the program was completed. The difference indicated the success of the program. A resident spokesperson responded: "You, sir, may be interested in the statistics; we want to know what happened to the mother whose baby just died."

Anecdotal evidence indicated a measure of success, ranging from a black dance group that is still in existence to a significant number of participants learning how to deal with the "establishment," and hence to obtain employment and move. From the vantage of the "establishment," many "movers and shakers" learned how their policies were blocking access to jobs and education, and many agreed to institute changes. Similarly, sensitivity training was made part of the training of police and sheriffs. Service delivery was further decentralized, so those needing help could obtain it. School curricula were broadened to include cultures other than those derived from northern European sources. And, of course, Denver did not burn during the riots of the 1960s.

Civil Rights in Employment

Congress had passed the Civil Rights Act of 1964, barring discrimination in the private sector on the basis of race, color, creed, gender, or national origin in employment, housing, and public accommodations. Parallel legislation barred such discrimination in education. At the time, F. Arnold McDermott was the personnel director heading the Denver Career Service Authority. He perceived that it was likely that these acts would be extended to the public sector, and he wanted to be prepared. To accomplish this, he created a position of research director within the career service authority, and offered it to Kurtz. She accepted.

Kurtz's first assignment was to analyze what, in the experience of running a public service careers program, could be used by the career service authority.[16] This report highlighted both the strong points and the weaknesses of the organization, and included recommendations for solving the latter. The U.S. Department of Labor (DOL) found the report to be helpful in lobbying Congress to continue funding the public service careers program.

How to Eliminate Cultural Bias from Employment Recruitment and Testing

In return, DOL funded a demonstration project for the Denver Career Service Authority on how to tailor civil service tests to eliminate or at least to minimize cultural biases.[17] When the project was completed, the DOL distributed the six-volume report nationwide.

Comprehensive Changes in Personnel Practices

Over the years, Kurtz's evaluations had an impact on every phase of the career service authority's activities: records, recruitment and selection, classification, pay, employee relations.

She used her legal training to update the personnel rules and install the needed adjustments when the city became subject to the Fair Labor Standards Act. She represented the city in administrative proceedings alleging discrimination before the U.S. Equal Employment Opportunity Commission (EEOC) and the Colorado Civil Rights Commission. She also represented the city in contesting unemployment compensation claims. For a time, she administered the career service appeal process. Also, she appeared as an expert witness for the city in court litigation.

"Uniform Guidelines on Employee Selection Procedures": Unintended Consequences

Kurtz became best known on a national scale on two issues. One dealt with the test validation standards issued by a combination of federal agencies.[18] The standards had initially been developed by the American Psychological Association for use in validating educational tests. There was no problem in getting enough students to have reliable test validation results on educational tests (generally a minimum of 60 to 100). In contrast, large civil service systems around the country, including Denver, averaged ten positions per class, and the vast majority of classes had only one to five positions. Statistically significant results could not be obtained with samples that small.

Some personnel consultants were using scare tactics to get merit systems to drop all testing, and substitute random selection, or other irrational bases. Their argument was essentially the EEOC will sue you if you continue to measure candidates for employment on the basis of relative competence. Personnel directors around the country seemed to be so frightened that they capitulated. Kurtz became frustrated with this tactic, and she told the director of the International Personnel Management Association (IPMA) that someone should let the personnel directors around the country know what a trial is really like. He responded that if she would prepare something to accomplish this end, IPMA would publish and distribute it. When Maxine returned to Denver, she joined with Glenn McClung, Denver's employment division director, in writing the transcript of a fictional court case alleging discriminatory testing.[19] IPMA distributed the result to all of its members and to others. That seemed to deflate many of the more unusual claims of the consultants.

The "Equal Pay for Equal Work" Movement and the "Lemons" Case

The other activity of national import had to do with the claim by the feminist movement that women were being discriminated against because of the practice of using prevailing market data to set pay for work. The term generally was defined by the proponents as "equal pay for work of equal value," although the terminology varied, and so did the definitions. The sifting sands of the argument even evoked a frustrated comment by the U.S. Supreme Court pointing out the difficulty in dealing with that issue.

One of the leading cases on the subject was *Lemons v. City and County of Denver.*[20] The plaintiffs framed the issue as comparing the pay received by nurses to the pay received by tree trimmers. In addition to helping prepare the city's defense, Maxine became a nationally recognized opponent of the system. In her view, as appealing as the notion may have been in theory, there was no objective way of making "comparable worth" determinations in the real world. Her activities included testifying before hearings of subcommittees of the U.S. House of Representatives,[21] giving talks to national organizations,[22] including the American Society for Public Administration, appearing on the *McNeil-Lehrer News Hour*,[23] and writing several articles.[24] Comparable worth has been negotiated in jurisdictions that have collective bargaining, but after several courts have vigorously rejected the concept, it seems to have died down as an issue in merit systems.

U.S. Commission on Civil Rights

For many years, Kurtz was a member of the Colorado advisory committee to the U.S. Commission on Civil Rights, and for four of those years she was chair of the committee. The committee addressed state civil rights issues ranging from police-community relations to English as a second language. She worked with Commission Chairman Clarence Pendleton to encourage advisory committees of several southwestern states to hold simultaneous public forums on immigration, thus providing the commission with information requested by Congress. Maxine also testified at oversight hearings on the commission held by a committee of the U.S. House of Representatives.[25]

Personal Management Style

Maxine combined the bottom-up style of management as practiced by such firms as SAS (Scandinavian Airlines) and Goretex (sports apparel) with the "walk-around" system used by Hewlett-Packard (computers) to encourage employees at all levels to assume responsibility for the quality of the work in the career service authority. At the same time, it promoted their personal careers.

Maxine's retirement from the City and County of Denver in 1990, after 43 years of service, was marked by a special resolution of appreciation by the Denver City Council, and by a farewell party attended by many of the men and women who had worked for and with her over the years. She was touched to see the diversity of those attending the party—Anglos, Hispanics, African Americans, Asians, Native Americans, and both men and women whose careers had been advanced by her support and encouragement.

For a few years following retirement from the city, Maxine conducted a mixed legal practice and consulting service on personnel issues. She currently is writing an historical memoir, which she calls "Knocking Down the Bars of the Invisible Cage."

Notes

Manuscript materials and notes on the numerous discussions between Kurtz and the author are omitted from this section.

1. "Project Knowledge 2000" was the National Science Foundation Bicentennial Project (1976). Forum I identified the need for knowledge, forum II was concerned with the generation of knowledge, and forum III dealt with the communication of knowledge. No generally available report was issued.

2. A settlement house was "a community center offering social and educational activities. The services are usually free and directed at the underprivileged element of the population." *Webster's New Twentieth Century Dictionary, unabridged*, 2d ed. (New York: Collins-World, 1975), 1662. At that time, most settlement houses were privately funded.

3. Robert S. Lynd, *Knowledge for What? The Place of Social Science in American Culture* (Princeton, NJ: Princeton University Press, 1939), 205–206.

4. George V. Kelly, *The Old Gray Mayors of Denver* (Boulder, CO: Pruett, 1974), 1.

5. Ibid., 26.

6. Ibid., 28.

7. Denver Planning Office, *General Street Plan: Denver Metropolitan Area* (Preliminary), 1952; Maxine Kurtz, "Research Aspects of an Annexation Study," *Journal of the American Institute of Planners* 23, no. 2 (1957): 58–63; Maxine Kurtz, "The Planning Aspects of Annexation and of Service Areas," *Urban Problems and Techniques, #1* (Denver: Chandler Davis, 1959), 7–30; Maxine Kurtz, "A Second Look at Annexation Fees and Financing," *Journal of the American Institute of Planners* 28, no. 2 (1962): 130–131; Maxine Kurtz, "The 1960 Census: A Workshop," *Planning, 1957* (Chicago: American Society of Planning Officials, 1957), 127–132.

8. Denver Planning Office, *Working Denver: An Economic Analysis by the Denver Planning Office, 1953* (out of print); Maxine Kurtz, "Denver Economic Survey," *Journal of the American Institute of Planners* 28, no. 2 (1962): 130–131.

9. *Denver Buick v. City and County of Denver*, 141 Colo. 121, 347 P.2d 919 (1959).

10. *Frankel v. City and County of Denver*, 147 Colo. 373, 363 P.2d 1063 (1961).

11. See, for example, Jules Witcover, *The Year the Dream Died: Revisiting 1968 in America* (New York: Warner Books, 1998).

12. Demonstration Cities and Metropolitan Development Act of 1966, Title I.

13. The "5–5–5 project" called for five cities, five counties, and five states to conduct experiments in the use of these management techniques. Denver was one of the five cities, and started its assigned project. However, the sponsors of the project were not able to recruit enough other governments to participate, and the project was dropped. Denver officials gained significant experience in the use of these techniques, however.

14. Camilla Stivers, *Bureau Men, Settlement Women: Constructing Public Administration in the Progressive Era* (Lawrence: University Press of Kansas, 2000), 132–133.

15. Ibid., 135.

16. Maxine Kurtz, *Self-Appraisal of the Denver Public Service Careers Program, 1970–1972* (Denver: Career Service Authority, 1972).

17. Maxine Kurtz et al., *A Report of the Denver Test Validation Project*, 6 vols. (Denver: Career Service Authority, 1972).

18. U.S. Equal Employment Coordinating Council, "Uniform Guidelines on Employee Selection Procedures," 29 CFR Part 1607, U.S. Equal Employment Opportunity Commission, 1995.

19. Maxine Kurtz and Glenn G. McClung, *Care and Feeding of Witnesses—Expert and Otherwise* (Personnel Employment Practices Bulletin #8) (Chicago: International Personnel Management Association, 1974).

20. *Lemons v. City and County of Denver*, 620 F.2d 228 (10th Cir., 1980), cert. denied. The trial court ordered that its decision not be published officially; however, the text can be found at 17 Fair Empl. Prac. Cas. (BNA) 906.

21. *Joint Hearings on Pay Equity Before the Subcommittees on Civil Service, Human Resources, and Compensation and Employee Benefits, Committee on Post Office and Civil Service*, House of Representatives, December 2, 1982.

22. Maxine Kurtz, panelist, American Bar Association, Section on Urban, State, and Local Law, "Roundtable A: Comparable Worth Problems and Concerns" annual meeting, August 5, 1984, Chicago; Maxine Kurtz, "Recent Court Decisions Affecting Personnel Practices of State and Local Governments," International Personnel Man-

agement Association International Conference on Public Personnel Management, October 7, 1981, Milwaukee; Maxine Kurtz, "Recent Legal Developments in Comparable Worth," International Personnel Management Association annual meeting, October 11, 1983, Washington, DC.

23. "The McNeil-Lehrer Reports: Pay Equity," THIRTEEN, Transcript #1876, Box 345, New York, December 6, 1982, 2–7.

24. Maxine Kurtz, "The Practical Problems of Comparable Worth," in *Equal Pay for Unequal Work*, ed. Phyllis Schlafly (Washington, DC: Eagle Forum Education and Legal Defense Fund, 1983), 171–183; Maxine Kurtz and E. Clyde Hocking, "Nurses v. Tree Trimmers," *Public Personnel Management* 12, no. 4 (Winter 1983): 369–381.

25. Maxine Kurtz, *Oversight Hearing Before the Subcommittee on Civil and Constitutional Rights*, House of Representatives, Serial no. 57, September 19, 1985, 74–78.

Afterword

We leave to others the intriguing task of turning the multifaceted lens of feminist theory to the lives of the women portrayed in this volume. We support and celebrate women in public administration, yet we hardly consider ourselves peers of the likes of Camilla Stivers, Mary Ellen Guy, and their scholarly cohorts in feminist theory.

We keep for ourselves two important tasks: First, to put forward several themes that link the lives of the women in this book with contemporary women—and by "contemporary women," we mean our collective selves in public administration and our daughters, whether by birth, relationship, or professional connection. We do not presume to offer what in today's parlance might be termed "lessons learned," although we see clearly qualities that connect many of these lived lives, one to another. And, in our second task, we urge others to join our authors in contributing to the shamefully small trove of research on women in public administration. Even beyond our admiration for these women as individuals, we believe that a failure to acknowledge and learn from the contributions of women as a significant force in the public service arena deprives our world of a crucial source of wisdom.

Linkages

In the process of editing this book and working with the authors, we have come to view the subjects of the chapters as "our women" rather than "these women." That said, we ask that our readers reflect on some of the themes that permeate the lives of our women. We see at least three linkages: willingness to do and a passion for pursuing whatever it took to get the job done; awareness of and responsiveness to the constraints of society in her time; and unwillingness to permit those constraints to define creative action in the public interest. We invite our readers to appreciate these and related themes in the lives of our women and to entertain the possibility that those qualities can be seen in your own lives as well as the lives of women you admire and revere.

Celebrating Outstanding Women in Public Administration

A fourth theme links our women. Not one among them has been sufficiently recognized for her contributions to public administration, and we as a society are less than we could be because of it. We are honored to have had the opportunity and encouragement for moving the recognition of women in public administration forward by some small amount. And we urge you who have taken the time to read these fascinating stories to add to the fine archive that our authors have begun.

Claire L. Felbinger and Wendy A. Haynes

About the Editors and Contributors

Claire L. Felbinger is the senior program officer for Transportation Policy and Management at the Transportation Research Board of the National Academies. She is also the founding editor of the peer-reviewed journal *Public Works Management & Policy: Research and Practice in Transportation, Infrastructure, and the Environment.* Her most recent book, *Evaluation in Practice: A Methodological Approach* (1989), is coauthored with Richard D. Bingham. Dr. Felbinger serves on eight editorial boards and holds leadership positions in professional associations in public administration, urban politics, and engineering. She also holds a position in the School of Public Policy and Center for Transportation at George Mason University.

Mary E. Guy holds the Jerry Collins Eminent Scholar Chair in Public Administration at the Askew School of Public Administration and Policy, Florida State University. She is a past president of the American Society for Public Administration (ASPA) and a past chair of ASPA's Section for Women in Public Administration. Professor Guy writes extensively about women in the workplace and the difference that gender makes.

Wendy A. Haynes has devoted over twenty-five years to the public service as a professional practitioner at all levels of government. Now as a consultant, practitioner, and scholar, Dr. Haynes's expertise resides in megaproject management; performance measurement, reporting, and auditing; policy and management analysis; and management/organizational assessment. Her' interests lie in both the quantifiable, measurable aspects of the organization as well as the less tangible issues surrounding leadership, management, coaching, organizational development, and change. She teaches, publishes, and speaks at seminars and conferences on an array of topics related to her fields of expertise. As an active leader in the ASPA, she serves as chair of the Section for Women in Public Administration, on several editorial boards, and on a variety of committees nationally and locally.

Van R. Johnston, now professor of Management and Public Policy at the Daniels College of Business at the University of Denver, also taught and conducted research at the University of Southern California, where he received his Ph.D. Dr. Johnston was elected to the National Council of the Policy Studies Organization and has been coeditor of *Policy Studies Review* and is associate editor of the *Review of Policy Research.* He has served in many leadership roles in ASPA, including election to the National Council. He has received numerous professional awards, grants, and fellowships, and authored dozens of refereed publications, conference papers, and books/ monographs, in addition to extensive consulting and training in the private and public sectors.

Meredith A. Newman is associate professor and chair of the Department of Public Administration, University of Illinois at Springfield. Her articles on public management, the gendered bureaucracy, and human resources appear in a number of scholarly journals, including *Public Administration Review* and *Women & Politics.* She is a past-National Council Representative of the ASPA and past chair of the Section for Women in Public Administration. She currently serves as vice-chair of the Section on Public Administration Research.

Linda K. Richter is professor of Political Science at Kansas State University where she teaches gender and politics, public administration, and public policy. Her field research is focused primarily on South and Southeast Asia. She has authored three books and numerous articles on these regions. She has also written widely on gender, female leadership, and travel and tourism policy. Her biographical articles include former Philippine President Corazon Aquino, Myanmar opposition leader and Nobel Peace Prize winner Aung San Suu Kyi, and former U.S. Senator Nancy Landon Kassebaum. She has held two fellowships from the East-West Center, two Fulbright scholarships, and an American Institute of Pakistan Studies Grant.

Hindy Lauer Schachter is a professor of Management at New Jersey Institute of Technology. She is the author of *Reinventing Government or Reinventing Ourselves: The Role of Citizen Owners in Making a Better Government* (1997), *Frederick Taylor and the Public Administration Community: A Reevaluation* (1989), and *Public Agency Communication: Theory and Practice* (1983). Her articles have appeared in *Public Administration Review*, *Administration and Society*, and other journals.

Teva J. Scheer received her Ph.D. in public administration from the University of Colorado at Denver's Graduate School of Public Affairs, where she is an adjunct faculty member. Dr. Scheer is also a full-time human resources analyst at the Department of the Treasury in Washington, DC. Her primary research interest is the history of public administration. As part of a 2002 symposium on Progressivism, she published a paper on American club women and public administration; she also presented a paper on the history of the merit system at the 2002 conference of ASPA. She is currently completing a book-length biography on Nellie Tayloe Ross.

Patricia M. Shields directs the Master of Public Administration Program at Texas State University. Her research interests include pragmatism and public administration, civil military relations (broadly defined), and women in the military. She has published over forty articles and book chapters in journals such as *Administration & Society*, *Armed Forces & Society*, *Public Administration Quarterly*, *The American Review of Public Administration*, *Society*, and *The Journal of Political and Military Sociology*. She is author of *Step by Step: Building a Research Paper*. Since 2000, she has been the editor of *Armed Forces & Society*.

Elizabeth G. Williams is an assistant professor of Political Science and MPA graduate faculty member at James Madison University. She teaches women and politics, American government, health policy, and public budgeting. She has a Ph.D. in political science (1997), graduate certificate in gender research (1995), and M.A. in public administration (1989). Her recent publications include "Meadowville Valley: Open For Business" an economic development case-study chapter based on Harrisonburg in *Managing Local Economic Development: Cases in Decision-Making* (2003); "Experiential Service-Learning in Undergraduate Women and Politics," *Undergraduate Educator*, July/August 2003; *POS 2112: State and Local Government* (1999); and "The Florida Legislature and the Legislative Process," a coauthored chapter in *Government and Politics in Florida* (1998).

Name Index